D0680570

The Cabinet and Congress

The Cabinet
and Congress

STEPHEN HORN

1960 New York

Columbia University Press

Copyright © 1960 Columbia University Press
Library of Congress Catalog Card Number: 60-13237
Published in Great Britain, India, and Pakistan
by the Oxford University Press
London, Bombay, and Karachi
Manufactured in the United States of America

Preface

AN INDIVIDUAL who engages in research quickly finds that he has many friends and interested people who go out of their way to assist him.

In the provision of research materials, valuable aid was rendered by Mrs. Hope H. Grace, chief of noncurrent records, office of the director of the budget; Miss Mary M. Pope, catalog assistant in the Stimson Collection at Yale's Sterling Library; Miss Bess Glenn, chief, and Mr. John E. Maddox, archivist, in the justice and executive branch of the National Archives; Mr. Joseph C. Vance, chief, recent manuscripts section of the Library of Congress; Mrs. Ruth Ballenger, manuscripts librarian, Rutherford B. Hayes Library; Mr. M. G. Toepel, chief, Wisconsin Legislative Reference Library; and Mr. Herman Kahn, director, Franklin D. Roosevelt Library.

Appreciation is also expressed to the several hundred legislators and present and former Cabinet members who took time out of their busy days to answer a letter or submit to an interview.

Part of the historical research was originally undertaken in a paper prepared for Professor Thomas A. Bailey, then chairman of the Department of History at Stanford University. I am grateful for Dr. Bailey's careful editing of that manuscript and his many thoughtful suggestions and continued interest. Much of the additional manuscript received the scholarly scrutiny of Professor Robert A. Walker, chairman of the Department of Political Science at Stanford, who—along with Professor Thomas S. Barclay—first interested me in the study of government during my undergraduate days. In addition, valuable advice has been provided by both Robert A. Horn and John H. Bunzel, members of the political science faculty at Stanford, as well as by Dr. Gene Lindstrom, a former colleague at Stanford.

At the Columbia University Press, a wonderful group of people has taught the author much about the intricacies of publishing. Robert J. Tilley, assistant to the director, has been particularly unsparing in his time and friendship. Both Mrs. Barbara Voorhis Levy, editor, and Miss Elisabeth L. Shoemaker, assistant editor, have educated me as to the imagination and creativity with which good editors pursue their task. To their skilled surgical abilities, I am indebted.

The assistance rendered by my mother, Mrs. Isabelle M. Horn, by my wife's parents, Mr. and Mrs. Clifton H. Moore, and by my aunt, Mrs. Mary Walen, permitted more extensive research than otherwise would have been possible.

To Nini, who has been a participant in the study from the beginning and whose advice, typing abilities, and good humor have made it possible, this work is affectionately dedicated.

STEPHEN HORN

Washington, D.C.
June, 1960

Contents

Figures

Tables

(1)

Introduction

THE CABINET AND CONGRESS is the study of an idea, an idea that
has waxed and waned intermittently since 1789. It centers on a
problem which is unlikely ever to be resolved, owing to the
structure of the American government. This problem involves
the relationships between the legislative and the executive
power of the federal government.

At various times in the nation's history the taut equilibrium
between the Chief Executive and Congress has shifted to favor
first one branch and then the other. Presidential and legislative
temperament, the prevailing level of communication, and the
demands for public policy which can be stimulated within the
society, all these—singly or in combination—have played their
role upon this moving stage. In the nineteenth century, as students of politics and reformers became concerned over the rise
of "Congressional government," several Speakers of the House
of Representatives acquired the label "czar." In the first half
of the twentieth century a handful of so-called strong Presidents
were accused of usurping legislative functions. In turn, the legislative branch has been condemned for becoming a "rubber
stamp" in ratifying—often with little change—the decisions
made in the great departments of government dominated by
the expert and the administrator.

Neither the Founding Fathers in Philadelphia nor the succeeding generations of voters in democracy's perpetual constitutional convention have ever reached agreement on the exact
dividing line between the domain of the Presidency and that
of Congress. The sentiment that exists for the structure which

separates "legislative" and "executive" power, on the one hand, and then brings them together again through a system of "checks and balances," on the other, has caused some individuals to seek a reconciliation of goals, not by merging the separate fiefdoms but by bringing the agents of the Chief Executive into a closer and more open relationship with the people's elected representatives. Since the First Congress and the era of Alexander Hamilton, the idea of seating the Cabinet in Congress to participate in debate or answer questions has been the recipient of both praise and scorn.

Support for this proposal has come from those who see in the procedure an opportunity to increase citizen visibility of how public policy is made. They have equated government conducted in a "goldfish bowl" with honest administration. With a strong belief in libertarian rationality, this group has held that the clash of minds in argument before the full houses of Congress would decrease the influence of small bodies of willful men who sit behind closed committee doors and engage in provincial bartering rather than a search for the national interest.

Others have taken a more utilitarian position than those who become embroiled in crusades of righteousness against corruption and cynicism in government. This more pragmatic group has viewed the federal government as a network of communications centers. For them the Presidency and Congress are collective decision-making units, operating at the apex of funnels into which have been poured all of the data, opinion, prejudice, and values which are the basis of public policy in a democracy. Under the Constitution no single individual makes a final decision. The President shares the legislative power through his authority to recommend measures for consideration and to veto acts of Congress. The legislative branch has often delved into minute administrative detail, not only at the annual appropriations hearings but throughout the congressional year, especially when departmental representatives have appeared before the substantive committees of the two houses. Both branches are subject to varying pressures arising from the vast number of interest groups which exist in our society. Confronted with these circumstances, the pragmatic group has argued that seating the Cabinet in Congress would provide unity within the executive branch, since the pressure of interrogation would compel prior consultation as to what was actually the presidential program.

Opponents of this reform have feared, in part, that a Cabinet member might attempt to ingratiate himself with Congress and thus become alienated from the Executive. Without doubt, Cabinet members have on occasion flanked the directives of the President and entered into collusion with members of Congress to thwart the Chief Executive. Following his service as the nation's first budget director, the late General Charles G. Dawes is said to have concluded as a result of the departmental–congressional committee collusion he witnessed: "Every member of the Cabinet is a natural enemy of the President." [1] At times the permanent career bureaucracy has joined forces with the elected bureaucracy coming from "safe districts" (Southern Democrats or Middle West Republicans) in curbing both presidential and agency policies.

Despite the broad phrase of the Constitution which vests "The executive Power . . . in a President of the United States of America," [2] no Chief Executive under modern conditions can remain master of his administration without reliance on his Cabinet appointees. Although a Cabinet was not mentioned in the Constitution, its gradual evolution has been sanctioned—like that of political parties—since the first administration of George Washington. Its use could not be dispensed with by the most aggressive of Presidents without jarring public confidence. The addition, by the Eisenhower administration, of both a secretary to the Cabinet and special Cabinet assistants in each department—who are charged with aiding the department head in the implementation of presidential decisions—has given new emphasis to the role of the Cabinet in developing "government-wide" as opposed to merely "departmental" policy. Traditionally, many Presidents have begun their terms with the intention of attempting to utilize the potential which the group process of the Cabinet offers, but as a result of departmental reluctance to share what each department regards as "its" problems with other agencies, most Chief Executives have gradually reverted to individual discussion with the Cabinet officer concerned when determining major governmental policy.

In recent years, the attempt to attain administrative unity within the Executive—through the increased use of the legislative clearance procedure and the enlargement of the White House staff—has been intensified. This emphasis on coordination and efficiency is a result, in part, of the more thorough understanding of the problems of the Presidency which has come from such reports as the President's Committee on Administrative Management and the First and Second Hoover Commissions. In 1945, the final year of the Second World War, Congress also undertook at least a partial self-analysis of its effectiveness in fulfilling the legislative function.

Both branches, however, have shied away from detailed attention to problems involving their relationships with each other. Thus new importance is provided for an analytical and historical study of the merits of the proposal to admit the Cabinet to Congress. Why was this reform suggested originally? What motivated its proponents to sponsor the measure? What were the overt and underlying reasons of those who opposed it? What conditions within our political society—and especially in our legislative-executive relations—have given impetus to this idea? Under what conditions might it function successfully? Can it ever be enacted?

For many throughout our nation's history, the idea of Cabinet participation in either congressional debate or a question period has seemed to be the one possible way of bridging the gap between Capitol Hill and the White House—that single mile which at times appears to be the longest in the world.

II

The Heritage of the Federalists

OVER TWO MONTHS had elapsed after March 4, 1789—the date set to mark the beginning of the new government of the United States under the Constitution—before the First Congress began consideration of the relationships which should exist between the executive departments, the President, and the legislative branch. Eight senators and thirteen representatives were present on March 4 at the new capital of New York City. But crude means of transportation, a failure on the part of two of the thirteen states to ratify the Constitution, and a lag in the holding of elections to fill the congressional seats delayed the arrival of the remaining legislators. Both houses were compelled to adjourn from day to day until a quorum was finally secured during the first week in April.

CREATION OF THE EXECUTIVE DEPARTMENTS

Revenue was the first consideration of the government then as it is today. From early in April until late in May, the House discussed legislation specifying the duties to be levied on imports. Since taxes and duties were uppermost in the legislators' thoughts and actions during this period, it is not surprising that the first executive department suggested was that responsible for finance.[1]

Elias Boudinot, a New Jersey federalist leader, proposed on May 19, 1789, that the House establish a department headed by a secretary of finance which would be charged with the care of the government's funds. After this function was provided for, said Boudinot, the House could then consider the creation of both a war department and a department of foreign affairs.[2]

Boudinot's informality in proposing the departments disturbed New York's Egbert Benson, who stated that Congress should first decide how many departments were needed. Without permitting an answer to the query he raised, Benson announced that three departments—foreign affairs, treasury, and war—should be established.[3] John Vining of Delaware added that the territorial possessions and domestic affairs of the new nation warranted the creation of a home department.[4] No member seemed certain as to how to proceed and there were few specific ideas about the actual functions that would be assigned to the suggested establishments.

James Madison, recognized by his colleagues as well as by succeeding generations as the "Father of the Constitution," focused the rambling debate by formally moving that first a department of foreign affairs be created, next the treasury, and then a department of war.[5] Several members disagreed with Madison's implied ranking since they believed that finance had a higher priority than foreign relations. But their protests were of no avail, and the seniority of the cabinet departments had been determined.

THE POWER OF REMOVAL

The actual content of the bills authorizing the three departments apparently was worked out in small *ad hoc* committees rather than on the floor of the House. Most of the debates concerning the new departments centered on the power of the President to remove the department heads. An analysis of those discussions offers an insight into the legislators' conception of the executive power and the relationship which they assumed existed between individual departments and the Congress.

The principal advocate for vesting the removal power solely

in the President was Madison.[6] Elbridge Gerry, a sometime erratic anti-federalist, was of a different opinion: the removal of an official must follow the same procedure as his appointment. Consequently, if the Senate agreed to the President's nomination of an individual for a particular position, then the Senate must be consulted when that officer was removed.[7] The Gerry view was disposed of rapidly when the House by a "considerable majority" approved the motion declaring that the power of removal rested with the President.[8] This was to be but the lull before the battle.

On May 21, 1789, an eleven-man committee was appointed to draft bills specifying in detail the functions of the three proposed departments. This action followed the defeat of a proposal by Gerry which would have provided a board of three commissioners to head the treasury, as had existed under the Articles of Confederation, instead of a single executive.[9]

A contested election, the disposal of Western lands, revenue collection problems, and new amendments to the Constitution occupied House time while the eleven committee members were meeting frequently to draft specific proposals as to department structure and functions. The House finally resolved itself on June 16, 1789, into a committee of the whole and began consideration of the bill to create a department of foreign affairs. At this time, the previous decision to exclude the Senate from participating in the removal of a department head came under renewed attack by the pro-Gerry group. Quotations from *The Federalist*—in the exposition of which Madison had played a major role—were used in an attempt to bolster the idea that the Senate should participate in the removal of those officials whose appointment it had originally ratified.[10]

Madison, however, vigorously objected, stating that such a scheme would cause the department heads to seek favor with the Senate, and that consequently the President would lose his control over and responsibility for them.[11] In a letter written two weeks earlier to his friend Edmund Randolph, who had authored the basic governmental plan discussed in the Constitutional Convention, Madison expressed his fears more specifically when he speculated that if the removal power were given the Senate, "a faction . . . might support them [the department heads] against the President, distract the Executive department, and obstruct the public business." [12] Montesquieu's overemphasis on the separation of powers provided the criterion for Madison, who stated that "the preservation of liberty" required that the legislative and executive "be constantly separated." [13]

Representative James Jackson commented that the Constitutional Convention could not have intended department heads to be merely instruments of presidential control; otherwise the delegates would not have inserted the provision authorizing the executive to request information in writing from the heads of departments. [14] Obviously exasperated by the drawn-out debate and firmly convinced of his own position, Samuel Livermore exclaimed: "Leave them [the executive] to do their duty, and let us do ours." [15] Verbal support came readily from several members who sought to conclude the argument and secure a vote on the controversial "removal" clause of the Foreign Affairs bill.

The next day, on Friday, June 19, the representatives had another opportunity to register their viewpoint on the various interpretations which had been voiced in the committee of the whole concerning the President's power to dismiss a department head. Despite an eloquent last-minute plea by Gerry that the departments were creatures of Congress and that presidential authority must be limited, the House, by a vote of 34 to 20, agreed to specify in the foreign affairs bill that the removal power was vested solely in the President. [16]

Further reflection over the weekend, however, resulted in a change of position. On Monday, June 22, a motion to strike out the pro-presidential removal clause approved the preceding Friday in committee of the whole was ratified 31 to 19 by the

House.[17] It was not that a majority of the House had decided to roar like a lion against the pretensions of an executive mouse; rather, their belief had grown that under the Constitution the President possessed the sole power of removal, and they did not want it to appear that the executive was dependent upon Congress for the exercise of this power. These men were wise enough to know that what one Congress granted another could take away.[18]

Despite the opinion of many later commentators that the greatest political fear of this period was that of presidential tyranny (a fear based on contemporary parallels with another single executive named George III), two distinguished House leaders believed that the real constitutional infringement would more likely be made by the Senate. James Madison, for example, was concerned with possible Senate domination and believed that the executive probably would be the weak branch of the government.[19] Fisher Ames, who was to remain a loyal Federalist long after Madison had been irrevocably lodged in the Jeffersonian camp, thought that "the meddling of the Senate in appointments is one of the least defensible parts of the Constitution" and did not want to extend that body's power any further.[20]

The legislation authorizing a department of foreign affairs with no removal clause finally was approved by the House of Representatives on June 24. Yet although the events which led to the elimination of the removal clause in the case of foreign affairs were very recent, a similar provision was inserted in the war department bill that very afternoon by the close division of 24 to 22.[21]

CABINET OFFICERS IN CONGRESS?

Early the following day, June 25, 1789, after approving the war department legislation, the House again resolved itself into

a committee of the whole to undertake the first intensive discussion of the relationship of the head of an executive department to Congress.

John Page, a Virginia anti-federalist, began the debate by
objecting to the second clause of the treasury bill recently reported by the committee designated to draw it up. This clause
made it the secretary's duty to "digest and report plans for the
improvement and management of the revenue, and the support
of the public credit." [22]

Although Page granted that it was legitimate for the head
of the treasury to prepare estimates, he thought that "to go
further would be a dangerous innovation upon the Constitutional privilege of this House." He predicted the creation of an
"undue influence" on the floor of the House, since, "by the deference commonly paid to men of abilities, who give an opinion
in a case they have thoroughly studied," representatives might
be led to support the department head against their own beliefs.
If the treasury secretary were admitted, the precedent must
lead to the presence of all department heads "to explain and
support the plans they have digested and reported." And that,
said this follower of Jefferson, would lay "a foundation for an
aristocracy or a detestable monarchy." [23] Page's views were
seconded by Thomas Tucker, who—though a South Carolina
federalist—saw no necessity for the proposed procedure.[24]

Egbert Benson, who was to become one of Alexander Hamilton's strongest House supporters, disagreed with his two Southern colleagues and thought that the clause was "essentially
necessary." [25] Another federalist, Benjamin Goodhue, believed
that the House would be carrying its dignity to an extreme if it
refused to receive information from outside sources.[26] Page
clarified his position by replying to Goodhue that while he had
no objection to calling on the secretary for information, he
believed that it was "certainly improper to have him authorized
by law to intrude upon us whatever he may think proper." [27]

The preliminary skirmishes completed, Fisher Ames—an able orator and at thirty-one one of the youngest and brightest advocates of the federalist cause—declared that he favored getting information directly from the secretary on the floor of the House. Foreshadowing a query raised by all later-day proponents of this idea, and specifically replying to an earlier statement of Page's, Ames asked: "What improper influence could a plan reported openly and officially have on the mind of any member, more than if the scheme and information were given privately at the Secretary's office?" [28]

Ames feared that the federal government would be inherently weak. If the new Constitution were to succeed, the central government must be able to attract the talented and act decisively. The attitude of many anti-federalists, who believed that the best government governed least, was one of constant amazement to Ames. Given these preconceptions, it is understandable why he was one of the most faithful supporters of Hamilton's financial and governmental policies. Both men abhorred the tendency of the people's representatives to base their policy decisions on other than what to them seemed purely "factual" information.[29]

Though Ames's position received firm support from Theodore Sedgwick, Elias Boudinot, and John Laurance, it was opposed just as vigorously by Samuel Livermore, Thomas Hartley, and Elbridge Gerry. Livermore had reservations as to the mental processes of the committee that had drafted the treasury bill. He suggested that the group was thinking of the statute which had enumerated the duties of the superintendent of finance under the Articles of Confederation.[30] The committee, he thought, had forgotten that then the executive and the legislative were merged, whereas under the Constitution they were specifically separated. Hartley, though in favor of receiving factual data provided that the House had requested it, objected to the secretary's being permitted to send information on his own initiative. Gerry's concern was the possible abdication of congressional responsibility for originating legislation.[31] He would not be the last representative alarmed at the possible consequences of executive encroachment.

Exhibiting his Irish good-fellowship, Thomas Fitzsimons sought to end the dispute by changing the wording of the controversial clause so that the secretary of the treasury would not "report" plans of revenue to the House but rather "prepare" plans for it.[32] This proposal failed to allay the concern of those who feared undue departmental influence. Yet a motion by Page to strike out the whole clause was defeated, and shortly before adjournment, the Fitzsimons amendment to the bill which substituted "prepare" for "report" was passed by "a great majority." [33]

That evening, Fisher Ames described the day's events in a letter to his friend George Richards Minot. He related that some progress had been made on the treasury bill and that a "puerile debate" had arisen over the admission of the secretary to the House, concluding:

The champions of liberty drew their swords, talked blank verse about treasury influence, a ministry, violation of the privileges of the House by giving him a hearing from time to time. They persevered so long and so furiously, that they lost all strength, and were left in a very small minority. The clause, permitting this liberty, passed.[34]

PRECEDENTS FOR THE CABINET IN CONGRESS

Meanwhile, for almost two months, the Senate had been primarily marking time with such pressing affairs of state as a suitable title of address for President Washington. By the middle of May, after long and careful pondering, a Senate committee suggested that the President be greeted as "His Highness, the President of the United States of America, and Protector of their Liberties." Such phraseology, however, sounded too haughty even to the supposedly aristocratic Senate, and the committee's recommendation was postponed in favor of the House's simple, although less value-ridden mode: "To the President of the United States." [35]

While the Senate continued to await House action on the departmental organization bills, the first of two events occurred which were to provide precedent for the future claim that members of the Cabinet had participated in Senate debate. On June 16, 1789, President Washington submitted to the senators for their advice and consent the nomination of William Short to replace Thomas Jefferson as minister to France. The message was taken to the Senate by John Jay, the secretary of foreign affairs for the Confederation, who had been retained by Washington until Jefferson could return from Paris to become the first secretary of state. The presidential message notified the senators that Jay had the relevant papers which would attest as to the "character" of Mr. Short. A resolution was approved which invited the secretary to come back the following day with the information.[36]

On June 17, Jay returned with the necessary information and orally gave it to the Senate. No objections were made as to the procedure. The main argument developed among the senators over the manner in which nominations should be approved: some advocated a secret ballot, others favored a voice or recorded vote. Then, before the secretary left the floor, the Senate invited the second precedent when they ordered Jay to examine, in terms of instructions issued under the Confederation, a consular convention between the United States and France which was before them for ratification and report his conclusions to them.[37]

The day after Independence Day, 1789, Madison wrote back to a Virginia friend that "the business goes on still very slowly.

We are in a wilderness without a single footstep to guide us." [38]
The three departmental bills finally were sent to the Senate by
the House early in July. While the treasury bill was still under
consideration, the second instance—"footstep"—occurred.

In accordance with the June 17 order to Jay, the Senate, on
July 21, requested that "the Secretary of Foreign Affairs attend
. . . to-morrow, and bring with him such papers as are requi-
site to give full information relative to the consular convention
between France and the United States." [39] On July 22, Jay
"attended, agreeably to order, and made the necessary explanations." [40] The whole afternoon was occupied with executive
business, but toward the end of the session a resolution was
approved which requested "the Secretary of Foreign Affairs
under the former Congress" to examine the proposed convention in terms of the actions and instructions of the Continental
Congress in considering a 1784 consular agreement between
the king of France and the United States.[41] On July 27, a written statement setting forth Jay's opinion and recommending
ratification was received by the Senators. That same day, President Washington signed into law the act authorizing a department of foreign affairs.[42]

Further historical confusion accumulated on August 7 when
General Henry Knox, the man whom Washington was to appoint secretary of war under the recent law, and who, like Jay,
had been a carry-over, appeared in the Senate chamber bearing
a message from the President requesting that body to consider
the disputes between the United States and certain southern
Indian tribes. Washington's message notified the Senators that
he had directed General Knox to lay his statements on Indian
relations before them for their information.[43] Knox again appeared on August 10, and delivered a presidential message.[44]
The lack of verbatim reporting, combined with the secrecy
which originally surrounded the Senate debates, creates doubt

as to whether Knox read the President's message to the Senate and responded to questions or merely served as a messenger between the executive mansion and Congress.

WASHINGTON AND THE SENATE

During this period as the new government was slowly evolving its procedures, President Washington formulated his views on the proper mode of communication between himself and the Senate. The Senate shared a portion of the Executive's powers by constitutional fiat since it was required to give "advice and consent" to many of his nominations and all of his treaties. In his letter book, Washington noted the result of two meetings with a Senate committee: that the manner of communication should vary depending on presidential inclination and subject matter. He anticipated that with reference to appointments the Senate could be summoned to the executive mansion. With treaties—which were more legislative in character—the President might either appear personally in the Senate chamber or send his opinion in writing.[45]

On August 21, 1789, the Senate by resolution sanctioned Washington's suggested procedure. The following day, the President, accompanied by Secretary of War Knox, entered the Senate chamber.[46] Washington provided Vice President John Adams, the presiding officer, with a statement further detailing the government's relations with several powerful Indian tribes in the southern part of the country. Adams then began to read seven questions concerning the proposed Indian treaty. After stating the first question, the vice president asked the "advice and consent" of the assembled legislators.

The account of what immediately followed has been left by Senator William Maclay, a vehement Pennsylvania antifederalist who regarded Washington and Adams—particularly Adams—as heading "the court party." [47] Maclay noted in his journal that the noise from the street combined with the complexity of the issues did not permit the careful consideration which he believed the treaty warranted. Besides, he desired that Washington—whose prestige overawed many—leave the chamber so that the Senate might arrive at its judgment without any undue influence exerted by the presence of the President and his secretary of war.

Maclay secured a vote postponing consideration until more facts were available. His Pennsylvania colleague, Robert Morris, went further and moved that all the papers be referred to a committee of five. Objections were raised by several of the President's supporters. One senator insisted that since the Senate was acting as a council it was improper to refer this matter to committee where the dictates of a few would predominate. Maclay then urged the utilization of committees.

At this, Washington started up in "a violent fret" and exclaimed: "This defeats every purpose of my coming here." The President, after reiterating that he had brought his secretary of war to answer any questions, "cooled by degrees" (according to Maclay), and offered no objection to putting the matter off until the following Monday.[48]

Washington had noted earlier, on August 8, the possible embarrassment that might confront the Executive in placing his nominations before the Senate when he wrote: "It could be no pleasing thing I conceive, for the President, on the one hand to be present and hear the propriety of his nominations questioned . . ."[49] It now appeared that treaties could cause similar vexation.

The Senate next met with Washington and Knox on Monday, August 24. That the meeting was unsatisfying for both the President and the senators there can be little doubt. Maclay reported that "a shamefacedness, or I know not what, flowing from the presence of the President, kept everybody silent." Never again did a Chief Executive appear before the Senate seeking—in a "give-and-take" discussion—their advice and consent.[50]

Congressional sensitivity regarding legislative prerogatives had made itself evident. The fear of being overawed by the Executive or his representatives has been prevalent ever since. It has been a constant factor in the consideration of proposals for seating Cabinet officers in Congress or allowing them to appear on the floor in order to submit to interrogation.

"IN WRITING, NOT IN PERSON"

Washington had carried over on an "acting" basis the major departmental officials who had been appointed by the last Congress of the Confederation. By the end of September, 1789, the permanent heads of departments under the new Constitution had been approved, and the Senate adjourned until January, 1790. Except for Secretary of State-designate Thomas Jefferson, who was in Paris closing out his affairs as American minister, the other officials—Alexander Hamilton at the treasury, Henry Knox as secretary of war, Edmund Randolph as attorney general, and Postmaster General Samuel Osgood (who did not officially preside over a department until 1792)—had an opportunity during this "breathing period" when Congress was not in session to examine their new functions and lay plans for the future.

The debates of the preceding summer had revealed that many members of Congress considered revenue and public credit to be the most important problems facing the infant nation. The provision in the treasury law permitting the secretary to "report in person or in writing" revealed that a different type of relationship was contemplated between the secretary of the treasury and Congress than that existing with the other departments.

Probably one reason for this special status was the constitu-

tional provision that "All bills for raising Revenue shall originate in the House of Representatives." [51] To decide properly on
the collection and allocation of the money required for both the
daily operation of governmental activities and long-term debt
retirement, the legislators needed facts. Lacking an executive
budget system, which would not appear until the third decade
of the twentieth century, the Chief Executive exerted little
influence over the financial requirements of the departments
supposedly under his control.

A second and possibly equally compelling reason for the
treasury's special status was Alexander Hamilton. Although
Hamilton was not confirmed as secretary of the treasury until
September 11, 1789,[52] there is substantial evidence to prove
that he was especially active during the early months of the
new government in meeting with both the President and
various legislators. Since Washington previously had expressed
his intention of appointing his young wartime aide to the
finance post, probably much of the treasury's structure and
function was suggested or approved by Hamilton.[53]

The relationship of the secretary to Congress was foreshad-
owed in a letter Hamilton had written to a friend almost a
decade before.[54] Later, he had favored a strong executive
during the Constitutional Convention.[55] As the first administration evolved, Hamilton—especially from the point of view of his
great antagonist Thomas Jefferson—seemed to regard the treasury secretary as the leader and advocator of governmental
policy, while the President would be relegated primarily to the
role of chief of state.

In the interim between the adjournment of the old Congress
and the meeting of the new, Hamilton studiously applied himself to preparing a report on the public credit in accord with
the September 21st resolution of the House of Representatives.
On Saturday, January 9, 1790, a letter from Hamilton was read
to the House notifying them that "he had prepared a plan for

the support of the Public Credit, and that he was ready to report the same to this House, when they should be ready to receive it." [56] A motion was immediately offered to assign the
following Thursday to hear Hamilton.

Elbridge Gerry, increasingly sensitive to what he regarded as
the antirepublican tendencies of the new government, offered
an amendment to specify that the report be submitted in writing. Objecting, Elias Boudinot—always ready to soothe irri-
tated feelings—rose and addressed the chair. He hoped that
"the Secretary of the Treasury might be permitted to make his
report in person, in order to answer such inquiries as the members might be disposed to make, for it was a justifiable surmise
that gentlemen would not be able clearly to comprehend so
intricate a subject without oral illustration." [57]

Disagreement with Boudinot's argument was voiced by
Pennsylvania federalist George Clymer, who had been a member of the Constitutional Convention. Siding with Gerry, he
doubted the "propriety" of oral delivery by a department head
and personally favored limiting to writing the communication
between the two branches. Surprisingly, Fisher Ames—certainly one of Hamilton's most vigorous defenders in the House
—effectively undercut any attempt to invite Cabinet officers
to the floor when he announced that he preferred the secretary's views in writing because then "they would obtain a degree of permanency . . . [and would] . . . be less liable to be
misunderstood." [58] Another administration supporter, Egbert
Benson, offered no resistance to the Gerry motion when he said
that either way would be acceptable to him. The Gerry resolution requesting Hamilton to submit his report on the public
credit in writing was passed without further discussion.[59]

Two weeks after this incident, Hamilton appeared in the
House with a report on the operations of the post office system
and a draft of remedial legislation. Immediately following the
reading of the secretary's report, Thomas Fitzsimons (usually

a firm federalist) interrupted before the clerk could proceed to the accompanying bill. Fitzsimons "thought there was a degree of indelicacy, not to say impropriety, in permitting the heads of departments to bring bills before the House." Statements of fact, the representative believed, would be sufficient unless the House specifically requested that the secretary frame a proposal. Hamilton's suggested measure was not read and both the report and draft bill were sent to a select committee.[60]

HAMILTON AND THE RISE OF THE CABINET

Alexander Hamilton's relationship with the Congress was disturbing not only to many of the federalists and antifederalists of the legislative branch, but also to his fellow Cabinet colleagues. Even though he had been prevented from taking his recommendations directly to the floor, the ambitious head of the treasury was successful in having both the Senate and the House refer many problems to his department for a written report. Great industry was shown in submitting detailed and comprehensive replies. Although Hamilton's aggressiveness caused violent outbursts in some sectors of the administration, his influence continued to remain substantial.[61]

With the exception of Hamilton's, relationships between the Cabinet and Congress had become more formal and routine. Reports were requested from the executive agencies and replies were submitted in writing by the responsible departmental official. General Knox still periodically renewed acquaintanceships with the legislators by bearing messages from President Washington to both houses. There is no evidence that he ever uttered a word in debate in either chamber.

As his first term progressed, President Washington came more and more to believe that in order to understand the various facets of a question before determining his course of action, it would be advantageous to bring together department heads for discussion. In the spring of 1791, upon leaving New York City for a journey to his home at Mt. Vernon, Washington wrote Jefferson, Hamilton, and Knox encouraging them to meet together "if any serious and important cases should arise" during his absence. The President added that the actions which they agreed upon would be ratified when he returned to the capital.[62] This is the first recorded instance where the Chief Executive authorized collective action by the Cabinet. Because of the constitutional power vested in the President alone and the specifications of Washington's directive, it was not the complete collective responsibility exercised by the British cabinet.

Upon Washington's return, additional meetings to consider foreign and military policy were held in November and December, 1791. The institutional evolution of the constitutionally unrecognized body of advisers had begun, a group whose power traditionally has depended on the whim of the President. Although the Cabinet at times has not been utilized to any great extent, no President would now be able to eliminate it from our governmental structure without a strong public reaction.

In 1793 the tension with France caused frequent and sometimes daily meetings of the heads of departments with President Washington. Further absences of Washington during the summer of 1794 resulted in more collective decision making by the three secretaries, this time meeting with the attorney general.[63]

Sir Isaac Newton once postulated that for every action in physics there is an equal and opposite reaction. The world of social phenomena has exhibited similar behavior. The growth of executive power during the Washington administration had not gone far when a further congressional reaction erupted.

THE ST. CLAIR INVESTIGATION

In September, 1791, out in northwestern Ohio, Governor Arthur St. Clair had taken to the field with a small army of men in an attempt to construct a ring of military posts which would provide protection against the numerous Indian attacks that threatened the pioneer settlements. The governor and his troops were ambushed and defeated on November 4, 1791, by a smaller body of their opponents. This severe defeat was to end the major punitive expeditions against the Indians until 1794, when General "Mad Anthony" Wayne and his force won the Battle of Fallen Timbers.[64]

On March 27, 1792, a House resolution was introduced by Anti-Federalist William Branch Giles requesting the President to begin an investigation "into the causes of the late defeat of the army under command of Major General St. Clair." John Vining inquired how Giles planned to accomplish the purpose of his resolution. Following an evasive reply, Vining suggested that the House call upon the department heads concerned "to give an account of their conduct." [65]

Representative William Smith noted that this was the first occasion when the House of Representatives had sought to examine the conduct of executive officers responsible to the President. Asserting that Vining's proposal was a violation of the separation of powers, Smith urged the House to wait until President Washington had conducted his own inquiry.[66]

One of Smith's Federalist colleagues, Hugh Williamson, agreed as to the doubtful "propriety of the resolution" and recommended that a select committee be appointed to report at a later date.[67] Giles's original motion that the President conduct the inquiry was voted down 25 to 21. The House then sanctioned Williamson's idea of referring the investigation to a select committee by a four to one ratio of 44 to 10.[68]

A committee of seven under the chairmanship of Thomas Fitzsimons commenced its study of the St. Clair debacle. From General Knox, who as secretary of war was St. Clair's responsible superior, they sought the original letters and instructions pertaining to the ill-fated expedition.

Since this was the first time that either House had demanded information from the executive branch concerning possible errors in judgment and management, President Washington called a Cabinet meeting for March 31, 1792. According to Secretary of State Jefferson, who described the meeting with great detail in his "Anas," Washington had no fixed opinion as to the proper course of action in what was the first instance of its kind. He did desire to establish a "correct" precedent. Thus the Chief Executive presented the various alternatives that could be taken in response to the committee's demand. But the three secretaries and the attorney general requested time to "think and inquire" before stating a definite position.[69]

By April 2, when the Cabinet met again with the President, there was unanimous agreement that while the House might undertake investigations and call for papers, the executive should use discretion and communicate only those documents which it believed would not injure the public good. The lone dissent came from Treasury Secretary Hamilton who differed with his colleagues' position that the House should direct its inquiries to the President alone, not to the department heads. While Hamilton urged that the act establishing the Treasury Department "made it subject to Congress on some points," the secretary held that he was not required to forward all papers which either House might conceivably demand.[70] This attitude caused Jefferson to confide in his diary that Hamilton "endeavored to place himself subject to the House, when the Executive should propose what he did not like, and subject to the Executive, when the House should propose anything disagreeable."[71]

The Cabinet agreed to furnish copies of the relevant St. Clair papers and, if the committee wished, to allow a clerk to verify them against the originals. They also decided to speak individually to the committee members and "bring them by persuasion into the right channel."[72]

Hamilton's reluctance to sever his link with Congress created resentment on all sides. The House had shown uncertainty during the past few months in regard to a definite policy either of calling for information through the President or of issuing their requests directly to the particular department head. Following a dinner meeting between Jefferson and several of his congressional supporters earlier on January 2, Fitzsimons and Gerry had declared their complete opposition to the procedure of referring matters to a department rather than to the Chief Executive.[73] Later, in attempting to prevent the House from continuing the practice, the Jeffersonian supporters were to be unsuccessful. On March 7, 1792, the House had held a lengthy debate on the issue, and Jefferson believed that "a great majority" would vote for his position. Before a vote could be reached, however, Hamilton's partisans secured an adjournment. Apparently the treasury had exerted a sufficient amount of pressure by the next afternoon as it won a close decision by a vote of 31 to 27 in favor of continuing the practice of individual reference. Although Jefferson noted that Gerry voted against his own previously expressed sentiment and for the treasury, he believed "that Treasury influence was tottering." [74] Further encouragement came within a week. After a meeting, on March 12, with the President, Jefferson recorded that Washington had voiced keen disapproval of the congressional habit of referring questions to department heads.[75]

THE ST. CLAIR DEBATE

The select committee charged with investigating the St. Clair mishap worked intermittently throughout the spring and summer of 1792. The report was submitted in time for the Second Session of the Second Congress.

On November 13, 1792, one week after the session commenced, a resolution was introduced in the House which provided that both Secretary of the Treasury Hamilton and Secretary of War Knox attend and "furnish such information as may be conducive to the due investigation of the matters stated" in the select committee's report on the St. Clair expedition.[76] Hugh Williamson, who had been originator of the committee, immediately moved to strike out the latter part of the resolution requiring attendance of the two Cabinet officers on the floor of the House. His action was supported by Abraham Venable, an active young Jeffersonian from Virginia, who argued that the House had no right to request the secretaries to appear in person unless they were being impeached. Besides, the House could get in writing all the information it needed from the departments.[77]

Jonathan Dayton, who at a youthful twenty-seven was a signer of the Constitution and within three years would be Speaker of the House, was the first Federalist to defend the resolution seeking admission of the two secretaries to the chamber. He emphasized the importance of the information which could be made available to the House in this manner, but did not grapple directly with the issue of whether the value of the information would be impaired if it were committed to writing, as opposed to being elicited orally.[78]

James Madison, though granting that he had not "thoroughly resolved the matter in his own mind," cautioned that the passage of the resolution "would form an innovation in the mode of conducting the business of this House, and introduce a precedent which would lead to perplexing and embarrassing consequences." [79] He then explicitly favored written as opposed to oral reports from the department officials.

Against this Republican torrent of words—the intensity of which had not been decreased by Dayton's mild rejoinder— ardent Hamiltonian Fisher Ames rose to stem the tide. He had long been inclined to the proposed procedure even though he advocated the submission in writing of Hamilton's *Report on the Public Credit*. Ames, with the eloquence which caused one biographer to describe him as "the greatest orator in the generation between Patrick Henry and Henry Clay," reminded his colleagues of the impression which St. Clair's failure had made on the public mind. If there were misconduct on the part of various officials then the blame should be properly assigned. A personal appearance before the House seemed to him the best way to obtain the needed information.[80]

Several Republicans and Federalists urged that the members first examine the committee report before considering whether or not additional information would be required from the secretaries of treasury and war. Mr. Boudinot disagreed. He believed that in order "to throw light on several parts of the report" the two officials should be heard first.[81]

John Page, who in 1789 had been the first to take offense at the clause in the treasury bill which provided that the secretary could report in person or in writing to Congress, strongly objected to the precedent that approval of the current resolution would establish. He believed that the appearance of department heads in Congress "would operate to clog the freedom of inquiry, and the freedom of debate." [82]

A temporary breach occurred in the Republican ranks when that unpredictable and aristocratic democrat, Elbridge Gerry, registered surprise at "the apprehension which some gentlemen appear to entertain of the measure of introducing the Heads of Departments into the House." This was the Gerry, who, besides telling Jefferson after their January dinner that he disapproved of Congress directing its inquiries to the department heads rather than the President, and then voting to do just that, had in January, 1790, swiftly and successfully moved to have Alexander Hamilton's *Report on the Public Credit* submitted in writing rather than allow the dynamic executive to deliver it orally.

"The Secretary," said Mr. Gerry to his fellow legislators, "will attend at the orders of the House merely to give such in-

formation as may be required, and not as members or ministers, to influence and govern the determinations of the
House." [83] Gerry sensed that in one situation the legislature
would be able to exert its power, while in the other, the agents
of the executive would tend to dominate. Since Gerry's political gyrations were by now well known, it is doubtful that he
exerted much influence among the members. At least his
support of the resolution showed that he no longer "objected to
everything he did not propose," as a fellow member of the
Constitutional Convention had once remarked.[84]

The Gerry distinction as to the circumstances under which
the Cabinet appeared in the House, encouraged Venable to
elaborate his earlier position against the introduction of departmental officials into legislative proceedings. It did not
matter whether they appeared for the purpose of giving information or of participating actively in debate: their intrusion
was nevertheless "influence." John Laurance made a futile attempt to follow up Gerry's dichotomy between providing information and leading House deliberations. The Williamson
amendment to strike out that portion of the resolution requiring the two officials to attend the House was carried and the
remainder of the resolution approved.[85]

Thomas Jefferson expressed his faction's joy by writing a
Virginia friend that he was greatly pleased by the action of the
House in supporting the Williamson amendment by a majority
of 35 to 11, and that the size of the majority "gives us some
hope of the increase of the republican vote." [86]

The following day, November 14, 1792, Speaker Jonathan
Trumbull presented a letter from Secretary of War Knox, who
expressed "solicitude and regret" at the House's recent action.
General Knox begged "the justice of the House" that some
procedure be devised so that he could "be present during the
course of the intended inquiry," hear the basis of charges in

the select committee's report, and "offer . . . information and explanations." [87]

Madison favored letting the committee restudy its report as well as consider the Knox letter.[88] Fisher Ames did not think this would be enough. He reviewed the nature of the accusations that the public might infer from the report and then raised a question that would be asked in the future by those who advocated hearing the Cabinet before the full House: "Shall they [the Cabinet officers] be sent to a Committee room, and make their defence against the allegations brought forward to their disadvantage, which have been published to the world, in the hearing of perhaps ten or a dozen persons only?" Ames hoped that this would not be the case as he urged that "justice to them and to the public required that they should be allowed to make their defence in the face of the world." [89] The world for Mr. Ames presumably began in that area circumscribed by the walls of the House of Representatives.

John Page, unmoved by the appeal to justice, answered that he would never agree to having the head of a department before the bar of the House unless the officer was being impeached. If the Cabinet came to give information, they would set "a precedent of a most dangerous nature, tending to a destruction of all freedom of inquiry by committees." A majority of the House agreed with Page and in a spirit of revolt that was to foreshadow control of the next Congress by the Republicans recommitted the report to the committee by a vote of 30 to 22.[90] Jefferson reflected his followers' sentiments when he wrote that "the tide of this government . . . [is] . . . now at the fullest, and . . . it will, from the commencement of the next session of Congress, return and subside into the true principles of the Constitution." [91]

The question of the appearance of Cabinet officers in Congress had been settled indirectly and a "precedent" was established. From that day to this, no member of the Cabinet has participated in debate or answered questions on the floor of either House.[92] A few last gasps from confirmed Federalists were heard during the remainder of Washington's second term,[93] but until 1864 no further attempt was made to admit department heads into the legislative sanctuary of the American Congress.

III

From Union to Disunion

DURING THE FIRST HALF of the nineteenth century, relations between the department heads and the legislative branch depended upon the amount of leadership exerted by the Chief Executive, the aggressiveness of an individual Cabinet member, and the temper of a particular Congress. Diaries of leading statesmen for the period reveal the increased dependence of the President on his constitutional advisers.

Little control was exerted over Congress by either President Thomas Jefferson, the first of the "Virginia dynasty," or most of his immediate successors. The House still had no definite practice concerning reference directly to the department versus calling on the President to provide the necessary information.[1] John Randolph, whose feeling for his fellow Virginian, Jefferson, changed from early admiration to anxious mistrust because of what he believed was a decrease in the President's republican sympathies, led a persistent drive to amend all resolutions making requests of a particular secretary by directing them to the President instead.

In the early nineteenth century there apparently was no concerted attempt by Cabinet secretaries to entertain socially members of Congress in order to secure a favorable hearing for departmental programs. The fact that many of Jefferson's Cabinet—notably James Madison—had not invited any of the legislators to dinner for two or three years caused Senator William Plumer, of New Hampshire, to comment with wistfulness in his diary that "these gentlemen do not live in a style suited to the dignity of their offices." [2]

The Age of Jackson brought recognition to the potential of the "kitchen cabinet." Chief Executives found that influential advisers in business and journalism might be more beneficial in the formulation of public policy than the executive heads of the major departments, whose selection was often due to a feeling of obligation for faithful work on the political hustings or to recognition of a dissident branch of the majority party.[3]

Between the eras of Jefferson and Lincoln, the principal evaluation of the Cabinet's legislative-executive relationships occurred during the Jackson administration. It involved a battle of verbal titans. The executive mansion was dominated by Old Hickory while the marble halls of the Senate resounded with the echoes of such voices as those of William Hart Benton, Henry Clay, and Daniel Webster.

The provocation of the issue was Jackson's removal of the federal deposits from the government-chartered but privately managed pro-Whig Bank of the United States and his distribution of them among various state banks. To attain this goal, the President had to fire Secretary of the Treasury William J. Duane and replace him with the more "cooperative" Roger Brooke Taney. Duane had balked at Jackson's wishes because of his interpretation of the original Treasury Act, which he believed—as had Hamilton—placed him in a special relationship with Congress. Jackson resolved the conflict of interpretation to his own satisfaction by removing the interpreter. The President then called a Cabinet meeting for September 18, 1833, and read a paper giving his reasons for dispersing the deposits. There were no objections raised by those present.

In the publication of the Jackson memorandum in a Washington newspaper, Senator Henry Clay saw an opening for beginning his badgering of the administration's financial motives and policy. In the Senate on December 11, 1833,

Clay introduced a resolution, directed to the President, which inquired whether the purported Cabinet paper that had been published was genuine. If it was—and Clay knew that it was—the President was asked to furnish the Senate with a copy. Launching the Whig attack, Clay expressed great dismay at the President's calling upon heads of departments for a purpose other than to hear their opinions and at his communicating to his Cabinet "reasons which ought to influence their judgment." [4]

Missouri's William Hart Benton, defending Jackson, held that if the Senate could demand a presidential paper, then it might also demand to know what the Chief Executive said orally to his Cabinet. Clay parried, expressing no interest in any paper which remained confidential; only those that were published disturbed him. A revised version of the Clay resolution passed 23 to 18 and was forwarded to the White House. [5]

An answer was not long in coming. The next day a terse message from the President awaited the senators. Jackson stated that he was aware of no constitutional authority held by the Senate to inquire of anything he told his Cabinet. While he was willing to explain his conduct on all occasions to the American people and on "proper" occasions to the Senate, he avowed that his own "self-respect and . . . rights secured by the Constitution to the executive branch" forced him to decline the Senate's request. [6]

With Kentucky graciousness, Clay awaited until Christmas was over, and then on December 26 attacked the President's views. The senator objected to Duane's removal, as well as to that of the deposits. He informed his colleagues with reference to the status of the Treasury Department:

Congress reserved to itself the control over that department. It refused to make it an executive department. Its whole structure manifests cautious jealousy and experienced wisdom. . . . The Secretary is to report to Congress, and to each branch of Congress. [7]

Objecting to the idea of collective ministerial advice, Clay said the President had no authority either in the Constitution or in law to go to the other Cabinet members and seek their opinion concerning an action which was "confided exclusively" to the discretion of the treasury secretary.[8] Later, in hunting for barbs in his dialectic fence, Clay chastised those department heads who objected to Jackson's removal of the deposits and still remained in the Cabinet.[9]

On January 17, 1834, Senator William C. Rives attempted to justify the administration's course of action by attacking Clay's position that the Treasury was not really an executive department because (1) it was not denominated as such and (2) the statute authorized the secretary to report in person or in writing to either house of Congress. Rives blamed historical accident for the failure to label the department "executive." Regarding the reporting function, Rives argued, by analogy, that although the President sends his message to Congress on the state of the union, no one would argue that this action places the executive in constitutional subservience to the legislative branch.[10]

The logic and illogic convinced neither group of antagonists, but the separation of powers combined with the will of Andrew Jackson determined that the question would not be resolved in favor of Congress. The constitutional impasse and inability of the Senate majority to enforce its reasoning with effective sanctions were to mean periodic renewal of such contests, depending on the assertiveness of a particular White House occupant.

In 1833, the year the argument over the removal of deposits had begun, the idea of admitting the Cabinet in Congress was revived when Justice Joseph Story published his *Commentaries on the Constitution of the United States*. Discussing the constitutional provision which disqualified those holding office under the United States from being members of either house during their continuance in office, Story argued that such a "universal exclusion" was "attended with some inconveniences." [11] If the Cabinet were not seated in Congress, executive irresponsibility would result, since "there never can be traced home to the executive any responsibility for the measures, which are planned, and carried at its suggestion." [12]

Although a Massachusetts Republican who had run against Federalist candidates for both national and state office, Justice Story was nevertheless an admirer of Hamilton and a member of the so-called nationalist school of American legal thought, whose greatest exponent was Story's mentor on the Supreme Court, Chief Justice Marshall. Behaving more like an advocate of Whiggery than a disciple of the Democracy whose early affiliation had been responsible for his appointment to the court by President Madison, Story became to President Jackson "the most dangerous man in America." [13]

Part of Story's discussion of seating the Cabinet in Congress was based on his reaction to the analysis of William Rawle, a Philadelphia attorney of conservative leanings who, although exhibiting decided Loyalist sympathies during the Revolution, did not believe that the American government should follow the example of the British executive and House of Commons. In 1825 Rawle first published his *A View of the Constitution of the United States of America.* Its demand as a textbook resulted in a second edition in 1829.

In a chapter entitled "Of Incompatible Offices," Rawle had stated that the Founding Fathers were wise to exclude as a matter of "general policy . . . some of the executive officers, below the president, from seats in either house." [14] Considering the English arrangement, he had noted that, while some benefit might be obtained from the information derived from executive officers in the House of Commons, "this small advantage is counterbalanced by the influence they possess there" and in particular by the fact that the Commons which once prided itself as "keeper of the purse" was now merely a vehicle by which those who drew up the budget might secure the ready approval of it.[15] In addition, Rawle held that "the executive acts of the president, except in the two instances where the senate participates, are unshared with others, and the highest officer under him can constitutionally no more explain or account for them than any other individual." [16] By communicating with Congress in writing, the President protected himself from "the misapprehensions of others" and "the sudden, and sometimes unguarded, answers returned to the verbal interrogations of the members of the house of commons in Great Britain." [17]

Rawle also voiced an argument which would be noted occasionally by future opponents of seating the Cabinet in Congress, namely, that if a department head had sufficient time to appear before either house to answer questions, then he did not have enough work to do. More work should be given him or his office should be combined with the work of another department.[18] To Story, the appearance of department heads in Congress meant not a waste of time, but rather an improvement in the quality of presidential appointments to the Cabinet. The Chief Executive would be compelled

to make appointments for the high departments of government, not from personal or party favourites, but from statesmen of high public character, talents, experience, and elevated services; from statesmen, who had earned public favour, and could command public confidence. At present, gross incapacity may be concealed under official forms, and ignorance silently escape by shifting the labours upon more intelligent subordinates in office. The nation would be, on the other plan, better served; and the executive sustained by more masculine eloquence, as well as more liberal learning.[19]

Despite such persuasive arguments as both scholars exhibited, little attention was given them by the men of public affairs who were devoting their efforts to the more immediate problems of the currency, public works, the tariff, and slavery. As the complexity of the nation's problems increased with wars, gains in population, and westward expansion, the departments of government grew in size. Departmental officials soon learned that the cultivation of friendly relations with the influential members of both the legislative and expenditure committees of Congress would have more favorable immediate results than if they subjected themselves totally to presidential policy. Since some Chief Executives were relatively "policy-less," such conduct was not only expedient but necessary as well.[20]

There was increasing congressional recognition of the Cabinet's permanent status and the influence of department heads on the President. During the debate over the creation of the Department of the Interior in 1849, Senator James Mason remarked that the secretary "is to be a member of the Cabinet, and his voice is to have authority in the councils of the administration of the Government, in the management of all its affairs." [21]

Though Congress was not yet ready to reconsider admitting Cabinet officers to its own floor, in 1853 an attempt was made to guarantee each Cabinet member a well-constructed pacing area of his own. An amendment was offered to the annual civil and diplomatic appropriation bill which, had it been approved, would have authorized "the purchase of ground and the erection of suitable residences" for the department heads, at that time seven in number.[22]

IV

The Confederate Experiment

DURING THE SOCIAL and military upheaval of the Civil War, both the Union and the Confederate governments included strong individuals who advocated a different type of relationship than that which had existed previously between the heads of departments and the elected representatives of the people.

OLD QUESTIONS IN A NEW SETTING

The original seven seceding states of the Confederacy met at Montgomery, Alabama, early in February, 1861, and drew up a constitution for a provisional government. It was almost exactly parallel to the Constitution of 1787, except for the provision of a unicameral congress and the guarantee of slavery. No change was made at this time concerning the cabinet. As in the Constitution of the United States, the Confederate president was authorized to "require the opinion, in writing, of the principal officer in each of the executive departments, upon any subject relating to the duties of their respective offices." [1]

Within the month a second convention assembled at Montgomery and, by March 11, 1861, had adopted a permanent Constitution of the Confederate States of America. Alexander H. Stephens, a delegate from Georgia and provisional vice president of the Confederacy, proposed that an exception be added to the clause which prohibited an executive official from serving as a member of the legislature during his term in office. At the vice president's instigation, the following was added:

But Congress may, by law, grant to the principal officer in each of the Executive Departments a seat upon the floor of either House, with the privilege of discussing any measures appertaining to his department.[2]

Stephens, who had served in the House of Representatives from 1843 to 1859, a period encompassing Polk's dominance and Buchanan's weakness, also personally favored a provision which would have compelled the Confederate president to choose his cabinet from among the membership of congress. This attempt to merge a feature of the parliamentary system with the presidential system, whereby a single executive is responsible to the electorate rather than to their representatives, was not acceptable to the other delegates.[3]

In May, 1861, at a secret session of the provisional congress, Louisiana's John Perkins, Jr. introduced a resolution authorizing members of President Jefferson Davis's cabinet to be admitted to the floor to discuss measures pertaining to their departments. Approval of the resolution was secured after four states voted in favor, two against, and one divided on it.[4]

The secrecy of debates combined with the destruction of Confederate records when the war ended has prevented a careful analysis of the operation of this privilege. An opponent of the proposal when it was considered in later Confederate congresses admitted after the war that during its use under the provisional government he had "seen information obtained then in fifteen minutes" which during later sessions was not available for a month.[5] The durability of the Perkins resolution was only as great as that of the provisional congress, and the latter ended early in 1862 when the Confederate senate and house began to function under the mandate of the March constitution.

On March 19, 1862, a short time after the switch to bi-cameralism under the permanent government, a bill similar to the Perkins resolution was presented in the house. Discussion was vigorous. One member stated "that if the bill was passed he washed his hands of any evil that might henceforth accrue from its adoption." [6] This view predominated, since, despite token support and further debate the following day, the measure was "buried" behind closed doors.

Enough of the debate had been held in open session to arouse the interest of the leading newspapers. The *Daily Richmond Examiner,* edited by John M. Daniel and Edward A. Pollard, had been critical of Davis's cabinet for its lack of military and political leadership. The *Examiner* editorialized that, regardless of the merits on either side of the resolution, there was an overriding reason for approving its passage: "that of weaning these officers from their desks and bringing them into relations with the people." The Confederate government was vigorously and variously labeled as a "rigid and feeble imitation of the abominable concern at Washington," one "of routine and form, without genius or intellect," and "a vast depository of papers of infinite variety, bound in red tape, and preserved by a small army of animated automatons." The seating of the department heads in congress would "force every President, however jealous of talent and reputation, to place the strongest men of the country in his Cabinet, in order that they might cope in debate with the strong minds delegated by the people to the halls of Congress." The newspaper held faint hope for positive action since it regarded the congress as dominated by "imitative statesmanship" of a very low caliber and thus likely to avoid any novel features which, ironically enough, had not been sanctioned previously by the Northern enemy.[7]

JEFFERSON DAVIS AND SENATOR WIGFALL

The failure of the forces of Robert E. Lee to pursue General John Pope's retreating federal army following the Battle of Manassas, on August 30, 1862, brought the Davis administration under increasing criticism not only from the newspapers but also from generals in the field and politicians at home. President Davis had been at the battlefield and taken part in the conference which prevented a follow-up of the victory.[8] The principal critic of Davis in the senate was Texas's Louis Trezevant Wigfall, whom R. M. T. Hunter, president pro tempore of the senate, described as "that erratic child of genius and misfortune."[9] Thomas R. R. Cobb, who wrote frequently to his wife between sessions of the Montgomery constitutional convention, characterized Wigfall as promising to be "troublesome," "half drunk all the time and bullies and blusters about everywhere."[10]

Though Wigfall's antagonists might deny him many of the virtues possessed by calmer men, they could not dismiss his great energy and activity. As a prewar senator in Washington, he had been one of the most extreme secessionists. When the first shot was fired at Fort Sumter, Wigfall was watching from the shore and even went to the beleaguered fortress to demand its surrender. Accompanying the newly inaugurated Jefferson Davis—with whom he would later violently disagree —Wigfall, as an aide-de-camp, received the cheers of the enthusiastic crowds that lined the tracks waiting for the presidential train. Still later, as a military hero and general, Wigfall led the Texas Brigade in battle against Union troops. But it was not long before the military opinions of the Texan "fire-eater" clashed with those of Davis. The president—as a graduate of West Point, aide to Zachary Taylor during the

Mexican War, and secretary of war under Franklin Pierce—
had definite strategic and tactical ideas of his own.[11]

When the opportunity came to be a senator from Texas,
Wigfall hastily transferred his field of battle from the front
to congress. His target was Davis, whom a number of
legislators desired to strip of military power. The senator was
in constant communication with many of the field generals,
such as P. G. T. Beauregard, Joseph E. Johnston, and James
Longstreet, toward all of whom the Richmond administration
was cool. In November, 1862, Longstreet, hearing that Wigfall
had had an unpleasant interview with Davis, urged him not
to antagonize the president: "We think that all of our hopes
rest upon you and the hopes of the country rest upon the Army
—you will readily perceive what weight you have to carry." [12]

During January, 1863, Wigfall submitted a bill (S. 6),
similar to the house resolution of the previous year, which
would allow the participation of cabinet members in senate
debate.[13] The measure was referred to the judiciary committee,
whose chairman was Georgia's Benjamin H. Hill.

If one could expect anything to be predictable, it would be
that Hill would show nothing but hostility to any idea that
had originally been sponsored by Vice President Alexander
Stephens. Back in 1856, a debate between Hill and Stephens
had resulted in a challenge to an "affair of honor" by the latter,
who though of frail body was of quick temper. At the time,
Hill told friends that he must decline, since he had both a
family to support and a soul to save, while the volatile Stephens
lacked both. Stephens's reply was to advertise in the local press
that Hill was "not only an impudent braggart but a despicable
poltroon besides." [14]

In addition to personal rivalry before the war, Hill and
Stephens differed on policy during the conflict. Although
Stephens was the vice president, and consequently had a duty
to preside over the senate, he often remained away from the

capital for months at a time owing to his disagreement with many of Davis's policies.[15] Hill had become the leading senate defender of the President.[16]

"Common sense" would expect Wigfall and Hill to be on opposite sides concerning the cabinet bill. But men's motivations cannot always be discerned by using such a simple and vague criterion. And men with differing ends—Wigfall and Stephens against the administration and Hill for it—often resort to similar means. Hill, as judiciary committee chairman, narrowly secured a favorable report for the legislation with a vote of 3 to 2.[17]

Floor debate did not occur until March, 1863. Then Landon C. Haynes, of Tennessee, offered an amendment which aimed at striking from the bill its essential clause giving the cabinet officer "the privilege of discussing any measures appertaining to his Department." The Haynes amendment was carried 14 to 10, with Wigfall and Hill both voting against it and for the original proposal. The senate then approved postponement of the legislation indefinitely.[18]

The primary argument of the bill's proponents was that it would bring the department heads into a more responsive relationship with public sentiment. The opposition, on the other hand, saw only "collisions in debate," "heated personal differences," and increasing partisanship if the Wigfall idea was put into operation.

Although Wigfall was obviously anti-administration, an analysis of the later voting patterns of the senators who supported his bill showed that most of them remained more loyal to President Davis than did those who voted against the measure. Of the ten senators who voted for allowing the cabinet to participate in debate, seven were still in office in 1865. Six of those could be expected to vote with the administration more often than against it. The seventh was Wigfall.

Fourteen senators had voted against the Wigfall bill. Of

these, eight were in office in 1865 and seven of these usually voted against the Davis program.[19] The eighth was Edward Sparrow who backed the president most of the time. Sparrow had cast his vote against the Wigfall bill, although he had introduced the motion which placed the clause authorizing such a procedure in the Confederate constitution.

Senator Landon C. Haynes, who had offered the amendment which effectively killed Wigfall's bill, a year previously had voted against the confirmation of Stephen R. Mallory as secretary of the navy and for reconsideration of Judah P. Benjamin's appointment as secretary of state. Interestingly enough, Wigfall had voted for the two men.[20] This fact and the previous analysis of the two groups' voting behavior suggests that the main opposition to Wigfall's bill came from those senators who intensely disliked the members of the Davis cabinet and possibly feared that the administration would gain in influence if its department heads were granted privileges of the floor. Wigfall's fiery nature certainly would not have been subdued by the presence of executive officers and, in fact, undoubtedly would have thrived on the opportunity for argument.

During the debates, the opinion of the executive branch never was revealed. In his memoirs, written over a decade after peace had come to the battlefields, Jefferson Davis hailed the constitutional clause that sanctioned Wigfall's procedure as a "wise and judicious provision, which would have tended to obviate much delay and misunderstanding." However, there is no record of his opinion while the discussion was taking place.[21]

Although the Southern senators were not willing to listen to the department heads debate, they raised no objection to the cabinet members' entering onto the floor and discussing departmental affairs with individual legislators. Even while the Wigfall bill was under consideration, a resolution had been approved which at least permitted the cabinet inside the senate railing.[22]

THE FIRST ATTEMPT TO LIMIT CABINET TENURE

Following the repulse of Robert E. Lee's once feared Army of Northern Virginia by Union forces at Gettysburg, in July, 1863, the ability of the South to impose its will on the North seemed indeed remote. When the Confederate congress re-assembled in the late autumn of 1863, they were "in a very bad humor," according to Robert Kean, head of the bureau of war.[23]

The ever present antagonism of many members toward the Davis cabinet exhibited itself in a bill (S. 150) offered by Senator Robert W. Johnson, of Arkansas, on December 10, 1863. The Johnson bill provided that the term of office of the department heads would be the same as that of members of the house, and though still subject to removal at the president's pleasure, would expire definitely at the conclusion of each congress.[24] If the bill passed, Davis would be required to renominate his cabinet at least once every two years. The intent was to compel the president to take into account public opinion and congressional sensitivity before forwarding his nominations for senate consideration.

The Johnson measure was correctly viewed by the bu-reaucracy and the administration as "a direct attack on Mr. Davis, so intended and regarded." Kean, whose position as head of the war department's administrative services placed him in close contact with the secretary, noted that Wigfall had informed him on December 13, 1863, that the bill would probably pass. It was an obvious move to make department heads dependent on the senate. Kean believed that Johnson had acted as a result of a "very foolish offense towards the

Secretary of War because the Trans-Mississippi was not referred to in his report of last year, prepared a few days after he came into office." [25] Though the legislation had perhaps resulted from such a petty motive, the responsive support it gained in the senate showed that there were deeper currents of discontent.

The Johnson bill was referred on December 17, 1863, to Hill's committee on the judiciary for study.[26] While the measure was being considered there during the Christmas and New Year holidays, some hope grew among administration supporters that the legislation would not clear the senate, though they admitted that the bill would have, had it been pressed when initially introduced. Wigfall, however, was still convinced that it would pass.[27]

On January 14, 1864, Senator Thomas J. Semmes, who had voted for the Wigfall bill the previous year, favorably reported the Johnson measure for the majority of the judiciary committee. There was also a minority report—a minority of one, Benjamin H. Hill, interestingly enough the committee chairman and faithful defender of Davis.

The majority report deserves consideration not merely because it proclaimed the full constitutionality of biennial congressional review of the cabinet, but more significantly because of the relationships it described between the congress, president, and department heads.[28] The senators denied that a "cabinet" in the sense of a council of state was authorized by either the constitution or law. Any such gatherings of department heads were "the mere creations of executive pleasure," and could be composed "of unofficial persons, or be dispensed with entirely." [29]

In retracing the evolution of the departments during the Washington administration, the committee—with argument strange to modern political science, although not to the reasoning of Henry Clay—stressed that the department heads were "legislative officers, and their offices were subject to regulation by Congress, in every respect whatever, except as to the power of removal." [30] Semmes's group did not concede much in admitting the president's power of removal when they held, concerning the resolution of the issue by the First Congress of the United States, that:

Many distinguished statesmen considered this legislative decision of an important constitutional question unsatisfactory, especially as it had been carried in the United States Senate only by the casting vote of the Vice President. [31]

Since the departments were subject to law and these laws were passed by congress, the committee concluded that the cabinet members were not "solely" the organs of the executive. [32] Despite the framework of legalistic and constitutional rationalization, the essence of the committee's action was well-stated in their own words: "This bill, if passed, will prevent the retention for a longer period than two years of the head of a department who may become obnoxious to the country." [33] Seemingly replying to the 1862 accusation in the *Examiner* of "imitative statesmanship," the committee decried the opinion which held that because a proposed measure is novel, it is also objectionable. In an eloquent conclusion, the majority expressed its frustration and discontent with the *status quo:*

While respecting the experience of our predecessors, the committee entertain no superstitious reverence for the past. In the present state of our knowledge, politics, so far from being a science, is one of the most backward of all the arts. Politicians should modify their schemes, not according to notions of their ancestors, but to the actual exigencies of the times; for men, urged by a sense of their own progress, are growing weary of the idle talk about the wisdom of their ancestors. [34]

The committee soon would find that what some viewed as exigencies of progress, others would view as schemes of disruption.

Benjamin Hill, in his minority report, while not arguing that Johnson's plan was clearly forbidden by the constitution, did object to what he regarded as an inconsistency with the time-honored separation of powers.[35] The president alone is responsible for the acts of his cabinet officers. To make the cabinet's tenure also dependent on the congress would result in a weakening of their accountability to the chief executive.[36]

Paradoxically, Hill relied on the arguments that had been used by the opponents of Wigfall's legislation to admit the cabinet officers to the senate—a plan which Hill favored. Now, he believed—apparently with the hope that the Confederacy might still survive following the defeat which even in early 1864 many could see coming—that the parties sure to evolve in peacetime would breed "strifes, acrimony, and bitterness." Then if the Johnson measure were in effect, the commencement of each congress would

witness a disgraceful struggle for the cabinet. If the President . . . [were not] of the dominant party, he may find himself without a cabinet, or be forced to accept one with whose feelings and opinions he is utterly at variance.[37]

For Hill, the measure was "radical, new, and untried." [38]

After intermittent discussion during January and February, 1864, the Johnson bill to limit cabinet tenure was postponed without ever having come to a vote.[39] There was no postponement, however, in the attempt to change the Davis cabinet.

THE LAST ATTEMPT

During the remainder of 1864, the dissatisfaction of the congress with Davis and his cabinet seemed to increase in direct proportion to the mounting pressure and sledge-hammer blows aimed at the contracting Southland by the Northern armies and their newly appointed commander, Ulysses S. Grant.[40] By the middle of January, 1865, the Confederate government was confronting not only military catastrophe in the field but a political crisis in Richmond.

War Bureau Chief Kean noted on January 21, 1865, that during the previous week, "matters seem to be coming to a head between Congress and the President." The Virginia delegation in congress had adopted resolutions calling for a complete change in the Davis cabinet. As a result, War Secretary James A. Seddon, a native of Virginia, submitted his resignation on January 18.[41]

Another Virginian, House Speaker Thomas S. Bocock, informed the president that there had "been some discussion among the members of Congress in relation to the propriety of declaring by resolution that the country wants confidence in the cabinet as an administration." The speaker believed that such a resolution was likely to be offered and that three fourths of the members of the house of representatives were ready to support it. He advised Davis that "something must be done, and that promptly, to restore confidence and revive the hopes. . . ." The president noted in the margin of Bocock's letter: "It now is a warning, if not a threat." [42]

Almost two weeks later, on February 1, 1865, Davis replied at length in a firm but friendly manner to Seddon's letter of resignation. The president absolutely denied the congress any power or right to control the tenure of his cabinet. Avowing, without offering a method, that he was always willing to respond to "enlightened public opinion," Davis also denied that the congress necessarily reflected with accuracy such sentiment. After a cogent explanation of the differences between the parliamentary and the presidential systems, Davis held that since both the president and the congress derived their existence directly from the electorate, "it would be quite as proper for the Executive Department to express want of confidence in the Legislative Department as for the latter to express distrust of the former." Apparently, the congress recognized the traditional separation of powers dogma, otherwise it certainly would have admitted "the Heads of Departments . . . to the right of debate on subjects appertaining to their Departments as contemplated by the Constitution." [43]

The editors of the *Examiner* read the exchange between Davis and Seddon and concluded that "the country is going to ruin under gross and palpable maladministration." Defending the congress's attempt "to put somebody into confidential relations with the President, who should possess the confidence and know the feelings of the country," they condémned Davis for dealing in abstractions and not actions.[44]

During this governmental crisis, as the armies of the Blue and the Gray were rallying for their final stand, one last attempt was made to bring the cabinet onto the senate floor. On February 8, 1865, Missouri's Waldo P. Johnson introduced legislation (S. 186) similar to the Wigfall plan of two years before.[45] By now many senators might well have wished to query the department heads on some of the decisions which had affected the conduct of the war. But it was too late, and the proposal was lost in the chaos of a government shortly to go into retreat and then soon to cease altogether.

As in the North, the necessities of war produced great conflict between the legislative and the executive. While there is confusion as to the actual success of cabinet contact with the Confederate congress, for a short period under the provisional government department heads did come to the floor to discuss legislation.[46] This procedure was not renewed in either the senate or the house once the permanent constitution took effect. Although congress was authorized by this constitution to pass legislation admitting the cabinet to the floor for debate, it never did; whereas, ironically, when such a procedure was not constitutionally sanctioned—as during the existence of the provisional government—congress invited the department heads to participate in its deliberations simply by approving a resolution.

(v)

The First Pendleton Bill

WAR—WITH ITS NECESSITY for rapid government expansion and the need to arrive at decisions which determine individuals' life or death and a nation's salvation—creates great tension not only on the battlefield but in the processes of government itself. Men and circumstances cause even greater inroads to be made into the myth that under the government of the United States the legislature "makes" the policy and the executive merely "implements" it.

The Civil War was no exception to this general pattern; on the contrary, it was an intensification of it. To maintain the Constitution, the Union itself must first be saved—and such a deliverance might have to be attained by means of doubtful constitutional validity.

A series of weak Presidents following James Polk had aided the ascendancy of Congress over the Executive. What schoolboy remembers Zachary Taylor, Franklin Pierce, and James Buchanan so well as Henry Clay, Daniel Webster, and Stephen A. Douglas?

LINCOLN AND CONGRESS

Then came the war, and the unequal *status quo* was reversed. Lincoln ordered money to be spent without prior congressional appropriation; in certain areas the privilege of the writ of habeas corpus was suspended; a call for troops was issued that exceeded by thousands the authorized allotment set by Congress. These were but a few of the major shifts in policy. In their wake came thousands of daily decisions by strong Cabinet leaders such as Secretary of State William Seward and a year later Secretary of War Edwin M. Stanton. The Congress's feeling of importance and responsibility was imposed upon further when the members were not even called into session until months after the shooting had started.[1]

The animosities within the Cabinet which were to manifest themselves in the relations between individual department heads and Congress have been described succinctly by Hilary A. Herbert, Cleveland's secretary of the navy, who drew upon the diaries of Gideon Welles, his wartime counterpart in the Lincoln administration:

The troubles Abraham Lincoln had with his advisers: his Secretary of State, Seward, assuming the airs and presuming to exercise the authority of a British premier until Mr. Lincoln's friends in Congress revolted and demanded the dismissal of the Secretary; Mr. Lincoln placating the Congressmen and retaining Seward; Seward and Secretary Stanton conspiring to obtain control; Secretary of the Treasury [Salmon P.] Chase counterplotting; Secretary Stanton giving or withholding from the President army news and plans at his own will and pleasure; Chase and Stanton each habitually taking President Lincoln into a corner of the room to whisper to him while the other members sat waiting around the cabinet table; Chase and Seward both candidates for the Presidency against Mr. Lincoln, and Mr. Lincoln retaining them both in office, although he well knew that each of them was using the patronage of his office to further his own ambitions.[2]

When Lincoln had announced his Cabinet selections to close friends on election night, 1860, someone replied: "They will eat you up." While Herbert's description might lead one to support that prophecy, Lincoln's response accurately predicted what did happen: "They will be just as likely to eat each other up."[3] He might have gone further and added, "Congressional leaders and the Cabinet will also attempt to devour each other."

The requirements of military secrecy—made more necessary

than usual with the enemy just across the Potomac River and spies infesting the capital city—meant that the decisions of the government could not always be aired in the halls or committee rooms of Congress. A few congressional leaders, such as the Republican chairmen of the various important committees, might be taken into confidence. But most of the senators and representatives had to discover the policy of the administration by reading the newspapers. It was obviously difficult for the typical congressman to adjust to such a reduction in status from the days of Webster, Clay, and Calhoun when issues were openly debated for several weeks or even months in an effort to decide national policy.

While the Republican leadership of Congress was better informed than the rest of the party's representatives, the assorted factions of Democrats—some of whose members were still "suspect"—were even less informed by the administration. It is not surprising then that a member of the minority party would attempt to create some mechanism by which Congress as a whole, and his party in particular, could become more knowledgeable regarding the policies of the government and perhaps even actively participate in the critical examination of those policies at the planning stage. Even if the policy was in process of implementation, an opportunity to remedy what the minority might regard as "grievances" would be fruitful. Hopefully, a large number of the majority party's followers would give tacit or even active support to the development of such a mechanism.

THE SUBMISSION OF PENDLETON'S BILL

On February 3, 1864, three months before Grant's lunge toward Richmond and over a year before the end of the war, Ohio Representative George Hunt Pendleton, one of the leaders of the Peace Democrats, rose in the House to make a unanimous consent request. The chair granted recognition and Pendleton asked permission "to introduce a bill to provide that the Secretaries of Executive Departments may occupy seats on the floor of the House of Representatives." A possible solution to securing information for Congress and reversing the trend of power toward the executive had appeared. The immediate objection of Representative William Steele Holman prevented either enthusiastic approval or vigorous dissent from being uttered, as the bill, at least momentarily, was blocked from introduction.[4] But the idea had been voiced, and the man who would be its most active sponsor in the House—and fifteen years later in the Senate—was revealed.

Pendleton, known to some as "Gentleman George" because of his unfailing courtesy and quiet dignity, had sat on the same platform as ex-Congressman Clement L. Vallandigham, the Ohio "Copperhead." In agreement with the latter, he believed that war between the states could have been averted. Pendleton had objected to such major administration actions as the suspension of the privilege of the writ of habeas corpus and the advocacy of legal tender. Attempts to subordinate the civil functions of government to those of the military were particularly onerous to his critical mind.[5]

Within a week, on February 8, 1864, Pendleton was able to introduce his bill (H.R. 214).[6] The measure was read twice, and on the following day the Speaker announced a special select committee of seven to which the proposal was referred for analysis and a report. Since Pendleton had authored the bill, he was selected to preside. Other members included Thaddeus Stevens, the aged chairman of the powerful Committee of Ways and Means; Justin Smith Morrill, author of the famed Land Grant Act of 1862; Robert Mallory, a representative from Kentucky; John Adam Kasson, who had been first assistant postmaster general when the Lincoln administration began and was now serving his first term in Congress; John Ganson, of New York, also serving his initial term; and James G. Blaine, now a newcomer, who in a few years would be Speaker, secretary of state, and a perennial candidate for the Presidency. Ganson and Mallory, like Pendleton, were Democrats.[7]

SUPPORT FROM THE PRESS

During the next two months the select committee met several times to consider the Pendleton bill. Two technical changes were made in the original suggestion, and the committee agreed to report the plan favorably to the House.

Before discussion had occurred on the floor, the New York *Times* in an editorial appearing on March 23, 1864, answered affirmatively its own question: "Shall cabinet officers have seats in the House?"[8] The editorial proclaimed that the Pendleton proposal "would remedy a great defect in our national system of legislation." The *Times* saw "no good reason why our Congress should be the only representative body of any nation that is deprived of personal communication with those to whom is intrusted the administration of the affairs upon which the body legislates."

Noting that historically a jealousy of the executive and fear of undue presidential influence had prevented the department heads from appearing before Congress, the editor stated that the enactment of the current scheme would reduce executive influence "because it would make the Executive power more directly accountable." This accountability would be achieved through interpellation before the full House, a more effective means of examining departmental policy than the numerous resolutions of inquiry now passed which so often elicited an inadequate response, if any. When Cabinet officers appeared on the floor, evasion could be exposed by alert questioning.

In addition, the *Times* saw a change that was of even higher value than the accountability of executive officials, and this was the promotion of "the enlightenment of Congress upon the subject-matter of its legislation." No longer would information come to the floor secondhand from a committee member who, no matter how interested, would usually be less informed than the department official who constantly grappled with the subject matter. "It is time," concluded the editor, "that this groping in the dark . . . should cease." [9]

Within a week additional editorial support was elicited in response to a letter from "S.J.B.," who questioned whether Congress could admit Cabinet officers to the floor even if they were not given the right to vote. Such a change would seem to violate "the letter and spirit" of the clause in the Constitution which reads "no Person holding any Office under the United States, shall be a member of either House during his Continuance in Office." [10] "S.J.B." urged that the Constitution was designed to prevent influence from a co-equal branch, and the presence of members of the administration would have no other reason than to influence.[11]

The editor disagreed that the Constitution sought to prevent such pressure by the executive. He reminded his reader that the Constitution provided that the President "shall" report to Congress on the state of the Union.[12] Since the end was clear, the means should be the most effective. Would it be any violation of the spirit of the Constitution if the President chose to provide Congress with the necessary information through his secretaries?

The *Times* further elaborated its position by stating that it would be quite willing to see each Cabinet member's right to speak limited to questions affecting his own department. "We do not believe that they ought to mingle in general debate." [13]

REPORT OF THE SELECT COMMITTEE

Pendleton reported to the House on April 6, 1864, that the select committee had completed its work and that he would like the majority and minority reports on H.R. 214 to be printed and recommitted to the committee. He assured his Democratic colleague from Indiana, William Steele Holman, that he did not propose any "hasty action" and would only call up the bill after due notice, when it suited the convenience of the House.[14]

Only the majority report was printed. It included an explanation of the purpose and benefits of the proposal, the procedure through which it would be implemented, and a discussion concerning the constitutionality of the plan. Also cited were alleged historical instances of the participation by department heads in congressional proceedings, a comparison of similar provisions in the constitutions of seventeen foreign countries, and some extracts from recent House debates which presumedly revealed how the Cabinet was currently influencing legislation.[15]

The essence of H.R. 214 was that Cabinet officers were to have the right to occupy seats on the floor of the House and participate in debate concerning the activities of their respective departments. At a minimum, the Cabinet would attend the House at the beginning of Monday and Thursday sessions in order "to give information in reply to questions which may be propounded to them under the rules of the House." The committee also submitted several amendments to the House Rules which would establish procedures for the handling of the Monday and Thursday appearances of the departmental executives.[16]

Under the revised Rules, the Clerk of the House would maintain a notice book containing resolutions and questions which required a response from any member of the Cabinet. The name of the representative who desired the information and the date on which the reply was scheduled would also be recorded. Answers were to be made by the Cabinet member the week following notification by the clerk, and no reply could be demanded in less than three days without securing the unanimous consent of the House. A duplicate of the notice book entry would be sent to the department so that the material could be prepared for the use of the secretary.

When the Monday or Thursday session came, the questions —except for unanimous consent requests—were to be taken up in the order in which they had been initially introduced. The sponsor of the query was to state the purpose of his particular resolution and then the Cabinet officer would either respond with the necessary information or provide his reasons for refusing to reply.

Regardless of the official's answer or lack of one, the House would vote on the resolution which requested the information unless the sponsor, satisfied with the reply, withdrew it. "No argument or opinion" was to be offered with reference to questions asked on the floor except as necessary to clarify the original query. Debate was to be avoided, and both executive and legislator would be required to state only those facts and opinions which aided in the explanation of the initial answer.

The Pendleton committee pointed out that the appearance of the officials on the floor of the House would not make them members of that body since they would have no vote; consequently, the constitutional provision against holding a dual office in both legislative and executive branches would not be violated. The constitutionally specified power of each House to determine the rules of its own proceedings was held to authorize the recommended deviation from precedent. The committee reminded the House that many nonmembers had the privilege of the floor and cited contestants in disputed elections, territorial delegates, and the secretary of the treasury under the law of 1789, which permitted him to provide information "in person or in writing."

As to the legality of the bill in terms of the supreme law,

the committee held "no doubt of the power of Congress to pass this resolution." The "separation of powers" argument was anticipated by noting that if absolute separation were intended, the framers would never have allowed the President to participate in legislative activity through his veto or State of the Union message.[17]

Congress must avail itself of the "best possible means of information," said the Pendleton group. More particularly, no doubt having various contemporary experiences in mind, the members suggested that the executive influence on the legislative branch "should be open, declared, and authorized, rather than secret, concealed, and unauthorized." [18] The debates on Civil War financial proposals were used as a timely illustration of the less desirable practice.[19]

The committee, like the *Times*, did not think that the executive would be able to exert more influence if H.R. 214 became law. Rather, by bringing executive pressure into the open, the President's advisers would be rendered more accountable and the current trend of diminishing congressional power would be reversed.[20]

A shaky historical limb provided the support for part of the report when it was held that:

In the early days of the government the propriety, even the right, of calling directly on the head of an executive department, was seriously questioned, and solemnly debated. The right was fully established, but the practice has generally been to call upon the President.[21]

While it was true that the provision authorizing the secretary of the treasury's appearance in person had never been repealed, it was equally correct that the first time an attempt was made to utilize this power, the effort was obstructed for various reasons. In any event, the law applied only to the treasury and not to the remainder of the departments.

Perhaps a more brittle twig was grasped when the committee detailed the various instances of Cabinet officers' appearing on the floor of Congress. That they were physically present, as has been shown, there can be no doubt. There is some question, however, as to the extent of their actual participation in the oral give-and-take of the legislative process. The incompleteness of the early records makes it uncertain for many of these appearances whether they were merely for the delivery of messages or involved active participation in discussion.[22]

PENDLETON AS A "LAME DUCK"

At this juncture the pressure of important legislation such as the currency bill and departmental appropriations as well as the quadrennial desire of the politicians to get out of Washington and to the political conventions combined to sidetrack the Pendleton bill. There was no time available on the crowded calendar for any proposal which, in the opinion of some, might—at the least—be considered utopian and—at the worst—subversive of what they regarded as fundamental institutions.

On May 30, 1864, over a month before the completion of the First Session of the Thirty-eighth Congress, Pendleton secured the approval of the House to continue the select committee during the remainder of the Congress.[23] The basis had been laid for debate on the measure in the Second or lameduck Session which would commence on December 5, 1864, following the fall elections.

Pendleton's activities were transferred to a new arena as the Democratic convention met in Chicago on August 29, 1864, to select its slate to compete for President. Although originally he had been opposed to the selection of "Tardy George" McClellan—formerly the cautious commander of the

Army of the Potomac—as the party nominee for the Presidency, "Gentleman George" agreed to be the general's running mate.

During the course of the 1864 campaign, some of Pendleton's legislative colleagues under the name of the Union [Republican] Congressional Committee issued—with definite partisan goals in view—a pamphlet charging the Democratic vice presidential candidate

upon the face of his record as a public man as having consented to a division of the country, . . . opposed the raising of armies to suppress the rebellion, . . . opposed the raising of revenue and loans to support our armies, . . . opposed the punishment of armed traitors and spies in the loyal States from the consequences of their crimes, by preventing the suspension of the writ of habeas corpus.[24]

By the middle of the nineteenth century, the House had become an institution in which it was possible for two legislators who had vehemently denounced each other on the floor over an issue of public policy to walk out together arm in arm to lunch. But the bitterness of the 1864 political campaign and the intensity of feeling which had been aroused by the Civil War created conditions such that one might expect a measure supported by a "Peace" Democrat to have difficulty securing approval, no matter what the particular merits of the proposal.

Further complications arose as the lameduck session (in which Pendleton, who had been defeated in his race for the House as well as for the vice presidency, was lamer than most) opened on December 5, 1864. Awaiting the arrival of the victorious Republicans and the unhappy Democrats when they straggled in to the opening meeting was a message from President Lincoln advocating the passage of a constitutional amendment abolishing slavery. The battle for adoption was led by Thaddeus Stevens, who though now seventy-two years of age was crossing the threshold of an era that would bear the unforgettable imprint of his actions.

Early in January, 1865, Pendleton, as minority leader in the House, took the floor and in one of his more impassioned addresses—looking directly at Stevens—defended the position of the South on the slavery issue. Two days later, on January 13, Stevens replied and in the course of his remarks prophesied that the Ohio representative's epitaph would read: "Here rests the ablest and most pertinacious defender of slavery and opponent of liberty." [25]

Despite undoubted personal antipathy for Pendleton, Stevens, who had served on the select committee which considered H.R. 214, never voiced an opinion in the House as to his position on the bill. Since he did not dissent vocally, as was the case with Representative Morrill, Stevens may be assumed to have given his tacit support, probably realizing that the bill had little chance of passing. During the Reconstruction period which was to come, he might well have regretted the inability to call members of the Johnson Cabinet to the floor for extensive interrogation. But in 1865, the coming firebrand of the radicals was too wily a politician to bother himself with what might be regarded as a very secondary matter, given the present necessities.

THE DEBATE

A week before Sherman began his march north from Georgia —as the power of the Confederate forces was rapidly being scattered and crushed—Pendleton after several interruptions called up H.R. 214. The debate had begun.

Single-termer John Ganson of New York, himself a member of the committee and a fellow Democrat, explained Pendleton's proposal to the representatives. The primary reason for approving the change, urged Ganson, was that the direct communication which developed between the House and the executive departments would mean more information, less behind-the-scenes solicitation, and an opportunity for Congress "to detect faithlessness in its officers." The Pendleton bill "is a direct step toward the people and the security of popular rights." [26]

The first opposition appeared when another member of the select committee, Vermont's Justin Smith Morrill, after apologizing for not having had time to prepare a written minority report, charged that the whole scheme "results from a study and admiration of the British example." Morrill believed that the plan was "opposed to the genius of our institutions" and that it would be "cumbrous, expensive, and unwarranted by the Constitution." [27]

Reflecting on the probable consequences if Cabinet officers were permitted to participate in discussions before the full House, Morrill predicted that either some of the opposition would delight in putting the administration through "the torture of a cross-examination" or, alternatively, the head of an executive department would exhibit such an amount of persuasive power that many bills would be passed which were really devoid of merit. Furthermore, should the services of capable executives be debarred because they might not be able to render an impressive performance in debate? The current difficulty with respect to information from the executive departments, believed Morrill, was that Congress had much which was "too voluminous and too minute to be reasonably read." [28] In this conclusion proponents of both the Pendleton and—eighty years later—the Kefauver plans would agree. But they would add that since the bulk of executive reports goes unread, the appearance of Cabinet officers on the floor of the House would provide the bridge necessary for an understanding of the great governmental functions by the overburdened congressman.

Turning to the constitutional issue, Morrill queried, "If the Secretary should refuse to appear, what are you going to do about it?" The Constitution had provided that only "members" could be punished by the House. Were department heads to be members? If so, another constitutional provision prevented an individual from holding an office in both the legislative and executive branches at the same time.[29] If not, he implied, what sanctions would Congress be able to impose to enforce compliance with the new rule?

Morrill passed over the possibility that Cabinet members did participate during the First Congress by holding that even if they did, the House and Senate were engaged in executive and not legislative sessions. Concerning the authorization under which the House could invite the secretary of the treasury to appear in person, Morrill held that since the practice had never been utilized, there could be little doubt regarding its wisdom. Then in a flowery conclusion, he avowed that the House should never debase "the luster of its republicanism" by departing from "fundamental law as well as . . . our most revered traditions" through contact with the "executive alloy." [30]

Maine Republican James G. Blaine took issue with his New England neighbor, Morrill, and chided him for the statement that the House would have no power to compel the attendance of Cabinet officers if it desired. What about impeachment? queried the "Man from Maine." Morrill failed to see how a refusal to talk was a misdemeanor, one of the constitutional criteria to be met in order to bring a charge. Answered Blaine, if a "contemptuous disregard and defiance of law does not constitute a misdemeanor, what does?"

James F. Wilson, who was chairman of the committee on the

judiciary, asked to what tribunal Blaine would take an action by the House against an executive officer. Nonlawyer Blaine responded to lawyer Wilson that the Constitution holds that a civil officer can be removed by impeachment and that the House and Senate would handle the case, one body bringing the charge, the other trying it as would a jury.[31] This statement provided an amusing exit, as Representative Robert C. Schenck inquired if Wilson considered the Secretary of War a "civil officer." Uproarious laughter greeted this jab at the unpopular, but vigorous, Edwin M. Stanton. Wilson replied that he did "not consider that a very civil question."[32]

The levity continued the next afternoon when Pendleton's fellow Ohioan and Democrat, Samuel Sullivan Cox, who also had been defeated for reelection, objected both seriously and jocularly to the proposal. He held that the enactment of H.R. 214 would violate the spirit if not the letter of the Constitution.[33]

Cox did not expect public debate to prevent secret intrigue. Certainly it would not reduce the influence of the executive upon the legislative; in fact, "it is a step toward the absorption of the power of Congress by the Executive."[34] Furthermore, he did not approve of the timing of the measure since during war the executive tended to enlarge its powers.

In a concluding half hour of emotionalism, Cox acclaimed the greatness of the American system of government and denounced that of the British. Possibly, such laudatory comments on the American republic came as a surprise to many Republicans who knew Cox only as a supporter of Vallandigham. They were not above suspecting that he might seek to undermine the Constitution and perhaps even plant some powder kegs under the Capitol's foundation. As Cox's fervor increased, he not only ridiculed the British cabinet, but also the Tower, the patronage of the crown, and past beheadings. It was also apparent that he was as worried over the temptation of his colleagues to succumb to lobbies, speculators, and men of wealth as to any overpowering influence of the Cabinet.[35]

The Ohioan continued in a lighter vein with his speculation as to a future meeting of the Cabinet and Congress if the Pendleton bill became law. The secretaries would be seated next to the committee chairmen who were concerned with the business of their departments. Cox asked his listeners to picture how "lovingly" the secretary of state and the chairman of the committee on foreign affairs would act at such close quarters: one for Juárez and the other for Maximilian. Within minutes, Cox had all but one of the Cabinet seated at his mythical session. But wait, who was missing? A thundering rumble would sound in the corridor as the door was thrown open for the secretary of war (obviously he was thinking of Stanton), whose "flowing beard and spectacled face, so familiar to our eyes 'Assume the god, affect the nod, and seem to shake the spheres!' (Laughter)." [36] The questions which Cox had his fancied legislators asking his make-believe Cabinet stressed provincial rather than national policies. He believed that each member would be primarily concerned with such issues as tariff adjustment for protection of a small industry in his district.

James A. Garfield, classics professor, major general, and within fifteen years to be an assassinated President, scolded Cox for the lightness with which he had treated such "a grave measure." Garfield, disregarding the politician's concern for the potential Irish vote, focused on Cox's Anglophobia and urged that the House "in the discussion of this subject be equally free from that international jealousy, that hereditary hatred, so frequently and unreasonably manifested against Great Britain." [37]

Recalling Morrill's explanation of the action of the First Congress, Garfield next clarified the facts by stating that the question had never been whether or not Cabinet officers should appear in Congress, but rather whether Alexander Hamilton should submit his report in writing so that the members might better understand it. As for the St. Clair debate of 1792—during which, according to Morrill, Madison raised objections to the appearance of the secretaries in the House—the fact was that the Father of the Constitution never elaborated what those grounds were. And for the final thrust at the revival of Madison's 1792 stand, Garfield added:

It is a little remarkable that he who had in 1789 spoke and voted for the Treasury act authorizing the Secretary to report in person or in writing, as either House might direct, should declare only three years later that it was unconstitutional to let the Secretary come before the House to give information or testimony.[38]

Garfield was too charitable to suggest that sometimes the interpretation of what was and was not constitutional depended on whether one's friend or one's enemy was in power. By 1792, Madison was no longer as closely identified with Hamilton as in the days when they had collaborated on the *Federalist Papers*.

As for the constitutionality of H.R. 214, Garfield continued, the department heads were already communicating all the information which the bill contemplated. "It is only a question of mode. They now communicate with the pen. This resolution proposes to add the tongue to the pen, the voice to the document, the explanation to the text, and nothing more." [39] He urged his colleagues to take advantage of an opportunity to get action on requests for information instead of tolerating the situation which then confronted the House where "our table is groaning under the weight of resolutions asking information from the several Departments that have not been answered." [40]

But the future President was advocating more than a need for information: there was also the need for responsibility. Garfield saw no chance for a return to prewar "do-nothing" governments. Government would be stronger, and he, for one, was glad. The talents of the ablest men must be enlisted. Men with ability would be proud to assume responsibility for their acts and be held accountable: the weak shrink from such a challenge. He estimated that the bulk of current executive information came from petty officials and chief clerks who were unknown to Congress. With the enactment of the Pendleton bill, the heads of departments would have to become "thoroughly acquainted with the details of their office." [41] In a stirring appeal which revealed some of the desires of the intellectual in politics, Garfield—referring to the Cabinet officer appearing before Congress—exclaimed:

I want that head of Department to tell me why; I want him to appeal to my reason; . . . it is the silent, secret influence that saps and undermines the fabric of republics, and not the open appeal, the collision between intellects, the array of facts.[42]

He sensed that the temper of the House—whose immediate concern was the problem of ending the war and punishing the rebels—was not ready for the change. Yet, Garfield was convinced that some day a proposal such as Pendleton's would be approved. "When that day comes, I expect to see a higher type of American statesmanship, not only in the Cabinet, but in the legislative halls." [43]

Martin Russell Thayer, a Pennsylvania lawyer and, like Wilson, a committee (Private Land Claims) chairman, took issue. If the Pendleton measure was approved, the members of the Cabinet would be dependent on the will of the House when constitutionally they were responsible to the President alone. Turning toward Pendleton, Thayer expressed mock surprise that the House's "strict constitutionalist" had authored such a bill.[44]

Thayer, unlike those who opposed the idea for fear of seeing Congress swallowed by the executive, objected that the Pendleton plan would bring about "the destruction of the legitimate influence of the executive office." [45] He wondered if the desire of the department heads to curry congressional favor would cause them to be less responsible to presidential policy and thus become mere tools of the dominant legislative majority. Noting the experiment—or lack of one—with Cabinet officers in Congress which was presumedly occurring south of the Mason and Dixon line, Thayer inquired: "Why, then, should we tinker . . . or substitute for a plan which has stood the test of time and experience, the imaginary improvements of the anarchist of Montgomery?" [46]

And with that the diversion had ended. For the next month the House preoccupied itself with the creation of the Freedman's Bureau and tax legislation.

On January 30, 1865, the New York *Times* reviewed the two-day airing of opinion in an editorial entitled "English Precedents and American Practice." Mr. Morrill was the target as the *Times* pointed out that far from being "incongruous to republican institutions," having the Cabinet officers give information in Congress would in reality be "a practice eminently democratic in its nature and bearings." "If anybody objects," continued the *Times,* "it ought to be on the ground that it is a step toward . . . pure democracy." [47]

INFORMAL DEFEAT

On March 2, 1865, after several unsuccessful attempts by Pendleton to gain the floor, Commerce Committee Chairman Elihu Washburne rose and reminded the House that Pendleton "has yielded to every member who requested him to do so," and added, "I think that we are crowding the gentleman from Ohio a little too far." Despite the diplomatic appeal of the future one-week secretary of state in the Grant administration, several Republican members objected to Pendleton's being allowed to speak for H.R. 214. A motion for the suspension of the rules so that Pendleton could address the House was passed by more than two thirds of the members present.[48]

The next day, March 3, 1865, the last day of the Thirty-eighth Congress, "Gentleman George" Pendleton addressed his colleagues at what was to be his last appearance in the Capitol for fourteen years, until he returned in 1879 as a senator from Ohio. He dealt at once with the question of his measure's constitutionality. For Pendleton, a favorable answer depended on the response to two questions, one involving the power of the House to invite to its floor anyone it chose, and the other, the power of Congress as a whole to impose appropriate duties on the heads of the executive departments.

In reply to those who were worried that the entry of the Cabinet onto the floor of Congress would violate the sacred province of the executive under the "separation of powers" doctrine, Pendleton reminded them that the executive in the United States was a single individual, the President. "He, and he alone, is the coordinate branch of the Government. Our law recognizes no council of state; our law recognizes no Cabinet. . . . The President, and he alone, is the responsible Executive" [49] Continuing, he recalled that although the President had the power of appointment of those officials, this privilege might be taken away from him by Congress. Department heads

are creatures of our law. Their offices are established, their duties prescribed, their term of office and their emoluments defined by our law; and they perform the duties we assign to them only by the powers we give them. We may repeal the law, and the offices fail.[50]

Basing his argument on authority, Pendleton cited excerpts from Henry Clay's speech delivered in the Senate when President Jackson removed the federal deposits from the Bank of the United States and placed them in various state banks. His ire aroused, the Great Compromiser had not been conciliatory concerning what he regarded as illegal action by an overly compliant secretary of the treasury. Said Clay:

Except the appointment of the officers with the cooperation of the Senate, and the power which is exercised of removing them, the President has neither by the Constitution nor by the law making the Department anything to do with it. The Secretary's reports and responsibility are directly to Congress. The whole scheme of the Department is one of checks, each officer acting as a control upon his associates. The Secretary is required to report, not to the President, but to Congress.[51]

Given this relationship between the departments and Congress and the precedent that information could be demanded from the various agencies, then the only remaining question was "the single one whether or not the means now used by resolutions of inquiry is preferable to that which the committee recommends." [52] For Pendleton, there could be only one answer to that question.

Ex-harness maker James F. Wilson, chairman of the powerful judiciary committee, climaxed the opposition arguments by describing the bill as an "infernal machine" that "out-Federals the Federalists" with its "open-browed, undisguised centralization." [53] Following his remarks, H.R. 214 was informally laid aside "according to the previous understanding that no action should be taken upon it." [54]

(VI)

The Tenure of Office Act

FOR ALMOST A DECADE and a half, the proposition that the heads of the executive departments should be allowed seats in both houses of Congress was to lie legislatively dormant, until George Hunt Pendleton—having spent ten years as president of the Kentucky Central Railroad—returned to Capitol Hill in 1879 as senator from Ohio. During this period there were infrequent letters in the newspapers from a handful of reformers who continued to advocate the idea. But the desire of the nation to return to "normalcy," the ascendancy of the Radicals in Congress over Johnson and Grant, and the increasing problems resulting from urbanization and industrialization caused people to concern themselves with matters closer to home, if they concerned themselves at all.

The breakdown in morality that frequently follows an era of tremendous national tension generated its own reaction. Reform movements, whether for temperance, change in the structure of state and local government, or just to "throw the rascals out," reasserted themselves. The "mugwumps" broke with the "standpat" Republicans. Democrats grew in numbers as the antipathies of the Civil War decreased and the "bloody shirt" dried.

A twenty-year period of potential congressional control over the Cabinet was enacted into law with the passage of the Tenure of Office Act in 1867. This statute, which had been introduced first into the House on December 3, 1866, was the handiwork of the congressional lion-tamer, Thaddeus Stevens.[1] It reversed the interpretation of the First Congress that the power of removal over executive appointments rested with the President alone. Now the power of removal was to be exercised only in concurrence with the Senate. During adjournment of the senators, the President was prohibited from removing a department head until he had called them back into special session.

The act was originally designed by the Radicals to insure that Lincoln's successor, Andrew Johnson, should not expel from his advisory council the obstreperous secretary of war, Edwin M. Stanton.[2] During the early winter of 1867 many pages of the *Congressional Globe* were filled with the opinions of senators as to the nature of both the President's and Congress's relationship with the heads of the executive departments. The principal advocate of closer ties between the Cabinet and Congress was Senator Timothy Otis Howe:

I deny that the Cabinet is the President's Cabinet, that it was intended so to be by law, that it ought to be in fact. It is the Cabinet of the people. . . . It is to enable him to exert powers and influences not given to him by the Constitution or by law that it is thought to be essential that he should have control of the tenure of these heads of Departments; and it is precisely because you cannot give him control of the terms of these officers, without giving him powers and influences which the Constitution never designed that he should have, that I object to leaving the control in his hands.[3]

Senator George H. Williams did not agree. He believed that the Cabinet was an integral part of the executive branch and that the President was responsible for any actions in which the department heads engaged.[4] Howe responded that it was more essential to the welfare of the nation to foster harmony between the Cabinet and the people (as represented by Congress) than between the Cabinet and a single individual, the President.[5] His position that "these heads of Departments ought to be independent of the power of the President"[6] was elaborated by Senator William Sprague in such emotional terms as adequately portray the temper of the Reconstructionist Congress. Sprague admonished:

When you have established a rule that the Cabinet officers of this Government must recognize the power of the Senate, subordinate officers will be relieved from the pressure that now unmans them and makes them slaves.[7]

The Tenure of Office Act was not officially repealed until 1887, after the Cleveland administration had been in power for two years. Even before this, the act's reason for existence had diminished following the failure of Johnson's impeachment, the election of Grant to the Presidency, the rise of factionalism within the Republican Party, and the consequent return to a more evenly balanced two-party system.

The revival of the Democratic Party as a national power was aided not only by factional fights within the Grand Old Party, but also by the removal of federal troops from the South and the dispersal of the militarily supported carpetbag governments. No longer would the Southern Negro vote be held for the party of Lincoln against the combined forces of the Klan's army and general apathy. Rutherford B. Hayes, who had withdrawn the last of the federal troops, was faced with a Democratic-controlled House during his whole term and, following the loss of a three-man Republican Senate majority, a Democratic Senate for his last two years in office.

Among the new senators returned to Washington by those midterm elections of 1878, which gave the Democrats control of both houses, was George Pendleton, who had put aside his railroad presidency for one more try at politics. In 1868, Pendleton had been deprived of the Democratic presidential nomination because of the obstinacy of the New York delegation who strongly objected to the Ohioan's conversion to "greenbacks." Under the well-known "two-thirds rule," which until its repeal in 1936 gave an organized minority powerful control in the Democratic convention, the views of New York prevailed. The following year, in 1869, Pendleton had been defeated for governor of Ohio by Rutherford B. Hayes, former Union general, now President.[8]

While out of office, Pendleton had continued his interest in the idea that Cabinet officers should be admitted to Congress. In 1878, he responded to a letter from President Hayes inquiring about his proposal.

Hayes's interest had been aroused following a meeting at the White House with the Boston reformer Gamaliel Bradford. Upon the latter's return home, he had written the President urging him to assume leadership in convincing the nation of the value of seating the Cabinet in Congress. Voicing many of the arguments used by the advocates in 1864, Bradford advised Hayes that "the appearance of Cabinet officers as private witnesses before the standing committees is inconsistent with the dignity of the executive, as a co-ordinate branch of the government."

Bradford, at that time still a Republican, hoped that the Chief Executive would "deprecate any reference to the report of Hon. Geo. H. Pendleton. That gentleman is a democrat and an inflationist." [9]

On March 1, 1878, Bradford again urged the reform on Hayes and hoped that the President would send a message to Congress stating "at some length the reasons for asking it so as to give the country an idea of what is wanted." The reformer granted that there might be little immediate effect, although he hopefully suggested "no one can tell what lightning it may draw from the cloud of public opinion." In any case, he reminded the President, such a message would "leave a splendid record for the future." [10]

A month later, on March 30, 1878, Hayes—overlooking Bradford's earlier admonition concerning Pendleton—wrote his former gubernatorial rival inquiring about the latter's 1864 bill. That evening the President noted in his diary that one of the four aspects of civil service reform which he might bring to the attention of the legislators included the seating of Cabinet officers in both houses so that they could participate in debate concerning their departments.[11]

Pendleton replied immediately. He emphasized that his measure was "clearly constitutional" both as to the letter and spirit since the bill had imposed on the Cabinet officers only "the *duty* of giving information, and the *privilege* of debating measures touching the subjects confided to their respective departments." Pendleton cited the argument of some of his friends who held that logically the proposal required the Cabinet to become members of Congress and also compelled them to resign their office when confronted with an adverse vote. With this reasoning he wholeheartedly disagreed. An outcome of that sort would require "an amendment of the Constitution and a very considerable change in the theory of our government as to the distribution of power." Concerning the advisability of reorganization along those lines, Pendleton believed "such amendment and change impracticable, even if they were clearly beneficial, which I cannot assert." [12]

No recommendation was ever made by President Hayes.

In April, 1878, before accepting the Senate bid, Pendleton had invited the rising New York Democrat, Perry Belmont, to Cincinnati to address the annual meeting of the American Social Science Association.[13] On May 22, 1878, Belmont gave his paper entitled "Executive Officers in Congress." It was very well received in the press.

Gamaliel Bradford, who had been converted to the proposal a decade earlier, also gave a paper advocating the same remedy.[14] Bradford generated more criticism, however, as one editor stated that his talk "hardly rose to the dignity and character of the occasion. The current newspapers of the day often have articles equally thoughtful." [15]

Pendleton was in the audience during both talks and supported the speakers from the floor. The Cincinnati *Daily Gazette,* which had been inclined favorably toward the Pendleton proposal in 1864–65, gave strong editorial support for the change. Although the editor believed that the practical implementation of the idea would have more far-reaching results than its advocates foresaw, he urged that the experiment be tried:

And the main reason is like that of the boys in the thunder storm, who declared that either praying or something had got to be done. Our Congress is now so lacking in rational organization, and so incapable of proceeding in a business way, that any change may be improvement.[16]

The *Gazette* objected to the Cabinet's becoming "like witnesses in a court, to be limited to categorical answers to questions, and to then have their answers left to the melee of the opposition attack, while they withdraw." Instead, the newspaper advocated the right of debate and predicted that a possible outcome of this privilege would be the President's selection of his Cabinet from the foremost leaders of his party in Congress. This development would mean "that the Executive is to take the leadership in the legislative body." And that change, the newspaper concluded, was both sound and long overdue.[17]

ing a sentiment that would have brought rapport with the ablest Grand Army of the Republic stump speaker, the former leader of the Peace Democrats recalled how Edwin Stanton, as secretary of war, had failed to reply to the House's request for data as to the exchange of prisoners. The War Department passed the resolution up and down its hierarchy while "the hearts of mothers and wives were bleeding and sick, emaciated prisoners, despairing because they believed they had been deserted, were dying, to whom this gleam of hope would have brought comfort and strength and health." [10]

Unlike proponents before and after him, Pendleton did not anticipate that the changes resulting from passage of his bill would "bring a higher order of intellect or morals into the public service." High caliber men were already in the public service. The problem was to bring the strongest of them into face-to-face contact with each other.[11] To those who argued that the department head was already overburdened and would not have the time necessary to appear before both houses, the senator's simple answer was that additional office help would have to be hired if necessary. Perhaps even an undersecretary who would be responsible for routine agency administration could be secured. He urged the secretaries to turn their full attention "to those duties which require intellectual activity and wise discretion" and away from "the harrowing and harassing cares of distributing clerkships." [12]

This would not be the Senator's last attack on the swarms of office seekers, one of whom, within a few years, would end the life of his fellow Ohioan, James A. Garfield. The spoilsmen, like locusts attacking an already drought-devoured field, descended on each incoming administration, virtually paralyzing the necessary government business in their quest for jobs and favors. Pendleton's interest in such civil service reform was to result in the perpetuation of his name as synonymous with the basic civil service act of the nation.

In closing his argument for S. 227, Pendleton denied the charge that the bill would mean "aping British ways." He then proceeded to deliver a major Anglophile oration.[13]

The old antagonist of 1864, Justin Smith Morrill, voiced his disapproval. Pendleton's pro-British eulogy that "the parliamentary history of England is the chief glory of the Anglo-Saxon race" probably added to the displeasure of Morrill, whose long dislike for Great Britain was reflected legislatively in his tariff views.[14]

Certainly another fundamental difference between the two men was that Morrill, solid as the granite of his native Vermont, consistently fought inflationary schemes such as legal tender legislation, while Pendleton now was a convert to "greenbackism." In addition, Morrill, who had already attained the half-way mark in his congressional career that was to span almost forty-four years and result in his being labeled "the Nestor of the Senate," was not about to tolerate a utopian scheme which might cause Congress "to drop to the plane of a theater for star performers drawn from the President's Cabinet." [15]

During his address, which "almost immediately completely emptied the Senators' and ladies' galleries," Morrill pledged not to repeat the objections he had made to the proposal over a decade and a half earlier.[16] But he then did just that.

Said the Vermonter: the bill would die now as it had before because it was "an unfragrant exotic, which here found no congenial soil or climate." [17] Morrill attacked Pendleton's logic and offered some illogic of his own. Where in the Constitution could one find warrant for this measure? A less courteous man than "Gentleman George" would have replied, "Right next to the spot which sanctioned your land grant colleges!"

Specifically, Morrill charged that while the House could make rules for its own members, it could not do so for outsiders. Territorial delegates were admitted under the power of Congress to regulate the territories, not under the power of both houses to make their own rules. Bubbling with analogies, Morrill compared Congress to a jury room. The intrusion of Cabinet officers onto the floor would be like admission of the rival attorneys into the jury's sanctuary.[18]

Assuming that Cabinet officers would have to be "members" of Congress in order to appear in either chamber, Morrill facetiously raised such questions as those concerning their privilege from arrest and protection against being questioned for what they said on the floor. His "insurmountable" objection was that the implementation of S. 227 would violate the constitutional clause prohibiting a person holding an office under the United States from concurrently being a member of the legislature.[19]

In concluding his predictions of the dire consequences which would ensue if the Pendleton plan were approved, Morrill offered a suggestion—probably in jest—which has been considered seriously by both students of government and leading politicians in the twentieth century. The senator advised that perhaps dual heads of the departments would be needed, "one for congressional service and another for departmental."[20]

The old gentleman saw no value in a scheme which he believed would result inevitably in a decline of congressional influence.

FURTHER SUPPORT FROM THE PRESS

A month before the debate had begun, one of Pendleton's hometown newspapers, the Cincinnati *Daily Gazette,* had given strong support to the senator's second attempt at passing his reform. The newspaper urged that the Cabinet be permitted to debate, and not merely be questioned. The *Gazette* predicted that if only the latter privilege were allowed, the result would be ridiculing of executives rather than granting them a position as "the natural leaders" of their party in Congress. The journal also believed that the quality of Chief Executives as well as department heads could be improved: invite the President himself to discuss his measures with the Congress.[21]

The Cincinnati *Commercial*, a rival of the *Gazette*, objected to having a "feature of the British system . . . engrafted on our own." The principal defect in American national government was not a dearth of information needed as a basis for congressional policy-making; rather the "chief defect is the neglect of Congressmen in availing themselves, by study, of the information furnished to their hands." [22]

The Washington *Post*, which was vociferously anti-Hayes, attacked the Anglophobia that had already manifested itself in some newspapers' comments on Pendleton's idea:

We can afford to borrow from any people, any government or any age, any governmental feature which experience has vindicated, and which may be adapted to our system with strong assurance of improving its general operations. With all its excellences, our governmental mechanism is not so good that no possible change in detail can make it better. Nor is the English system so bad that it may not be studied with profit by the most advanced statesmen of this Republic.[23]

The New York press provided powerful editorial support, just as they had during the Civil War. Horace White wrote in the *Nation* that the Pendleton measure was in the "highest class of political questions." The *Nation* labeled the bill's opponents as monarchical and noted with irony that those opposed usually favored the election of Grant to a third term. In that age of Social Darwinism, White foresaw that there was more to the idea than "a mere change of vehicles for the conveyance of information from the Departments to Congress." If the plan were approved, he predicted that a process of natural selection would evolve by which the party's "best interests" would be chosen for the Cabinet; the Senate and House provided the logical training area in which to develop this much-needed talent.[24]

In the period between the submission of the bill and the Pendleton-Morrill debate on it, the New York *Times* viewed the legislation with favor. The *Times* believed that S. 227 was not radical but "very moderate in its scope." The power which the bill sought to exercise already existed since the functions of the departments had been established and defined by Congress. Not envisioning any other consequences than those the proponents claimed, this newspaper viewed the possible change as a mere matter of improved communication.[25]

The day following the Pendleton-Morrill speeches, the *Times* abstracted the reasons for and against S. 227. Editorial comment, however, was reserved for April 30, 1879, when the illogical nature of Morrill's reasoning—especially with regard to his statements concerning the relationship of the Constitution to the different departments—was scrutinized. Pendleton's analysis appeared reasonable to the *Times,* which could not understand why anyone would object—under the pretense of preserving the separation of powers—to bringing into the open the communication already daily taking place between the departments and Congress.[26]

James Gordon Bennett's adventurous and erratic New York *Herald* devoted considerable editorial space to a summary of Pendleton's position in the debate. Although the *Herald* did not expect an early adoption of the legislation, it fully agreed with the arguments advanced by the Ohio senator. Granting that the bill could be easily misunderstood "as an aping of monarchical institutions," the editor urged Mr. Pendleton "to show that he is not assailing that division of powers established by the American Constitution." [27]

The Boston *Daily Advertiser* found fault with Morrill's objection that because other governments allowed Cabinet participation in legislative debate there was no reason why such a change should be permitted in the United States. The *Advertiser* granted that while Morrill had correctly demonstrated the flaw in the argument, it did not follow that his criticism was sufficient to preclude a trial of the plan. "It might be a very Yankee-like principle to have nothing like anybody else, but it is not wisdom."

After carefully analyzing the existing attitude of Congress and the parochial concern of the standing committees and their chairmen for what they regarded as their prerogatives, the newspaper concluded that such resistance eventually would yield. In a city which prided itself on tight thinking, shrewdness, and conservatism, at least one of its printed voices believed that the Pendleton bill must succeed because it was "in harmony with common sense." [28]

The transcontinental telegraph passed the news of the debate across the prairies westward to Sacramento, where many good citizens were being exposed to torchlight parades, fights, and speeches the week before the voters were to approve the second California constitution. An item in the Sacramento *Daily Record-Union* reported a Washington correspondent's analysis that the Pendleton bill "was not a political issue." Referring to the Confederate experiment with the plan, the reporter noted:

It is probable that some of the Southern Congressmen will oppose it on the ground of unfavorable experience. The plan was tried in the Confederate Congress, and for a time worked well, but the attendance on Congress soon became a bore to the Cabinet officers, while the familiarity bred a species of contempt on both sides.[29]

Here was a novel interpretation of what really happened. It is unlikely that much contempt was bred on the floor of the Confederate senate or house because of the presence of the cabinet. No legislation was ever approved by the Confederate congress operating under the permanent constitution which sanctioned the participation of those department officials. The contempt that existed was not caused by the mere existence of a procedural mechanism. Rather, it resulted from fundamental differences of policy over the proper course of governmental action. It is true that members of the cabinet did circulate among the legislators at various times in an attempt to secure support for administration projects. Such contact has also been practiced occasionally on the floor, though more frequently in the cloakrooms, of the United States Congress since 1789.

A NEW SELECT COMMITTEE

On May 28, 1879, a month after his encounter with Morrill, Pendleton moved that S. 227 be referred to a select committee of ten.[30] A day later, President pro tempore Allen G. Thurman, Ohio's senior senator, announced the appointments to the committee.[31] An indication of the attempt at bipartisanship was the selection of five members from each party.

Besides Pendleton, who became chairman, the Democrats included Daniel W. Voorhees, of Indiana, who although a member of the House in 1865 had not voiced an opinion on the proposal; Delaware's Thomas Francis Bayard, well regarded after twelve years in the Senate, and within a few years to become Cleveland's secretary of state; former Confederate General Matthew C. Butler, of South Carolina; and from the Far West, James T. Farley, who was just beginning his first year as senator from California.

The five Republicans were led in seniority by the shrewd and powerful Roscoe Conkling, who eventually left the committee when he resigned his Senate seat in protest against President Garfield's patronage policies. Much to his surprise and to his enemies' delight, Conkling was not reelected to the position by the New York legislature. William B. Allison, like Conkling, had served in the House during the consideration of the first Pendleton bill but had made no formal statement of his opinion. The Grand Old Party's growing luminary, James G. Blaine, was the only other committee member besides Pendleton who previously had been recorded in favor of the idea (in 1865, Blaine had engaged Morrill in a spirited debate). John J. Ingalls, of Kansas, and Orville Platt, of Connecticut, completed the Republican group on the committee.[32]

ELECTION OF PRESIDENT GARFIELD

As 1879 drew to a close and the presidential election year of 1880 became actuality, further discussion of Pendleton's bill was sidetracked. Both parties sought issues and scandals with which to besmirch each other during the months ahead.

Early in June, the Republican convention was held in Chicago. Representative James A. Garfield, who had given the most eloquent and reasoned argument for the Pendleton bill during the Civil War, was in attendance as head of the Ohio delegation. Former President Grant was being boomed for a third term by a substantial bloc of Republicans, who were not above hoping for another easy ride into office on the coattails of the "hero of Appomattox." There was coolness to the renomination of Rutherford B. Hayes since many party regulars believed that four years were enough of the somewhat puritanical President and his First Lady, "Lemonade Lucy."

Garfield's main goal was to stop Grant and prevent a third term tradition from being established; his secondary goal was to secure the nomination for Senator John Sherman, his fellow Ohioan and the brother of the ruthless general who had led the "blue bellies" through Georgia.

For thirty-five ballots, the convention remained stalemated between the forces of Grant and an opposition divided among Blaine, Edmunds, and Washburne. On the thirty-sixth ballot, the delegates broke ranks, and gave a majority to Garfield, who had impressed them with his address nominating Sherman. The selection was then made unanimous.[33]

Garfield's victory in November brought with it slim Republican control of the Congress. Possibly Pendleton was hoping for success in bringing the Cabinet and Congress together now that a former advocate of his idea was in the Presidency. If such a thought influenced the senator, his actions did not indicate it. On February 4, 1881 a whole month before the lameduck Democratic Congress was to end, Pendleton notified the Senate that the committee report was available. He informed his colleagues that the bill would be called up for discussion as soon as possible.[34]

Only eight of the ten committee members had signed. Bayard and Conkling were not listed. Since further debate on the bill did not arise during the session and no minority report was filed, the actual opinion of these two senators remains ambiguous. Conkling, who did not resign from the Senate until May 16, 1881, was reported to favor the legislation while Bayard was said to be opposed.[35]

The report itself turned over no new furrow. Congress's power to create departments and specify the duties of the Cabinet members was reaffirmed, and the various constitutional arguments supporting the bill were again detailed. The committee accepted Morrill's suggestion—although he probably had not offered it to be helpful—that each department should appoint an undersecretary who would handle the routine administration while the executive head gave his "attention to those duties which require wise discretion and intellectual activity." [36]

A deluding fallacy was voiced in equating a "strong" secretary with one who could hold his own in debate on the floor of Congress. This assertion had been criticized previously and would be attacked in the future. Obviously there was no inevitable correlation between actual executive capacity in running a large, complex organization and the ability to handle the possibly "loaded" questions which might ensue from congressional interrogation. On the contrary, there was a fundamental question whether a Cabinet member should be primarily a party leader and inspirer of programs—a role in which the oratorical attributes would play a prominent part—or mainly an administrator whose principal contacts were intra-departmental rather than interdepartmental or national in scope. This problem was not analyzed by the committee and since then has rarely been considered.

Newspaper support again was both favorable and wide-spread. A notable convert had joined the ranks. Less than two years before, the Cincinnati *Commercial* had objected to graft-ing what it regarded as a feature of the British system onto the American governmental structure. Now in the issue of Febru-ary 9, 1881, it could "not see any substantial reason for opposi-tion accompanying the bill." [37] Murat Halstead, the publisher, was in attendance at the Senate session of April 29, 1879, when Pendleton explained the measure.[38] The newspaper's attack on the idea had come a month prior to the address. It did not occur again.

Within two weeks of the *Commercial's* switch, on February 17, 1881, the *Nation's* editor, E. L. Godkin, reviewed the "unani-mous" report issued by the Pendleton group. After summarizing the usual objections that had been raised, especially the one concerning possible executive dominance of Congress, Godkin concluded that on balance the measure would do more good than harm. The great evil was secret government:

In fact, all reforms now of necessity take the shape of an increase of publicity, or of increased means of knowing, on the part of the people, why and in what manner things are done, while nearly every abuse of which the public now complain has its roots in privacy, or in the exclusion of the people from all means of know-ing why and in what manner things are done.[39]

Enactment of the Pendleton bill would revive congressional responsibility, whereas now the legislators "shield themselves from all responsibility behind the caucus, and gain their own ends by private management." [40]

In the same issue of the *Nation,* a letter from "J." of Norwalk,

Connecticut, hoped that the magazine "was not finally committed to a support of the Pendleton bill." The correspondent argued that "the Confederate Congress was almost a nonentity." He warned that "it may fairly behoove us to think of these things diligently before trying a similar experiment." [41] Reader "J.D.J." answered "J." and congratulated the *Nation* on its advocacy of the Pendleton measure and on being the "original suggester" of the proposal.[42]

A breach in the front of journalistic support appeared in the February 26 issue of *Harper's Weekly,* a reformist Republican magazine which proclaimed itself "a Journal of Civilization." *Harper's* admitted the advantages of the Pendleton legislation, but added that there was something to be said against it: the appearance of Cabinet officers before Congress to be "catechized" without a right to vote was "an unnecessary derogation of dignity." Under the American system, a written and detailed reply was preferable. If it was wise to bring department heads before the legislature, said civilization's mentor, then the Cabinet ought to resign when they were defeated on an issue. Strangely enough, despite their initial conservative hesitance, *Harper's* had arrived at a solution more radical than that of the Pendleton reform's strongest Senate proponents.[43]

With the conclusion of the Third Session of the Forty-sixth Congress, the life of the Pendleton bill (S. 227) expired. Again it had not come to a vote, although a distinguished and apparently powerful committee of senators had recommended the idea. More widespread newspaper support had been obtained, but such an issue of procedural reform was not likely to inspire extensive vocal support from the electorate.

PENDLETON'S FINAL ATTEMPT

Shortly after the commencement of the Forty-seventh Congress in December, 1881, Senator Pendleton offered S. 307, which was almost identical to his S. 227 of the previous Congress. Another select committee of ten was appointed, and the third cycle seemed well on its way.[44]

On December 13, 1881, David Davis, the president pro tempore, designated Pendleton as chairman. Three Southerners were named to the group, including Charles W. Jones, of Florida; John Tyler Morgan, of Alabama; and Howell E. Jackson, of Tennessee. The only Democrat from west of the Mississippi was a former Oregon governor, Lafayette Grover. The five Republicans on the evenly divided committee were all committee chairmen. William Windom, of Minnesota, presided over the committee on foreign relations. Eugene Hale chaired the select committee on the census. Henry L. Dawes (Indian affairs) and Joseph Roswell Hawley (civil service and retrenchment) came from Massachusetts and Connecticut, respectively. Public Lands' chairman Preston B. Plumb, of Kansas, completed the membership.[45]

A report from this committee would have been an invaluable aid in determining the effect of holding a committee chairmanship on advocacy of the proposal. Although the Senate approved the hiring of a clerk to aid the group, no report was ever issued.[46] There is no record as to the fate of the committee. Evidently, it formally ended with the Forty-seventh Congress, if it had not expired informally long before.

Pendleton was now concerning himself with a revision of the procedures used in selecting federal employees. In the summer of 1881, Garfield's assassination by a rejected office seeker had centered the public's attention on the plight of government in maintaining a semblance of efficiency against the quadrennial, if not perennial, droves of spoilsmen. Public pressure finally forced Congress to approve legislation extending the merit system to slightly over ten thousand employees. This basic civil service act was guided through the Senate by Senator Pendleton and is rightfully and properly known as the Pendleton Act of 1883.[47]

Pendleton's vigorous championing of civil service reform

was partially responsible for his losing the 1884 renomination from the party which he had served so long and faithfully. Following the political retribution which the Democratic spoilsmen in Ohio had dealt Pendleton, Grover Cleveland—the first Democratic President in twenty-four years—appointed the former senator minister to Germany. Pendleton died abroad in 1889.[48] With him passed substantial congressional agitation for seating the Cabinet officers in Congress. It did not reach that pitch again until the fifth decade of the twentieth century.

VIII

The Efforts of Bradford and Belmont

EXCEPT FOR the introduction of one lone bill into the House hopper after George Pendleton's term in the Senate, legislative attention to bringing the department heads before Congress was on the wane until after the first decade of the twentieth century. Only then was governmental interest in the spurned proposal revived by outgoing President William Howard Taft, who had been repudiated a few months previously by the voters and—as a result of the Bull Moose movement of 1912—by a substantial segment of his own Republican Party. Between 1881 and 1912, however, the Pendleton idea was kept before the public, primarily by two reformers, Gamaliel Bradford and Perry Belmont.

GAMALIEL BRADFORD

Gamaliel Bradford was a direct descendant of William Bradford, governor of Plymouth Colony. As a proper Bostonian so directly descended from other proper Bostonians, he attended Harvard College. In 1849 he graduated with Phi Beta Kappa honors, sixth in his class.

While some men were going West in that memorable year, young Bradford divided his time between working for a Cambridge firm that published the *Nautical Almanac* and making two trips to Europe. Following his second voyage to the Old World, he entered a cousin's banking house to begin a career which would establish him as an authority on finance and bonds.[1]

Bradford later wrote that during the Civil War he had seen many of his closest friends go off to war and felt a great "self reproach for not joining them." Yet if he lived and acquired some independent means, he hoped to retire and engage in the study of public affairs: "I would do more for my country, than by throwing away my life on the battle-field." [2] Nineteen years out of Harvard, he retired and was able to fulfill that desire by devoting the remainder of his life to reform.

His role as a reformer was not a new one, even though it now occupied his full time. Early in life, Bradford was an abolitionist like his father before him. As a financier, Bradford had been critical of the Legal Tender Acts. Though a Republican until 1884, he, as had George Hunt Pendleton decades before, broke with the family tradition to enlist in the ranks of the Democratic Party. Unlike Pendleton, who was identified with the greenback movement, Bradford was a hard-money man. He even ran as a gubernatorial candidate for the Gold-Standard Democrats of Massachusetts, but was notably unsuccessful. [3]

Bradford was an avid reader of modern history, law, and political science. Much of the influence which he exerted was the result of prolific letter writing (several thousand letters in all) to the leading newspapers and magazines of his day.

The measure that Bradford advocated the longest and that meant the most to him was Pendleton's plan calling for Cabinet officers to appear in Congress in order to provide information and submit to questioning. He developed the idea two steps further when he advocated it as a cure to the ills of secret government, not only at the national, but also at the state and local levels. But the latter move was urged only after "ten years of unremitting effort proved that the national field was too extensive to be reached." "A fatal obstacle . . . [had at once arisen] . . . from the Congressional politicians whose schemes and methods of operation would be thwarted by it." [4]

Following his early retirement from the world of materialism, the reformer had spent a winter in Washington at the end of the 1860s. He often sat in the galleries of the Senate and House analyzing the proceedings in an attempt to discover the reasons for what he considered irresponsible congressional action. Although his main interest at that time was financial legislation and the development of a national monetary system similar to that provided by the later Federal Reserve Act, Bradford's attention was drawn to a fault in the mechanism:

Many of the members had views of their own, but there was nobody to reconcile them, to put them into shape, or to bring them to any practical result. Everything which any member saw fit to propose was massed with everything else and distributed to the different committees, composed of local representatives, selected at hap-hazard, wholly irresponsible for administrative results, and which yet formed the only guidance for the houses to come to any conclusion whatever.[5]

Bradford's active letter writing on the national scene began in response to one of Godkin's editorials in the *Nation* on the *Alabama* Claims. In 1872, Godkin had described the President and the State Department as being "almost as secure from all enquiries as the Venetian Council of Ten in its palmiest days." Bradford answered praising this stand and suggesting that executive responsibility could be attained through better communication with Congress.[6]

A year later, in 1873, Bradford delivered a Boston lecture in which he specified the advantages to be gained by seating the Cabinet officers in Congress. Among them were: continuity in legislation, development of candidates for higher executive office, improvement in the tone of congressional debate, an increase in administrative responsibility, and the growth of a more effective opposition.[7]

The *Nation*—differing from its stand a half dozen years later when Senator Pendleton reintroduced the issue—took the position that the proposal was quite naive. The weekly could see "no sensible alteration in our conditions" from the installation of such a procedure.[8] The executive powers would only be further debilitated. Another objection to "the proposed panacea" was that "it was an attempted graft from a foreign stock."[9] As far as the *Nation* was concerned, allowing the department heads in Congress to solve the ills of government was as unreasonable as planting a few trees on a mountain top to stop the geologic forces from crumbling away the side of the hill.

Before embarking for Ohio in order to attend the 1878 meeting of the American Social Science Association, Bradford attacked what he regarded as the despotic power of the Speaker and stated his belief that Cabinet officers should lead the administration's policy in the House of Representatives. He argued that the proper function of the Speaker was to guide the procedures and not the substance of the legislative business.[10] By now Bradford had concluded that the only way to secure sanction for his proposal, as long as so many petty jealousies existed in Congress, was for someone to take the issue to the people.[11]

Bradford's paper, "Congress and the President," delivered at the meeting of social scientists in Cincinnati, May 22, 1878, hinted that if the Pendleton experiment were tried it might develop—though not necessarily—that the Cabinet would resign singly or as a group upon suffering a reversal in Congress. He saw the "irrepressible conflict of the future" as existing between the Chief Executive and the legislature.

George Pendleton, then a railroad president and soon to return to Washington as a senator, was in the audience. Twenty-seven-year-old Perry Belmont—whose father had been Democratic national chairman during the Civil War and was still an active force in New York politics—turned up as a fellow believer when he read his thesis on "Executive Officers in Congress." The following day, Bradford participated in a panel on the "Elective Franchise," with Judge Alphonso Taft, father of the future President, who in three and a half decades would recommend the Pendleton-Bradford plan to Congress.[12]

PERRY BELMONT

Whether congressman, horseman, or yachtsman, wealthy Perry Belmont was never long "off the track" or "at sea" concerning advocacy of seating the Cabinet in Congress. Like Bradford, Belmont was a son of Harvard (1872); like Pendleton, he had studied in Germany. Following his scholarly presentation of the reform to the Cincinnati convention in 1878, Belmont returned to New York City. Within two years, no doubt aided by both the Belmont name and his father's influence, Perry Belmont was elected to the Forty-seventh Congress, which began in 1881. In 1888, by now chairman of the House committee on foreign affairs, Belmont resigned to accept an appointment as minister to Spain.[13] Although an advocate of the Pendleton measure three years prior to his election to the House of Representatives—an advocacy he would maintain well into the fourth decade of the twentieth century—it is interesting to note that during his seven years in Congress, Perry Belmont never once introduced legislation which would implement that reform. Nor did he speak in favor of such a reform on the floor. Belmont's interest in such legislation, however, did grow more intense as he saw America becoming involved in the First World War.

CONSISTENT ADVOCACY

Gamaliel Bradford always abhorred the thought of Congress's choosing the Cabinet.[14] He believed in the wisdom of a single executive elected by and responsible to all of the people. As an able student of European, and especially French, history, Bradford was fearful of Cabinet instability if policy were totally dependent on the whim of legislators who were responsible not to the people at large, but to numerous local segments of society. His disdain for legislative caprice was undoubtedly increased by Congress's constant chipping away of presidential power in the post-Civil War era.

Agreeing with modern students of public administration, Bradford resented the parceling out of the state's executive power among a half dozen or more officials elected directly by the people. Such schemes of governing were not harbingers of democracy, but progenitors of chaos. At the national, state, and local levels, he favored a single elected executive whose actions the electorate could carefully observe, eventually ratifying or rejecting the official's policies. This responsible administrator would be able to choose department heads who reflected his policy orientation. So that the Chief Executive's program might be translated effectively into law, Bradford urged that the agency directors be invited to participate in their respective representative assemblies: Congress, state legislature, and city council.[15]

No doubt underlying Bradford's support of Pendleton's proposal was a basic belief that legislators were "bad" and executives "good." This attitude found its source in his explicit assumption that since the representatives were elected by local interests in small geographic areas, they could not adequately represent the national interest. Department heads, on the other hand, presumably reflected the broader interest since they were appointed by the Chief Executive whose tenure was passed on by the total polity. The equation of the forces of "goodness" with the executive and those of "badness" with the legislature was an obvious oversimplification. But on such simplifications many reforms are based and developed, and public attention focused and maintained.

An additional equation in Bradford's calculus was his belief that a great man plus public opinion would equal good government. Repeatedly, the reformer pleaded in the columns of the *Nation* and other communications media for a President or governor to go forth and take to the people an issue such as the admission of the department heads to the legislature.[16] Such abiding faith in the rationality of the citizenry spoke well for the democratic values held by this hard-money Boston aristocrat. But it also revealed Bradford's lack of political awareness that "the people" usually do not become vigorously agitated over changes in governmental mechanics unless there is a widespread feeling that the procedures have thwarted a substantive policy proposal about which there have been deeply rooted convictions.

For Bradford, the antagonistic forces which prevented the enactment of such a reasonable scheme consisted of the lobbies, the Speaker of the House, and that phenomenon known as congressional jealousy.[17] He focused on England and concluded that there the lobby did not exist owing to the presence of a cabinet which took responsibility for all governmental policy. Some would hold that if Bradford had scrutinized the House of Commons with greater care, he would have realized that there was no need for the leader of a private interest group to lurk in the corridors when he had a seat on the floor. In addition, he overlooked the possibility that if the Cabinet became influential in guiding congressional activity, there would be no barrier to prevent the lobbies from transferring their attention to this new source of influence.

Bradford many times repeated his conviction that a great advantage of the American system was that the Cabinet officer was solely responsible to the President. But he did hint that, if his idea were placed in operation, only the future could tell whether the department heads would become responsible to Congress, even to the point of resigning if defeated on a policy. Bradford appeared to depart from his belief in presidential responsibility as achieved through party responsibility when he suggested that the Chief Executive should be "a dignified citizen, in a measure independent of party." If the opposition party controlled Congress, then the President should select his Cabinet from its ranks.[18]

At times the lack of enthusiastic popular response to a proposition which seemed so reasonable and workable must have discouraged "G.B." Bradford's dejection was evident in his reply to one of the few critics who wrote to the *Nation* and differed with him: "In political discussion, an opponent is almost as valuable as a supporter. The most discouraging thing is (*crede experto*) to go on for years and find nobody paying any attention to anything you say." [19] He thanked the *Nation* for letting him ride his "hobby" in its columns.

Gamaliel Bradford occasionally viewed with humor his seriousness about this "hobby." He once remarked that he could imagine some people saying, "If the President had a toothache, G.B. would say that it was because the Cabinet officers were not in Congress." [20]

WILSON AND BRYCE

The analyses of Woodrow Wilson and James Bryce provided both target and additional ammunition for Gamaliel Bradford's reform cannon. The Boston reformer had reached the political conclusions of President Wilson while young Professor Wilson was still in the process of formulating them. In 1879, as a senior at Princeton College, Wilson had published an essay advocating for the United States a cabinet government on the prevailing British model. This would cure the evil

which Wilson and most political observers of the time agreed
was the irresponsible government resulting from the dominance
of public policy formulation by the standing committees of
Congress.[21]

Bradford had always favored a strong President responsible
to the whole electorate. He supported the Pendleton plan in
the belief that an open discussion of major governmental policy
by the Cabinet before Congress would increase the accountability of both branches to the people. But it would still be
a Cabinet chosen by the President and dependent for its
tenure on him alone. It would not be an executive committee
of Congress dependent upon the continuing approval of their
elected colleagues.

Wilson, on the other hand, would not only permit the
Cabinet to have seats in Congress and initiate legislation, but
he would hold that the principle of ministerial responsibility
whereby "resignation upon defeat is the essence of responsible
government" must sooner or later be recognized.[22] For Wilson,
the Cabinet officers could not merely be department heads
chosen from private life and seated in Congress, since that
would be at variance with republican principles. The highest
order of responsibility would be established only when the
President selected his Cabinet from among the representatives
already chosen by the people. Such a change did not seem
revolutionary to Wilson.[23]

A naive faith in the effectiveness of open debate was exhibited by the Princeton senior who avowed that the presence
of the department heads in Congress would mean that

in this open sifting of debate, when every feature of every measure, even to the motives which prompted it, is the subject of out-
spoken discussion and keen scrutiny, no chicanery, no party craft,
no questionable principles can long hide themselves.[24]

His belief in debate as a prerequisite to democracy was
equaled only by his abhorrence of Congress as a collection

of those who represented local and thus special interests. What was needed was a "guiding or harmonizing power" and this would be the responsible Cabinet which had the strength of a party at its command.[25] However, it was not the party with its conventions and platforms which provided the binding link in Wilson's conception of legislative-executive relations. Rather, it was the Cabinet which was to serve as the hyphen between the President and Congress.

The "degradation of our political parties" was summarized by Wilson in eight words: *"No leaders, no principles; no principles, no parties."* [26] His remedy for localism was to change the leadership so that it might develop a national party policy. Such leadership could not be offered by the standing committees operating behind the scenes in a constant bartering and trading of local interests which preceded the enactment of public policy. Such leadership could come only from the President and his Cabinet—even if, should the opposite party be in control of Congress, the Cabinet were to be chosen from its ranks. Wilson urged that it was better for the President to preside over a Cabinet of political opponents who could secure legislative action than over "a Cabinet of political friends who are compelled to act in all matters of importance according to the dictation of Standing Committees which are ruled by the opposite party." [27] No concern was expressed that the Cabinet might assume control over both the legislative and executive branches. In part, the fixed election system would prevent such aggrandizement and, even if it did not, Wilson believed that such centralization certainly could not be any worse than that exhibited by the irresponsible power of the standing committees and their chairmen.[28]

After a frustrating year during which he had attempted the practice of law, Wilson entered upon graduate study in political science at the newly established Johns Hopkins University in Baltimore, Maryland. In 1884, just prior to completing his doctoral dissertation, Wilson published an article delineating the choice between committee and cabinet government. Little new had been added to his senior thesis of five years before. He did suggest, however, two constitutional changes. The first was a four word amendment to alter the latter part of the clause which prohibited those holding an office under the United States from being a member of either house of Congress to read "and no person holding any *other than a Cabinet* office under the United States shall be a member of either House during his continuance in office." [29] To prevent the government from being "capricious and unstable" he advocated a lengthening of both the presidential and congressional terms.[30]

Wilson's faith in the value of debate had not waned. On the contrary, he saw free debate by a responsible ministry as providing a needed spur to the opposition in the "contest for ascendancy":

To stand the tests of discussion they [the majority and minority parties] must needs have champions strong of intellect, pure of reputation, exalted in character, and cogent in speech. . . . Nominating conventions would hardly dare, under such circumstances, to send to Congress scheming wire-pullers or incompetent and double-faced tricksters, who would damn their party by displays of folly and suspicions of corruption.[31]

In the process, Congress would be transformed into "a grand national inquisition." [32]

Similarly, a transition would take place in the executive departments. Although the Cabinet officer might well be of a different party than the President, Wilson, who foresaw only greater effectiveness in departmental management under his system, argued that "as chiefs of the executive bureau, the ministers would have a personal interest in preserving the prerogatives of the Executive; and as official leaders of their party in Congress, they would be zealous to protect the rights and vindicate the authority of the Houses." [33]

But perhaps most important was Wilson's major assumption of continued congressional supremacy. Regardless of schemes of reorganization

Congress will always be master, and will always enforce its commands on the administration. The only wise plan, therefore, is to facilitate its direction of the government, and to make it at the same time responsible, in the persons of its leaders, for its acts of control, and for the manner in which its plans and commands are executed.[34]

The doctoral dissertation, entitled *Congressional Government,* which Woodrow Wilson completed in 1884 rapidly became a classic following its publication in 1885. Although the advocacy was still prevalent, Wilson no longer concerned himself with concentrating on recommending a semi-parliamentary system to restore integrity to the political process. It would be almost two full decades before he fully grasped the leadership potential inherent in the Presidency.[35]

Shortly after the appearance of *Congressional Government,* Bradford scolded the future President and his work for not admitting the merits of the Pendleton scheme and yet preferring a form of parliamentary government which could only be attained through constitutional amendment.[36] In the future Wilson was to grant the merits of seating the Cabinet in Congress but not to battle for it.

The publication of Lord Bryce's *The American Commonwealth* in 1889 gave a spurt of intellectual stimulation to the Pendleton proposal in the nineties. Opponents of the plan had often argued that since the main feature of British government was the cabinet in Parliament and since the Founding Fathers had obtained most of their conceptions of government from Great Britain or the colonial charters which were patterned after English models, the Constitutional Convention must have deliberately intended *not* to have cabinet government. This position was held by legislative critics such as Justin Morrill and scholarly commentators such as Walter Bagehot.[37]

Bryce, however, argued that since there was no mention of cabinet government as practiced in modern times by either Blackstone or Montesquieu, the leading governmental authorities in the late eighteenth century, it was impossible for the members of the Constitutional Convention really to have taken a position on the issue.[38] He suggested, perhaps mistakenly, that you cannot reject something unless you are consciously aware of what you are rejecting.

Bradford regarded Bryce's reasoning as support for his own position. William W. Hudson disagreed. Hudson held that Bryce really believed the Pendleton-Bradford formula inadequate. Hudson offered his own solution to improve legislative-executive relations. He advocated the creation of a "governing committee" chosen from the majority party in Congress. This body was to be provided with an adequate staff who would aid it in the formulation of policy. Following the abolition of specialized standing committees, the House would be divided into several large committees of forty or fifty members, each of which would have the authority to consider legislation in all areas. The governing committee, which would participate in Cabinet meetings, could be constantly subject to the will of the House majority. As with the cabinet in Parliament, the governing committee would have to resign and be reconstituted if it were defeated on a major issue. Hudson believed that everyone would profit from such a reorganization. The administrative functions would still remain with department heads chosen by and responsible to the President. Yet the congressional opposition now would confront a group which offered both a constant challenge and a prize in the struggle for political control.[39]

Bradford replied that Hudson had misquoted Bryce. And

anyway, the governing committee was a useless institution since it would be "composed wholly of local representatives having no national authority." [40]

Another dissident, Harvard's Freeman Snow, attacked Bradford for proposing "a revolution in our methods of legislation" by having the Cabinet members take the initiative in preparing and introducing bills into the Senate and House. He tried to draw a distinction between the Pendleton proposals which would change a mode of communication and the secrecy of committees that seemed to worry Bradford. The Harvard professor accused Bradford of being unrealistic in assuming that the President was above the same party interests and exigencies which influence congressmen. Snow agreed that the "vicious practices of the caucus," "spoils system," and the "overgrown power of the Speaker" were contemporary evils which must be eradicated. With a final thrust at G.B.'s penchant for procedural reform, Snow queried: "Is not this a waste of energy that would be better employed in a direct attack upon the evils complained of?" [41]

Bradford answered that his proposal offered "the only effective and available way of escape" from an otherwise inevitable civil war between the executive and the legislative.[42] Harking back to 1790, he analyzed the motion which requested Hamilton to submit his *Report on the Public Credit* in writing (thus denying him an opportunity to appear in person) and found that "the true spirit of legislative jealousy" had revealed itself as the "members shrank instinctively from an agency which would compel them to personal and public responsibility." [43]

Bradford devoted most of the 1890s to writing his two-volume *The Lesson of Popular Government*. Drawing on a broad knowledge of European and American history, he offered an analytical and historical survey emphasizing the need for executive responsibility. Here, Bradford summarized the various advantages of the Pendleton proposal which he had noted during the past thirty years in his incessant letter writing to newspapers. It was fitting that he dedicated his book to Wendell Phillips Garrison of the *Nation,* Edward Henry Clement of the Boston *Transcript,* and John Henry Holmes of the Boston *Herald* in appreciation of the "liberality with which their journals were placed at my disposal during the many years in which the views herein expressed were taking shape." [44]

America's territorial expansion abroad, following the successful conclusion of the Spanish-American War, provided one last cause to which Bradford could apply his energies in the first decade of the new century. Bradford's new quixotic thrust at the corrupting windmill of imperialism was noted in a New York *Sun* editorial entitled "The Bobbing-Up of Gamaliel":

The asylum chosen for his reappearance was the Massachusetts Reform Club. At a dinner of the inmates last week Mr. Bradford, after a successful struggle with some rival steam which insisted upon hissing at him from an alley nearby, put forth his declaration: "It is an open question whether we shall sink under the tide of militarism or remain free. I believe that the reelection of McKinley in 1900 means Empire in place of the Republic." [45]

The *Sun's* ridicule of Bradford, including the suggestion that he "be brought to New York and exhibited in the Madison Square Garden," seemed to have little effect on the reformer since he dutifully clipped the item and pasted it in his scrapbook.

In 1900, Gamaliel Bradford was elected president of the Massachusetts Anti-Imperialist League and found himself in the midst of a nationwide movement, which included William Jennings Bryan and David Starr Jordan. Bradford's tussle with the menace of imperialism still allowed him time to toss his fedora into the ring of tophats that signified competition for the Massachusetts Democratic gubernatorial nomination of 1901. The Boston *Herald* greeted the reformer's entry as a non-machine candidate for the Democratic nomination with a cartoon captioned "The Volunteer Furnishes Fun for the Regulars." The caricature of Bradford showed him trotting along with wooden sword and broom as the chairman of the Democratic State Committee leaned over the fence to suggest, "You need a machine 'Gam.'" [46]

After one other attempt at the gubernatorial nomination in 1906, when he issued an open letter "To the Voters of Massachusetts" urging that the governor and his department heads have seats on the floor, Bradford made no more political forays. He devoted his remaining years to attending meetings of his familiar Boston clubs and to corresponding with public officials and like-minded reformers. [47]

A vigorous speech by Bradford on his favorite idea before the sedate membership of the Massachusetts Historical Society brought a terse note from its president, Charles Francis Adams. Adams refused to approve publication of the address in the society's proceedings since it was politics and controversy, not history. [48]

After an address to the Governors' Conference in Louisville, Kentucky, in December, 1910, Bradford renewed his acquaintance with Woodrow Wilson, who was no longer a professor of politics but a practitioner, bound for the Presidency by way of the governorship of New Jersey. Wilson's position on the idea of seating the Cabinet in Congress remained ambiguous or at least fluctuating. His youthful thesis urging parliamentary government as a salve for the nation's ills seemed to wane as he acquired political power. Perhaps he was too occupied with more substantive matters of policy to battle the entrenched resistance to such procedural reforms. Although during his college teaching days, Wilson had differed with Bradford on the advantages of a single executive as opposed to collective responsibility, while he was governor he apparently supported the adaptability of Bradford's proposal to the state level.[49] Later, when Wilson was President of the United States, he allegedly endorsed the Pendleton plan at a White House luncheon which included former President William Howard Taft and Elihu Root.[50]

Additional support for the idea came from a New York attorney, Henry L. Stimson, from Henry Jones Ford, a professor of politics at Princeton, and from Kentucky Governor Augustus E. Willson.[51]

In his later years, Gamaliel Bradford's enthusiasm for his idea never slackened, but on August 20, 1911, this leading advocate for changing the relationship between the Cabinet and Congress died within a few hours after being critically injured by a trolley car.[52]

BELMONT'S FINAL ENDEAVORS

The scepter of reform passed to Perry Belmont, who upon returning from his Spanish diplomatic post had devoted himself to various civic affairs. Belmont was the principal initiator in the movement which demanded legislation requiring publicity for expenditures made during state and national political campaigns. His efforts partially succeeded, in 1911, when the Congress approved a statute meeting that demand. In January, 1913, within a year and a half after Bradford had passed on, Belmont submitted an article to the *North American Review* seconding President Taft's address to the Lotos Club of New York, in which the Chief Executive had urged adoption of the Pendleton plan.[53]

Belmont spoke to the American Club of Paris, on July 2, 1914, elaborating his reasons for favoring the proposal. The position of a Cabinet officer had changed in the last century, he declared, especially since the passage of the Tenure of

Office Act in 1867 (he overlooked the fact that this act had been repealed), which made the removal of a department head subject to Senate approval and not just to presidential whim. Belmont feared what he labeled "personal government" in which the President is "unrestrained by Congress." To assure presidential responsibility to the American people, the President's Cabinet should be responsive to Congress for questioning.[54]

Belmont made three more endeavors to influence Congress in passing the proposal before summing up his position in his recollections, published seven years before his death in 1947.[55] The first occurred on March 25, 1916, when Vice President Thomas Marshall laid before the Senate a letter which he had received from Belmont. In this message, Belmont reviewed the constitutional and governmental reasons for supporting the seating of the Cabinet in Congress.[56] Since a bill implementing the idea had again been introduced in the House, there was some relevancy for Belmont's appeal. No action, however, was taken by the Senate. In the House, the bill, which had been offered by Representative Andrew J. Montague, a former governor of Virginia, remained buried and unnoticed.

Belmont's second major effort came in 1925 when he wrote Senator Key Pittman of Nevada. Besides stressing the favorable constitutional arguments, he reviewed the attempts that had been made since the action of the Confederate constitutional convention to implement the Pendleton proposal in the United States.[57]

Finally in 1935, Belmont engaged in a two-year correspondence with Representative Byron B. Harlan, who had introduced a bill which would allow the Cabinet to debate departmental policies before the full House.[58] The effort was fruitless.

With the arrival of the Second World War and the crusade

for a question period led by Representative Estes Kefauver of Tennessee, the isolated "letters to the editor" by such devotees of the Pendleton plan as Belmont and Bradford would no longer be a major means of the idea's support. Now, a much larger segment of the American press would advocate the reform. This enthusiasm indicated that the work of the two reformers had not been completely wasted. Bradford and Belmont were important both in laying the foundation for the broader support which later developed and in enlisting the sponsorship of various outstanding public figures.

IX

Growing Congressional Interest

BY THE END of the nineteenth century, despite the efforts of Grover Cleveland, Congress had regained its dominant policy formulation role, which had been encroached upon only temporarily by the necessities of the Civil War. Between 1881, which marked Pendleton's last attempt, and 1913, a year when several legislators showed renewed interest, only one bill authorizing Cabinet officers to participate in congressional proceedings was offered in the House of Representatives. This was strange indeed, considering the extensive activity of such reformers as Gamaliel Bradford and Perry Belmont in the last quarter of the century. The single bill was sponsored by John Long, a former governor of Massachusetts, member of Congress from 1883 to 1889, and secretary of the navy in the McKinley Cabinet. The idea that the Chief Executive's advisers should be permitted to debate policies which affected their departments had been urged by Long during his governorship. The arguments of Bradford seem to have sparked his interest then just as they were to prod him into submission of a bill when he later served in the House.

In his annual message to the Massachusetts General Court (senate and house) delivered on January 6, 1881, Governor Long urged that the legislature grant his department heads the privilege of the floor "with the right to speak upon questions affecting their departments, but, of course, without the right to vote." [1] The Boston *Daily Advertiser* thought that the suggestion deserved favorable consideration; but "we foresee the conservative opposition it will encounter." [2]

Newspapers in Boston were also commenting affirmatively during this period on the work of the Pendleton select committee which was studying the parent proposal in the United States Senate. Despite this additional publicity, the recommendation of the governor was not enacted. Long again urged its adoption in his last annual message, presented on January 5, 1882.[3] This effort was as futile as his earlier ones had been.

Almost four years later, on November 30, 1885, Gamaliel Bradford in a letter to Representative Long recalled "gratefully" his endorsement of the Pendleton plan when he was governor and added: "I hope the time may come when you will be ready to take the same ground in relation to the Cabinet and Congress."[4] During December, Long was involved in a vigorous debate to prevent the dispersal of the power of the committee on appropriations among the legislative committees. He defended the authority of a single committee to coordinate the financial policies of the House and concluded with a barb which accurately reflected his conservatism: "It is a first-rate thing to fill the reform bucket, but not to fill it to such an extent that it slops over."[5]

Shortly before Christmas, Bradford goaded Long further when he inquired in response to the recent debate: "Was there ever anything which showed more strongly that the Secretary of the Treasury ought to be heard?"[6] On January 5, 1886, Long responded by introducing H.R. 1081, which, in essence, was similar to the previous Pendleton bills.[7]

Bradford wrote immediately expressing his pleasure at this action. But he believed it was "utterly hopeless to expect that Congress of its own motion will give the matter any attention." The reformer advised that support would have to be gathered either from the executive or "from outside agitation." To create the latter, Bradford proposed that Long call a meeting in his district so that the measure could be explained and a following developed. "The greatest political weapon in this

country . . . [is] . . . awaiting the hand that has the bold-
ness to seize and the skill to grasp it." [8]

Although Long was to maintain an interest in the idea for
many years after he left Congress, he took no further action
during his tenure in the House.[9]

THE TAFT MESSAGE

In 1898, the destruction of an Old World power's naval
forces by the upstart Yankee turned attention at home and
abroad to the role the United States might play in global
affairs. The growing industrial society of iron and steel which
had produced the machines of war that pummeled the Spanish
at the close of the century was itself being subjected to
ruthless attack from within. Grangers, Populists, labor, and
a rising lower middle class sought more from government
than the services of the policeman with his nightstick.

William McKinley's assassination in 1901 brought Theodore
Roosevelt to the Presidency.[10] As Roosevelt strengthened his
political stature for the nominating convention which lay
ahead in 1904, his deference to Congress decreased. Politics
and administration became charged with vitality as the Pan-
ama Canal, trusts, food and drug regulation, coal strikes, and
foreign potentates were all tackled by the dynamo from
Sagamore Hill. By the astute molding and guidance of public
sentiment, T.R. secured congressional approval for more
measures than one normally would expect possible from a
Senate and House whose leadership was largely made up of
the conservative ranks of his own Republican Party.

Even as Roosevelt, in 1909, was packing his pith helmet,
spare glasses, and elephant gun for the voyage to Africa—to
begin after his hand-picked successor, Secretary of War William Howard Taft, was sworn in as President—congressional
resentment at growing executive domination was rising. On

March 1, 1909, Senator Joseph W. Bailey, of Texas, offered a resolution directing the Senate secretary to examine the records and return to the department head concerned all those communications in which the chamber's right to demand papers and information held by the agency had been denied. Although two days later Bailey's resolution was sidetracked and buried by a 52 to 25 roll call vote which referred it to the judiciary committee, it was, nevertheless, a warning signal for the new President of pitfalls to come.[11]

The amiable Taft bore the brunt of congressional opposition which had been nurtured by the actions of his predecessor. In May, 1911, to soothe some of the factional resentment which was manifesting discontent in his own party, Taft appointed Henry L. Stimson, a New York Republican leader and confidant of Roosevelt, as his secretary of war.[12]

A great influence on Stimson's thinking with regard to executive-legislative relations was Henry Jones Ford, professor of politics at Princeton. In the January, 1911, issue of *Scribner's Magazine,* Ford had presented his thesis that the basic cause of corruption in American public life was not so much individual license as the underlying weakness of the governmental system: "A government of separated powers is plainly incapable of responding to demands for greater efficiency of administration." [13] He noted favorably the movement that was then taking place in Oregon to seat the governor and his cabinet in the legislature with the right to debate and introduce legislation.[14]

Although Ford effectively demolished Montesquieu's erroneous reasoning concerning the separation of powers, he was not an advocate of parliamentary government based on the British model. Over a decade before, Ford had predicted that while eventually the Presidency would become more ceremonial and actual administration would "tend to pass into the hands of groups of statesmen trained to their work by gradations of public service," the future American govern-ment would not be parliamentary in nature but would ex-hibit closer cooperation between executive and legislative.[15]

In January, 1911, Stimson had traveled to Cleveland to speak before a dinner meeting of leading Republicans. During the course of his address, he stated: "We should frankly abandon the theory of the separation of the executive and the legislative functions and our state constitutions should be changed to accomplish that end." Stimson believed that keep-ing the governor from participating in legislative discussion was a tremendous block to efficiency in an era when the so-called representative bodies were becoming increasingly a less accurate reflection of public opinion.[16]

Shortly after making this speech, Stimson answered Gama-liel Bradford, who had written him urging that department heads as well as the governor should appear in the legislature. Stimson stated that he was "very much interested" in the suggestions and that they followed "the line upon which my own mind has been traveling." [17]

Following his appointment as secretary of war, Stimson devoted most of his energies to mastering departmental detail. In 1912, after a year's experience of relations with Congress concerning defense legislation and appropriations, Stimson mentioned the early efforts of Senator Pendleton and his select committee to President Taft.

Stimson's suggestion fell on receptive ears. Over two years before, Taft had greeted a meeting of the state governors at the White House with the phrase "fellow executives and fellow sufferers." The Chief Executive admitted to his state counterparts that the British parliamentary system presented

a good many opportunities that you and I would like to seize upon to argue out questions to the legislature, and not only to argue out questions, but to save them time by giving them considerable information on subjects in regard to which they are not advised. It shortens, I am sure, the course of legislation. But we have not got that system; we haven't it in any state and we are not going to have it, so there is no need of mourning over the fact that we cannot have it.[18]

Although Taft was now engaged in the throes of a bitterly contested campaign with his former mentor, Theodore Roosevelt, he took time to write a short note to Senator Henry Cabot Lodge informing him of the existence of the Pendleton report.[19]

The President was decisively defeated in the autumn election of 1912. Theodore Roosevelt and his Bull Moose Progressives had sufficiently divided the Republican Party so that Woodrow Wilson gained office with a plurality of the votes. On November 11, 1912, Stimson again broached the Pendleton proposal to Taft:

I desire to urge very strongly upon you the advisability of incorporating in your annual message to Congress a recommendation for legislation which will give to cabinet officers seats upon the floor of the Houses of Congress, for the purpose of answering questions and discussing matters within the purview of the business of their departments. . . . I think it would be particularly appropriate now in connection with your proposal of a national budget. . . . Indeed without giving them [the Cabinet officers] some such power as that, a budget presented by the executive would carry very little distance into the debates of Congress. There is no other practical way in which it could be explained to Congress and defined before it.[20]

The secretary then referred the President to Pendleton's 1864 report, which he had discovered since mentioning the idea in August. Stimson also noted Professor Ford's article in *Scribner's*, discussing "the evils of our system of separating the legislative from the executive." That same day, Stimson wrote two of his Cabinet colleagues, Attorney General George W. Wickersham and Secretary of the Interior Walter L.

Fisher, concerning the reform and noting the relevant literature on the subject.[21]

In a special message to Congress on December 12, 1912, President Taft formally recommended Stimson's suggestion. The future chief justice stated that a rigid separation of powers was neither intended constitutionally nor of practical benefit to the executive and legislative branches. The need was for a face-to-face meeting where the administration's policies could be clarified in advance of congressional criticism. Taft added that the seating of the Cabinet in Congress would "spur" each department head to take greater interest in the detail and goals of his establishment.[22] Three years later in his work on the Presidency, Taft predicted that the actual implementation of the Pendleton plan probably would encourage a Chief Executive to favor for his Cabinet individuals with prior legislative experience.[23]

On February 18, 1913—shortly before the completion of the lameduck session of the Sixty-second Congress—Representative Henry Schermerhorn DeForest submitted House Resolution 846, which sought to enact the Taft recommendation.[24] DeForest, who was a friend of War Secretary Stimson, had been defeated in his quest for reelection in 1912. Thus the "cause" remained for others to further.

ACTIVITY AT THE STATE LEVEL

As the discontent of the farmer, small businessman, and laborer had swelled, political movements in both major parties evolved in response. First Wisconsin under Governor Robert La Follette, then New York and California led by Charles Evans Hughes and Hiram Johnson were captured by the Progressives, operating primarily through the Republican Party. The oft-repeated phrase of students of government and Supreme Court justices that the states were social laboratories came to have real meaning as La Follette and his followers passed regulatory legislation, reorganized the various state departments, and alleviated at least temporarily the entrapment of the state by the forces of privilege. The men of talent and the men of votes were united when members of the University of Wisconsin and the practicing state politicians pooled their resources to serve the people of their state in an action program that was labeled "The Wisconsin Idea."

One of La Follette's active disciples was Charles McCarthy, who served as the chief of the Wisconsin Legislative Reference Department. In 1911, while Perry Belmont and Gamaliel Bradford were exchanging letters agreeing that the Pendleton plan had its greatest chance of success at the state level, McCarthy was a frequent correspondent of the Boston reformer. In his book *The Wisconsin Idea,* which was published in 1912, McCarthy wrote: "There should be some means whereby commissions may be called before the legislature in the same manner in which members of the English cabinet are subjected to questions or interpellation in the British parliament." [25]

At a session of the conference of governors which was held at Madison, Wisconsin, in November, 1914, McCarthy elaborated on his position. He urged that members of the state administrative commissions be subjected to questioning before the legislature where failure to secure a vote of confidence would be sufficient to eliminate the commission.[26]

In 1915, State Senator William M. Bray, Republican of Oshkosh, secured approval of a statute providing for interrogation of members of the Wisconsin Conservation Commission. By 1917, the provision had been extended to all appointive state officials and has remained in force to this day.[27]

The Wisconsin interpellation procedure has been resorted to only occasionally. The last time it was invoked was on March 12, 1941, when a member of the state Conservation

Commission was queried for almost forty-five minutes.[28] While the Wisconsin procedure could not be described as "punitive" since no official has ever been removed as a result of submitting himself to questioning, "it undoubtedly is an unpleasant experience." [29]

This method is not the one envisioned by the advocates of the Pendleton plan. A principal goal of men such as Bradford, Taft, and Stimson was to devise a system of executive-legislative communication in which there would be an exchange of views with a minimum of built-in hostility or advantage to either side.

Although the advent of the Wilson administration had brought with it Stimson's compulsory return to his New York law practice, he continued his interest in government at all levels. His temporary retirement from the national scene where he was to serve in the Cabinets of four Presidents—two from each party—provided Stimson with the opportunity to engage more extensively in sharing his reflections on government with his fellow citizens.[30]

On May 27, 1913, Stimson addressed the Philadelphia Law Academy on "Initiative and Responsibility of the Executive: A Remedy for Inefficient Legislation." He began with a thesis similar to that of Rousseau, who believed that individuals were basically good but that the system made them bad. Holding that Congress had a higher morality than the business world which surrounded it, Stimson advocated the admission of the Cabinet to legislative deliberations. Such action, he prophesied, would overcome the provincialism which was exhibited by the district-oriented representatives.[31]

The result of keeping the executive out of Congress because of the "dead line of separation" had been a system of committee government where "tremendous powers are exercised in secret and by men who, neither as committeemen nor as congressmen, are responsible to the country at large." [32] This was not only invisible government, but inefficient government.

The former war secretary recalled for his audience how a conference committee had inserted in the 1912 Army Appropriation Bill items which limited the choice of the President in selecting the chief of staff and curtailed the power of the secretary to supervise the construction of army posts. Neither item had been brought out in the open floor debate held in the House and Senate. This situation forced Stimson to lay aside any pretense of respect for the so-called separation of powers and borrow from a "friendly Senator" a Capitol room in which the secretary could "interview privately such Senators as would care to discuss the matter with him." [33]

Stimson believed that his reform would enhance "the importance and opportunities of legislators." Seating the Cabinet in Congress would increase party effectiveness since it meant inherently that there would be a well-defined program by the administration and the challenge of an alert opposition to meet it.[34] The new procedure would also

strike a death blow at the power of wealth and privilege which clings around the committee rooms and finally, by giving to the people of this country effective means by which their deliberate desires can be enacted into law, would terminate much of the dangerous criticism which is now aimed at our system of representative government.[35]

During the next year some influential support backed Stimson's position. In the summer of 1914, as war clouds were gathering in Europe, James W. Wadsworth, Jr., a former speaker of the New York Assembly, agreed that the Pendleton plan was desirable and practicable at the state level.[36] Ogden L. Mills, then a state senator-elect from the Seventeenth District of New York and later secretary of the treasury in the Hoover administration, argued that the "separation of powers" should not be confused with the "isolation of powers." "The former may or may not be wise; the latter is fatal, yet it is to the latter that we have been steadily and constantly tending." [37]

Stimson's ideas attracted more attention as the time neared for the beginning of the New York State Constitutional Convention of 1915. Prior to the meeting, the convention commission published studies strongly supporting the Pendleton proposal because it would make "unnecessary those subterranean relations between the two branches which inevitably spring up when official lines of communication are forbidden." [38]

The convention assembled on April 6, 1915, and its members divided into a number of committees where the detail of various amendments could be worked out. Stimson was chairman of the committee on state finances, which had the demanding task of formulating a provision to inaugurate an executive budget. On May 26, John J. Fitzgerald, chairman of the appropriations committee of the House of Representatives, testified. During the course of Fitzgerald's remarks, Representative Herbert Parsons, who was a close friend of both Taft and Stimson, asked him to comment on the idea of seating the Cabinet in Congress. Fitzgerald completely disapproved of the proposal. He argued that the House was too large to carry on effective interrogation and that the net result would be for department heads to overawe all but the most "unusual crank or persiferous individual." [39]

Two weeks later, Taft took direct issue with Fitzgerald, who had held that the Cabinet members would not want to appear and subject themselves to possible criticism. Taft was convinced that the Cabinet should be present to defend the administration since they did not enjoy "being pounded at the other end of the avenue without having an opportunity to explain." [40]

Stimson, on behalf of the committee on state finances, favorably reported a constitutional amendment which authorized the governor, controller, and department heads, "when requested by either house, to appear and be heard and to answer inquiries relative to the budget." [41] The proposal was never heard from again.[42]

Two years after New York considered a state version of the Pendleton plan, the idea was briefly revived in Massachusetts. During the summer of 1917, Governor Samuel W. McCall expanded on the remarks which he had made before the Massachusetts Constitutional Convention. Denying that he favored a change to the British cabinet system, the governor held, nevertheless, that an administration should have "the right to present its policies in an authoritative manner." He believed that the granting of seats in the legislature to the department heads along with the right to present and defend measures was essential if democracy was to continue to grow.[43]

A year later, on July 16, 1918, Josiah Quincy, the chairman of the committee on the executive, reported his group's recommendations to the full convention. Among them was the proposal to permit the governor to attend either house and speak upon any pending bill. Upon a written request from the governor or either branch of the legislature, any department head might also be admitted and have the right to speak, but not vote, on a matter within his official jurisdiction. The General Court (Massachusetts' legislature consisting of the house and senate) was to have the right to call upon the governor, or through him on his department heads, to furnish in writing information concerning the various departments. If the governor decided that the communication would be incompatible with the public interest, then it did not have to be forwarded.[44]

During the brief debate, Quincy, a former Boston mayor, stressed that the sole object of the proposal was "to bring these two branches of our government—which now operate very often too much at arms' length, with too little under-

standing on the part of each of the position of the other,—
into closer relations." [45] Various objections were voiced including the charges that passage would place "party government inside these legislative walls" and that it would be "adopt-
ing the English system." [46]

Although over half of the 319 delegates were Republicans,
the convention decided issues primarily as a result of individual inclination rather than party alignment. There was
a decided cleavage between the conservatives and the progressives in both parties but the outcome of the convention leaves
little doubt that it was the conservatives who were in control.[47]
Using two key votes—the selection of the convention president
and the initiative and referendum—as the criteria for determining conservative-progressive leanings, it is interesting
to note that all but one of the seven proponents during the
floor debate were progressives. Fourteen delegates had debated
the recommendation, seven for and seven against. Of the
seven opposed, four were conservatives, two were progressives,
and one split his vote on the guideline issues.[48]

The committee recommendation was refused a third reading
by a vote of 124 to 37 and thus another attempt to bridge the
alleged gap between the executive and the legislature was
effectively sidetracked.[49] Although in their various editions of
A Model State Constitution the Committee on State Government of the National Municipal League has continued to
endorse the Pendleton-type proposal, there has been no
further debate on the matter at the state level.[50]

ANDREW JACKSON MONTAGUE

With the conclusion of the Sixty-second Congress, the
DeForest resolution to implement President Taft's recommendation had expired. The "cause" was not long in being
resumed. Arriving from across the Potomac, former Virginia

Governor Andrew Jackson Montague was sworn in for his initial term in the House of Representatives. That same day he offered the first of his many bills which, if approved, would have authorized Cabinet participation in debate.[51]

Montague was to be reelected each term by his constituents until he passed away in office in 1937. During his twenty-four-year incumbency, he introduced eleven Pendleton-type bills. Strangely, Montague never advocated his own measures on the floor, although once in debate he did support a similar bill presented by a colleague.

Montague had publicly sanctioned the reform more than a year before Taft's attention was specifically focused on it by Stimson. At a dinner meeting of the Pennsylvania Bar Association, on June 27, 1911, Montague delivered a stirring appeal: "The Executive can perforce no longer regard the separation of powers; he must fight for his measures in the domain of the Legislature or see them quickly done to death." [52]

Holding that "this hiatus between executive and legislative powers is the demoralizing gap in our Government," Montague denied that the Founding Fathers intended it to be so.[53] He claimed the functioning of the modern British cabinet could not possibly have been discerned in 1787. "So not knowing, the Convention could not consider; and in the absence of consideration, no limitation upon such Cabinet activity can be inferred as a governmental policy." [54]

For Montague, opponents who bemoaned an engrafting of the British system onto our own were holding up "a man of straw." [55] The Cabinet would not become members of either house. No resignations would follow the tides of congressional displeasure. He did admit, however, that individual department heads might be pressured out of office through sheer unpleasantness.[56]

No longer would Cabinet members merely be administrators.

Now they would become "originators, formulators, and ex-
pounders of policies as well." [57] And this result, Montague
believed, was healthy for the survival of both the executive
and the legislative in a democracy.

In 1925, writing a one-page article for a popular magazine,
Montague, who had also served as attorney general of Virginia
and was a distinguished attorney in his own right, upheld the
constitutionality of the proposed procedure by noting Justice
Story's views that the separation of powers did not mean
"absolute" separation, but only that the "whole" power of any
one of the three branches should not be exercised by either
of the other two. Like Pendleton, Bradford, and Taft before
him, Montague believed the primary advantages to be derived
from enactment would be publicity and direct cooperation
in the place of privacy and indirect cooperation. [58]

RISING TENSIONS

Following America's entrance into the First World War,
two other legislators expressed an interest in the problem of
Cabinet-congressional relations by submitting bills to bring
more closely together the two branches of the government. On
June 18, 1917, Senator George Payne McLean, joining the
current efforts of Montague in the House, offered similar
legislation in the Senate.

McLean, a Connecticut Republican, was concerned about
the sweeping power over "production, distribution and con-
sumption" which Congress was then granting to the Wilson
administration. Noting Pendleton's Senate report of 1881—
and stressing in an obvious appeal for nonpartisan support
that the select committee had been composed of many of the
leading Democrats of that period—McLean recommended
that Congress "ought, if possible, to harmonize the thoughts

and actions of those who make the law with those who interpret and administer it." [59]

An interesting evolution in the McLean bill as opposed to its predecessors was that besides the regular Cabinet membership, the executive heads of the Federal Reserve Board, Tariff Commission, Federal Trade Commission, Shipping Board, Bureau of Efficiency, and Civil Service Commission would also be privileged to enter the legislative sanctuary and present the case for their own agencies. Here was recognition not only of emergency war offices, but also of that great and extensive so-called fourth branch of the government, consisting primarily of regulatory agencies which had developed outside the traditional line departments dating from the establishment of the Interstate Commerce Commission in 1887.

Senator McLean asked the chair to refer his bill to the committee on the judiciary. Discussion at once ensued concerning the proper reference of the measure. Lee Slater Overman, of North Carolina, urged that the presiding officer refer the bill to the committee on rules—of which Overman was chairman. Idaho Republican William Borah disagreed with both suggestions. He believed that the legislation never would be approved by the country unless the Cabinet were elected to office. After further exchange of opinion, another Republican, New Hampshire's eighty-year-old Jacob Gallinger, the chairman of the minority conference, made a suggestion which undoubtedly reflected the opinion of much of the Senate's majority and minority leadership: Gallinger hoped that the bill would be sent to the "Committee on the Disposition of Useless Papers in the Executive Departments."

McLean answered that while he had no doubt that the same influences which defeated the Pendleton plan in 1881 would defeat his own measure, he believed that the problem the proposal attempted to solve should be seriously considered by

Congress. Congress, as a whole, showed no inclination to take the New Englander's advice.[60]

On the House side of the Capitol, Representative Philip Campbell, of Kansas, sought to alleviate the growing executive domination of policy formulation when he offered his only public bill of the session. In early May, 1917, he had defended a fellow Kansan against what he regarded as the War Department "militarists" who favored the conscription act.[61] On the last day in July, Campbell introduced legislation providing for selection of the President's Cabinet from among the membership of the House. His effort was referred to the judiciary committee and, like its related proposals, remained buried by opposition, apathy, and what some regarded as more urgent measures.[62]

APPROVAL FROM HARDING

In the two decades between the First and Second World Wars, there was an increase in the number of proposals to rearrange Cabinet-congressional relations along the Pendleton line. President Warren G. Harding, a former senator, thoroughly approved of the admission of the Cabinet to legislative debates. The idea was discussed at a Cabinet meeting and it received "decided sympathy." [63] Harding's secretary of state, Charles Evans Hughes, proved to be an active supporter in many of his public addresses.[64] Enthusiastic approval also was provided by Nicholas Murray Butler, the president of Columbia University.[65] In addition, many magazines and newspapers urged what an author in the *Nation* described as the "One Immediate Reform." [66]

In the Senate and House, new "converts" sponsored various bills applying the Pendleton remedy to what they regarded as an inexcusable situation. On January 27, 1920, Representative Charles A. Mooney, an Ohio Democrat, introduced the first of what eventually were to amount to four bills endorsing the traditional solution.[67]

The following year, Pennsylvania's Melville Clyde Kelly joined Mooney's efforts with his first of six attempts between 1921 and 1933.[68] Kelly, an ex-newspaperman, who wavered between party affiliation with the Republican and a combination of the Roosevelt-Progressive, Democratic, and Prohibitionist elements in his district, never swerved in his advocacy of seating the Cabinet in Congress. With Kelly, as with Gamaliel Bradford, the plan became a consistent "hobby."

Kelly wrote each member of the Harding Cabinet to elicit their opinions on his proposal. The reaction of the department heads was very favorable. President Harding, who voiced no objection to the procedure, even raised the subject at a Cabinet meeting on June 22, 1922. Kelly was advised to amend his bill so that the whole Cabinet did not have to be present on the floor at the same time. The officials preferred to appear and answer questions only when business of their department was under discussion.[69] Already, congressional criticism had been voiced against Attorney General Harry M. Daugherty. The attorney general was said to have complained about the lack of opportunity to challenge personally his Senate inquisitors on the floor.[70]

Three years later, in January, 1925, Representative Meyer Jacobstein—in an action in which few of the recent proponents had engaged—spoke on the House floor in favor of the Pendleton plan. He had become disturbed by the impotency of the House "in getting at the facts and policies of the various Federal Departments." As had Kelly with the Harding Cabinet, Jacobstein wrote to several of President Coolidge's department heads, enclosing a copy of his proposed bill, and asking for comments. The favorable replies he received encouraged him to submit his bill.[71]

In the debate on January 6, 1925, Jacobstein quoted Secretary of State Hughes to the effect that "an ounce of fact is worth many pounds of talk." Missouri's Ralph F. Lozier objected to the bill as a "radical departure from our scheme of Government" and predicted that its passage would mean the beginning of a new era of executive influence through coercion and duress in Congress. Jacobstein retorted that he would rather have open coercion attempted before the whole House than "that sort of intimidation which comes through White House breakfasts." [72]

Besides that of McLean, the only other officially recorded Senate interest which occurred during the two interwar decades was that of Senator James Couzens. Even though Couzens was chairman of the Senate committee on civil service, no hearings or debate were ever held on the version of the Pendleton bill which he introduced on March 4, 1926.[73]

TWO ALTERNATIVES

Apart from the traditional attempts to rectify what some regarded as a lack of communication between the legislative and the executive, two other suggestions which deserve mention were made in the House of Representatives in the 1920s. The first alternative was presented on April 22, 1924. In the course of a debate over the merits of an appropriation for the investigation of insects which affected truck crops, Representative William D. Upshaw—a self-styled,[74] triple-threat "Successor to Bryan," "Abe Lincoln of the South," and "Billy Sunday of Congress"—pleaded that the presidential responsibilities had become "increasingly intolerable." A possible solution, urged Upshaw, was to elect Cabinet officers on the same ticket as the President.[75] How this solution would ease the presidential burden Upshaw never made clear. He proceeded to note approvingly that on the state level many of the department heads were elected separately by the people—a thought, even then, undoubtedly disconcerting to both students of public administration and reformers, who were advocating the merits of a single executive whom the people could hold politically accountable.

Upshaw believed the public could evaluate the presidential candidate better if they knew in advance who would work with him. He hoped that his suggestions would relieve the party's standard-bearer of preelection obligations and even remove the necessity for large contributions—another thought that would not be well received, but this time by the party hopefuls and "fat cats" who quadrennially attempt to obligate the potential Chief Executive to their will. Upshaw was not concerned, however, with either the few students of politics or the many students of influence. For him, it was: "The people! The people! They would be in the saddle as never before, first-hand and forever. This vital change would help to strike the fetters from our present executive system and prove a practical safeguard in the march of real democracy." [76]

This final flutter of oratory was applauded by the House, not an uncommon practice during particularly dull sessions. After some further sparring, the members again turned their attention to the less flamboyant, but more urgent problem of an appropriation to "investigate and encourage the adoption of improved methods of farm management and practice."

The second alternative was offered in 1926 when Representative Loring M. Black, Jr. introduced a bill providing for the printing of reports of the Cabinet sessions in the *Congressional Record*.[77] On February 10, 1926, Black presented his reasons. A stenographic summary, he argued, would reveal "the mysteries of the White House" and more specifically the reasoning processes of the department heads. Black objected to the idea of seating the Cabinet in Congress as being too time-consuming and of little benefit. Instead, if Congress knew what the Cabinet had said to the President as well as to each other, it could discover "what they are driving at." Applause greeted Black's remarks just as it had those of Upshaw. As with so many other applauded speeches, no action was taken.[78]

HARLAN'S BILL

A good example of the receptivity of some members of the House to the appearance of Cabinet officers on the floor—even if they remained silent—occurred in the late twenties. On March 15, 1928, Representative George Huddleston, of Alabama, interrupted a debate on the annual Naval Appropriations Bill by remarking that "to-day must be a holiday of the Navy Department." Huddleston pointed out that the secretary of the navy, Curtis Wilbur, was seated on the front bench. The congressman granted that while this was in accordance with the Rules, he desired his colleagues to know that during his fourteen years in the House, no Cabinet officer ever had been on the floor when a bill pertaining to his department was under consideration. Huddleston also noted that the assistant secretary, judge advocate, and numerous other naval officials were in the gallery.[79]

Although many members were receptive to the Alabaman's complaint, a fellow Democrat, Charles L. Abernethy, objected to Huddleston's "poor taste" in raising the issue. The Republican majority leader, John Q. Tilson, finally rose to defend his party's Cabinet officer. Tilson expressed regret that the members of the Cabinet did not come more often. Several members supported Tilson's position by recalling in turn how Secretary of War William Howard Taft in the Roosevelt administration and Wilson's secretary of the navy, Josephus Daniels, had both appeared on the floor.[80]

Some of the Democratic minority continued to snipe at Secretary Wilbur by broadcasting their objection to any department head's being present when legislation from his agency was under discussion. The withdrawal of the secretary ended the debate.[81] Congressional sensitivity to suspected—or at least, overt—executive "pressure" was still acute. The New Deal of 1933 was to increase this sensitivity.

Although bills advocating the Pendleton remedy were introduced periodically in both the Senate and House throughout the interwar period, it was not until the middle thirties that an attempt received more than an apathetic response. On February 6, 1935, Byron B. Harlan, an Ohio congressman, offered a bill following the usual pattern.[82] Within a week, on February 14—during a lull in a "pork barrel" debate over the feasibility of the army engineers' construction of a waterway across Florida and the full legislative attention required to pass a resolution authorizing celebration of the 150th anniversary of the writing of the American Constitution—Harlan received an opportunity to present his argument.

The Republican minority heckled Harlan. The stalwarts of the Grand Old Party were not alone in their denunciation of what they regarded as the executive encroachments of the New Deal. Unhappy Democrats also engaged in a round of catharsis as they vented their feelings against the executive. Said Warren Duffey, an Ohio Democrat who came and went with the New Deal's first term: "There are some members of the Cabinet we would not want on the floor of the House." [83] California Republican John Henry Hoeppel, editor of the *Retired Men's News*—an enterprise to which he could devote every effort following his compulsory retirement by the voters a year later—suggested that the Cabinet should be "muzzled" and not encouraged to flood the representatives of the people with further propaganda.[84]

When a noninflammatory question was finally raised, Harlan, who had become very disconcerted by the previous badgering, replied: "Oh, I want to go ahead with my address, and I wish the gentleman would not take up so much time." [85] The excursion from "pork barrel" politics was ended a few days later when one congressman became more interested in challenging Harlan's tariff views on wrapper tobacco than in hearing the merits of seating the Cabinet in Congress.[86]

Despite the distractions which he faced, Harlan did add some refinements to the reasoning which had been presented previously by those interested in improving Cabinet-congressional relations. Harlan agreed that executive actions would be bathed in publicity; in addition, he believed that many of the "purely sectional and bloc bills" which representatives now sponsored would never be introduced since they could not stand the exposure to which a Cabinet officer might subject them. He anticipated that with more active leadership in Congress, the platforms of both parties would be better implemented and responsibility assumed.

Harlan was not discouraged by the floor reception given to his measure. On March 16, 1935, he wrote Perry Belmont, who had been advocating the proposal since 1878, that he would continue to seek support for the bill.[87] Belmont was recruited to write to the chairman of the judiciary committee, Hatton Sumners, who presumably favored giving the legislation a public hearing. No hearing resulted. Although the bill was reintroduced during the next Congress, in 1937, Sumners's committee had by that time become more and more involved in the so-called Roosevelt Court Packing Bill and the evolving Constitutional Revolution of 1937 to the exclusion of all other issues. For some members of Congress, no longer was it a question of coordinating two of the three branches of government, but of saving one from utter destruction.

Also in 1937, another Ohioan continued the efforts of those who had preceded him from his native state, including Pendleton, Garfield, Taft, Mooney, and Harlan. William R. Thom submitted his bill on July 15, 1937.[88]

Five months later, Thom was joined by Texas's contribution

to both politics and the dictionary, Maury Maverick. "Maverick" Maverick offered two resolutions, one to extend the privilege of debate and another to provide for a question hour during which department heads would appear and respond to inquiries directed to them by the legislators.[89] It was this latter plan which gained the attention of Representative Estes Kefauver in the next decade and which was to secure the most widespread public approval.

The "Roaring Twenties" and the "Depressing Thirties" thus ended with no more legislative progress toward seating the Cabinet in Congress than had occurred in 1864. There was, however, increasing sympathy in Congress and among influential individuals in the public at large. The most noteworthy attempt to restructure Cabinet-congressional relations was yet to come.

The Kefauver Question Period

THE REPUBLICANS recouped some of their earlier losses in the 1942 congressional elections, but not enough to secure control of either house. The political appeal of Franklin Roosevelt and his New Deal was to keep them from power until "That Man" was no longer in the Presidency. Realistically, neither party as such had won in November, 1942; rather, the conservative elements in both political groupings had increased their power. Discontent grew as the people watched disheartening defeats in the early months following America's entry into the Second World War. Wake, Bataan, and Corregidor, combined with such governmental webs as rationing and price controls, provided ready targets for the anti-administration forces.

An increasing number of legislators were tugging at the executive reins which had constricted the scope of congressional activity since the early New Deal. One did not need a crystal ball to forecast that the reaction would erupt momentarily as the legislative "onlooker" attempted to pry open the front door which had shielded executive policy-makers from scrutiny.

With such a course of action in mind, Representative William Thom, the Ohio Democrat, again introduced his Cabinet bill on December 3, 1942.[1] Anticipating that the "conservative" Congress would be more liberal in the number of committee investigations which it undertook, Thom argued that the privileges of the floor should be given the Cabinet so that the whole House membership could witness the charges and defense— rather than merely a small group sitting in a closed committee session in a back room of the Capitol or House Office Building. Both logically and politically, Thom also insisted that the right to interrogate the administration representatives belonged to the legislature and not just to members of the Washington press corps.[2]

Thom first became interested in the possibilities of the question hour when he was touring England in 1924. While visiting the House of Commons he had acquired a daily question sheet on which were listed inquiries to be asked of the cabinet on a specific day. He immediately realized that "it was an admirable way of getting concise and intelligent answers on current public questions." As a representative, Thom was interested in raising the declining congressional prestige as well as providing information to clarify public discussion. Closer relations between the Cabinet and Congress also would mean a "better Cabinet," since the President would select the department heads "with the thought that they must be so trained in government that they could meet the challenges of the members . . . in the question and answer period."[3]

Estes Kefauver, then completing his third year in Congress as a representative from Tennessee, expressed interest in Thom's arguments. A little over a month later, Kefauver submitted a similar bill.[4] This proposal, which was drafted along the traditional line of granting the Cabinet privileges of debate on the floor, apparently gained little backing. Consequently, in October, 1943, Kefauver offered a resolution which provided for a question period in the House.[5]

The new proposal (H. Res. 327) was received more agreeably. Reports earlier in the year indicated that President Roosevelt had lost his control over the House.[6] In the fall, the administration attempted conciliation by asking various legislative leaders to participate in discussions on both financial and foreign affairs.[7]

Floor time was granted to Kefauver on November 12, 1943,

so that he could advocate the advantages of his measure. The Tennessee representative demonstrated a thorough knowledge of the idea's history, as he discoursed on the appearance of the department heads in the First Congress, the two Pendleton bills, and such distinguished advocates as John W. Davis—a former Democratic presidential candidate and leading constitutional authority—Elihu Root, and William Howard Taft.[8]

Though some constitutional uncertainties were expressed in the discussion which followed Kefauver's presentation, many Democrats and Republicans gave verbal support to the resolution. John Vorys, an Ohio Republican, offered the interesting analogy that no one seemed to have an objection to the attorney general, a member of the Cabinet, appearing before and being questioned by the Supreme Court—a branch co-equal with Congress and the Executive under the separation of powers doctrine.[9]

That Anglophobia had not died was apparent in Kefauver's sensitivity to the old charge of "aping the English." He carefully assured his colleagues that the United States possessed "the best form of government . . . ever devised" and that "the writers of our Constitution had almost divine inspiration." [10] The resolution would merely inaugurate "a good American practice." [11]

As had Thom the year before, Kefauver viewed the current status of Congress as similar to that of a legitimate theater which had been run out of business by the organ grinder and his monkey up the street. Face-to-face contact meant that many useless investigations might be avoided and that "news" concerning new public policies would be made in Congress rather than almost solely during an executive press conference. Ghost-writing might prove much less effective since the department head would have to be responsive to inquiries and often would be asked additional questions to clarify his original statement. The whole process, reflected the lanky Tennesseean, meant improvement of the executive's accountability to the House.[12]

The historic appearance of Secretary of State Hull before a joint session of Congress on November 18, 1943, following his return from the Moscow conference, gave unexpected impetus to the Kefauver resolution.[13] But many representatives wanted the opportunity to ask questions, rather than merely be subjected to executive pronouncements from the pulpit of their own church.

Simultaneous with the Hull appearance a House Democratic leader—his face livid with anger—who preferred to remain unidentified, denounced the Kefauver plan as a scheme which would bring about "ridiculous debate."[14] The New York *Times* Washington pundit, Arthur Krock, sagely predicted that the House "leadership must change in personnel as well as in viewpoint if the reform is to come."[15]

More debate—ridiculous and otherwise—ensued in late November. The Republican minority was worried that the Kefauver proposal would limit their opportunity to ask questions, since the queries were to be filtered through the various standing committees where decisions were made by majority rule on a party basis.[16]

Other procedural details were explored, as a few members inquired of the resolution's sponsor how Congress could compel a Cabinet member to appear if he declined. Kefauver replied that a sufficient stimulant existed in the force of public opinion. He also ventured that Congress would become more powerful if the measure secured approval. Military Affairs Chairman Andrew May—who in a few years perhaps came to realize that some types of influence send one to jail—disagreed. He expressed the belief that the gain in power accrued to the President and his agents.[17]

DISCUSSION WITHIN THE BUREAU OF THE BUDGET

On November 26, 1943, Representative Kefauver, pleased with the reception his question period idea had elicited from the newspapers and many members of Congress, wrote to each member of the Cabinet and the heads of the independent agencies and offices. He enclosed a copy of his resolution and explained that the proposed procedure was

intended to be beneficial to both Congress and the Executive Departments, by bringing about an open and frank consultation. It is not intended to permit any immaterial or picayune questions—it is not to be a heckling period, but an honest effort to improve teamwork.[18]

The department heads were asked to express an opinion on the legislation and to notify Kefauver if they were willing to appear before a hearing of the House rules committee and testify concerning the measure.

When the Executive Office of the President was organized in the fall of 1939, the function of coordinating and clearing the views on legislative policy held by the myriad of federal establishments—ranging from the vast departments of Cabinet rank down to the smallest independent office—was given to the Division of Legislative Reference, one of the five major operating units of the Bureau of the Budget.[19]

The impetus for centralized control over legislative clearance had developed out of the findings of the President's Committee on Administrative Management, which submitted its report in 1937. This group, presided over by Louis Brownlow, a former journalist and distinguished authority on public administration, held that the major need in American government was to provide the President, as Chief Executive, with the authority to supervise the executive branch commensurate with the responsibility granted him by the Constitution.[20] Besides coordinating the annual presidential budget which forced an agency to justify its financial and policy program within the executive branch prior to the program's submission to Congress, the aim of the Budget Bureau's legislative clearance function was to seek a continuing semblance of unity within the administration throughout the year. The stamp of approval that the views expressed were "In Accord with the Program of the President" aided in achieving this goal.

In the autumn of 1943, the Legislative Reference Division consisted of a small staff of career civil servants headed by F. J. Bailey, who served as an assistant director of the budget and chief of the division. Bailey's principal aide was Virgil L. Almond, the chief legislative analyst.

Kefauver's letter to the various departments and independent agencies of the executive branch requesting an opinion on his question period resolution brought the Bureau of the Budget and ultimately the President into the picture. On December 2, 1943, F. J. Bailey was notified that the United States Maritime Commission, at its regular meeting on November 30, had unanimously endorsed Kefauver's proposal. Admiral Emory S. Land, the chairman, drafted a letter to Kefauver explaining the favorable action. Before sending the reply, clearance was attempted by telephone from Legislative Reference in accordance with the established directives.

Bailey drafted an intraoffice memorandum to Budget Director Harold D. Smith explaining the nature of the proposal and asking: "Do you think it would be safe enough to clear out favorable reports . . . without waiting for a Presidential determination in the matter?" [21]

No decision was immediately forthcoming from Director Smith, who was preoccupied with the final weeks of preparation on the presidential budget for the 1945 fiscal year. On December 1, Kefauver had written Smith seeking an affirmative endorsement from him at "an early hearing" of the House Rules Committee.[22]

On December 7, 1943—five days after Bailey had first sought the advice of the director—Virgil L. Almond sent a memorandum to the assistant directors in charge of the Fiscal, Estimates, and Administrative Management divisions. At 9:30 that morn-

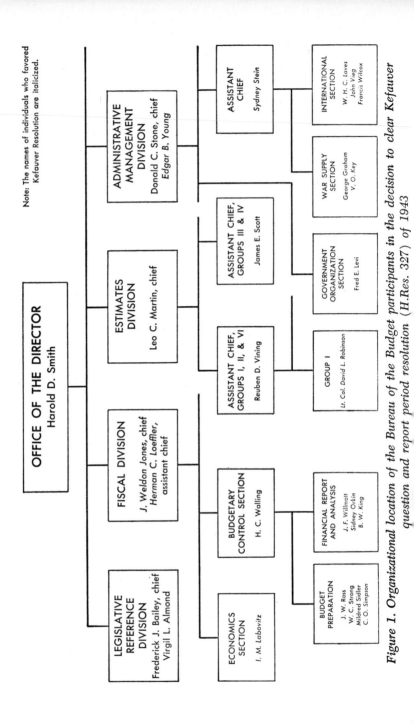

Note: The names of individuals who favored Kefauver Resolution are italicized.

OFFICE OF THE DIRECTOR
Harold D. Smith

LEGISLATIVE REFERENCE DIVISION
Frederick J. Bailey, chief
Virgil L. Almond

FISCAL DIVISION
J. Weldon Jones, chief
Herman C. Loeffler, assistant chief

ESTIMATES DIVISION
Leo C. Martin, chief

ADMINISTRATIVE MANAGEMENT DIVISION
Donald C. Stone, chief
Edgar B. Young

ECONOMICS SECTION
I. M. Labovitz

BUDGETARY CONTROL SECTION
H. C. Walling

ASSISTANT CHIEF, GROUPS I, II, & VI
Reuben D. Vining

ASSISTANT CHIEF, GROUPS III & IV
James E. Scott

ASSISTANT CHIEF
Sydney Stein

BUDGET PREPARATION
J. W. Ross
W. C. Strong
Mildred Sidler
C. O. Simpson

FINANCIAL REPORT AND ANALYSIS
J. F. Willmott
Sidney Orkin
B. W. King

GROUP I
Lt. Col. David L. Robinson

GOVERNMENT ORGANIZATION SECTION
Fred E. Levi

WAR SUPPLY SECTION
George Graham
V. O. Key

INTERNATIONAL SECTION
W. H. C. Laves
John Vieg
Francis Wilcox

Figure 1. Organizational location of the Bureau of the Budget participants in the decision to clear Kefauver question and report period resolution (H.Res. 327) of 1943

ing a proposed draft reply to Kefauver had arrived in Legislative Reference from H. A. Millis, chairman of the National Labor Relations Board. Interestingly enough, of the ten answers submitted to the Bureau of the Budget during the next month, this was the only negative reply. Yet it was this response which Almond circulated with his memorandum asking the three division chiefs for the position that the bureau should take in clearing the reports.[23]

Although Millis granted that the value of a question period might have "very real" advantages for executive departments and independent agencies which were not charged primarily with quasi-judicial functions, he did not concede any benefit for an independent agency such as the National Labor Relations Board. While "sympathetic" to Kefauver's resolution, Millis thought

that in respect to an independent agency like the National Labor Relations Board, the great preponderance of whose work lies in the consideration and determination of contested issues of fact and of law, the utilization of a question period directed to a member would not be feasible nor in the best interests of an impartial administration of the law. It will, I think, readily be appreciated that a member of such a quasi-judicial agency would find it well-nigh impossible to discuss issues in the abstract and without giving ground for a belief that such a discussion reflected a pre-judgment of issues which might in whole or in part then be involved in cases awaiting adjudication before the agency.[24]

In all three divisions, the impetus of the Almond memorandum started active discussions as to the feasibility of the Kefauver resolution. The first evaluation took place in the Budgetary Control Section of J. Weldon Jones's Fiscal Division. The budget control staff was divided equally on the desirability of the bureau's supporting the proposed legislation. Four members held that the size of Congress prevented it from effectively exploring departmental policy and administration in a question period before the full House. This group believed that "the

proposed questioning might be very embarrassing to department heads." Their solution was a "more searching questioning
of executive officials by Congressional committees."

The other four members favored Kefauver's plan with various degrees of modification. Two thought that the idea was a
good one if Congress would "forego the temptation to utilize
the questioning period for political sniping." A third condemned
the resolution as an attempt to make the Cabinet members
directly accountable to Congress. Instead, this staff member
advocated that the President be called before Congress with
the privilege of either sending the department heads in his
place or bringing them with him to aid in answering the questions.

John F. Willmott, who summarized the staff discussions, was
wholeheartedly and without reservations in favor of Kefauver's
proposal. He predicted that enactment of the procedure would
result in a Congress which was better informed and department
heads who were "more alert and conscientious."

Commenting on the possible "embarrassment" which four
members had feared the departmental officials would suffer,
Willmott's reaction was that "it would do some of them good to
get a well-aimed harpoon now and then." He concluded:

If some administrators are forced to display a humiliating ignorance
of their own agencies, they may exert themselves so as not to be
caught in that status next time. And if Congressmen deal in triviali-
ties, let that fact be highlighted for the entire Nation to see. By all
means broadcast the proceedings over the radio.[25]

On December 10, Herman C. Loeffler, the assistant chief of
the Fiscal Division, forwarded Willmott's summary to his su-
pervisor, J. Weldon Jones. Loeffler added some comments of
his own in addition to those of I. M. Labovitz in the Economics
Section. Labovitz was "quite favorably inclined" although he
was concerned over the possibilities for heckling the administration. Loeffler favored the resolution "mildly" and, like Labo-

vitz, was concerned with the "possible circus performances, particularly if the Executive happens to be of a different political party than the one in control of the House." But he granted that "this additional horseplay, if it occurs, would only be 'more of the same,'" and the proposed procedure offered the hope that accurate information might be received by a large proportion of the House. He suggested that a legislative clearance procedure be applied to the replies which Cabinet members provided in response to questioning from the floor so that Congress could ascertain whether the statement was an individual opinion or "in accordance with the program of the President." [26]

Jones immediately forwarded the opinions of his division to Bailey with the notation, "I would vote for the Bill." [27] The result was that of the eleven people who had offered an opinion in the Fiscal Division on Kefauver's resolution, seven favored it (including the chief and assistant chief of the division) and four opposed it.

The report from the Division of Estimates which arrived three days later did not reveal any extensive discussion among the staff. One reason for the seeming lack of consultation was probably the last-minute pressure created by the nearness of the annual date for submission of the bulky executive budget to Congress.

R. D. Vining, who was one of several assistant division chiefs, preferred to answer Almond's query on practical rather than theoretical grounds. He advised that regardless of the particular agency views, all replies that the Bureau of the Budget received should "be cleared without objection" since the resolution "deals with a policy of Congress and not with a policy of the President." The finding as to whether or not Kefauver's remedy would be effective in solving the problems of contemporary legislative-executive relations should not be the principal factor in determining the bureau's position. The realistic view suggested that the bureau, no matter what the opinion might be, could not oppose the Kefauver idea as lacking accord with the President's program. To do this "would give good grounds for charges that the Administration was covering up" and attempting to screen the Senate and House from the opportunity to receive needed information upon which to base legislative decisions.[28]

Another Estimates Division assistant chief, J. E. Scott, penned a note on Vining's memorandum with the somewhat cynical comment that if the legislation was adopted Congress would "soon learn that the heads of the agencies are not best qualified to answer the questions." The division head, Leo C. Martin, forwarded the statement to Almond without adding any comment of his own.[29]

In the meantime three more drafts and requests for clearance had been received in Legislative Reference. Major General Philip B. Fleming, the administrator of the Federal Works Agency, expressed his willingness to appear before the Committee on Rules since he believed Kefauver's suggested procedure was "a healthy one." [30]

The second to arrive was the favorable reply of the unanimous Maritime Commission, whose response had originally initiated the current legislative clearance activity.[31]

The most interesting of the three answers was the one from Secretary of Labor Frances Perkins. Miss Perkins was "disposed to endorse the resolution" because she believed that the procedure would be more efficient than the present system where a department head often repeated essentially the same testimony before different committees of the same chamber. Although she thought that "harmonious relations" would ensue, the secretary desired Representative Kefauver to amend the language of his resolution to permit the executive official the right "to refuse to answer questions when, in his discretion, the public interest would not be served by disclosure." Desiring to have her discretion and at times keep her distance too, Miss

Perkins also believed that the resolution should be amended to permit subordinate officials to appear in place of the Cabinet member because "the information sought is frequently of a highly technical nature." [32]

Having received the opinions he had sought initially from two of the three Budget divisions, Chief Legislative Analyst Almond prepared a summary of the reactions for Harold D. Smith, the director of the Budget. Although the Fiscal Division had supported the Kefauver plan seven to four, Almond concluded that it did "not appear to be very enthusiastic over the proposal either one way or the other." His own view teetered between the position that the question period "might be helpful in giving the entire membership of the House first-hand information" and that of fear that various blocs and parties would "heckle" the administrators. Almond doubted that the department head would be able "to answer impromptu the questions that are put to him." The result would be embarrassment for the executive branch. He finally resolved the dilemma by agreeing with the suggestion of the Estimates Division that no position be taken for or against the Kefauver idea and that the reports from the various government establishments be forwarded automatically to Representative Kefauver for his information.[33]

THE VIEWS OF THE POLITICAL SCIENTISTS

Although the Division of Administrative Management had been slow to answer Almond's initial memorandum seeking advice concerning the Kefauver resolution, the tardiness was not due to a lack of talent or interest in expressing an opinion among its personnel. The primary function of this division of the bureau was to strengthen and improve management practices in all parts of the executive branch. The staff, however, did not consist solely of technicians trained in the mysteries of flow charts and time and motion studies. In order to provide an "over-all" view of the annoying minutiae of federal administration, a small but select group of political scientists had been assembled under the efficient leadership of Donald C. Stone, who, in 1939, was appointed assistant director in charge of administrative management. Of the ten individuals from Administrative Management who took part in the discussions on the Kefauver idea, nine were members of the American Political Science Association.[34] Although this professional affiliation did not assure unanimous opinion one way or another, it did guarantee vigorous debate.

One of the participants has recalled that Stone made it a practice to consult the political science group on the long-range implications of many governmental policies. This action maintained not only professional, but organizational efficiency.

The initial catalyzing move on the Kefauver proposal was made by George A. Graham, the chief of the War Supply Section. Stone had charged Graham and V. O. Key, Jr., of the same section, with the task of preparing for a staff meeting a general statement of the issues involved in the enactment of the proposed question period. Graham's own reaction was highly favorable. Face-to-face discussions between members of the administration and Congress were needed. His thesis was that relations between the two branches were unsatisfactory because of a dependence on written as opposed to personal contact.

The hiatus between the separate fiefdoms at opposite ends of Pennsylvania Avenue supposedly was bridged by having control of both the White House and the Capitol in the hands of the same political party. But for Graham, this supposed link was wanting even with single party control, let alone the simultaneous placement of both Republicans and Democrats in positions of power. The party was not an effective link; Graham believed that there existed a "considerable portion of the Government's business which is not necessarily a matter of organization politics or campaign strategy."

The opportunity for personal contact provided by the Kefauver plan would "increase the understanding and mutual respect of the Executive and Legislative Branches." He held this view on the basis of the bureau's own experience in dealing with numerous federal agencies. Often, these almost rival principalities exhibited suspicion toward a legally sanctioned integrator such as the Bureau of the Budget, which acted on behalf of the Chief Executive. The frequent contact between the bureau's staff and the departmental administrators had resulted in a feeling of confidence that could not be achieved "by means of memoranda and written reports alone."

Graham also urged that a section be incorporated into the resolution indicating the differences between "proper" and "improper" types of questions. The presiding officer would have to maintain "fair play" and "rule out questions which were in themselves speeches or harangues by members of the House."

Graham believed, with reforming zeal, that the Kefauver plan gave the bureau an opportunity to advocate placement of the quasi-judicial agencies within the Cabinet departments.[35] This reform had originally been proposed by the President's Committee on Administrative Management. It would even allay the fears of the chairman of the National Labor Relations Board who had objected to the possibility that legislators might equate the general answers given to policy questions with future specific case decisions.

On December 18, 1943, Stone called a 2 p.m. meeting in his office to discuss the implications of the Kefauver resolution and what recommendation the staff of Administrative Management should make to Almond and the director. Besides Stone, Graham, and Key, the meeting included Sydney Stein, Jr., the assistant chief of the division; Edgar B. Young, chief administrative assistant; Fred E. Levi, head of the Government Organization Section; and Lieutenant Colonel David L. Robinson, who was not responsible to Stone as he was a group head in the Estimates Division. Of the seven present at the meeting, only Graham and Key were university political scientists. Three others were affiliated political scientists who had made their careers in either consulting or practice at the state and local levels. Before Harold D. Smith brought him to the bureau in 1939, Stone had been executive director of the Public Administration Service located in Chicago. He was associated closely with the Public Administration Clearing House whose director was Louis Brownlow, former chairman of the President's Committee on Administrative Management. Levi had served with Smith for two years when the latter was Michigan's director of the budget. In 1939 Roosevelt appointed Smith to the important budget post, and the director brought Levi along. Stein had been head of his own investment consulting firm in Chicago.

Five of the participants thought that "not much harm and possibly some good" might come of Kefauver's proposal. Stone described Levi and himself as being "very bearish" concerning the idea. The majority of the group believed that the direct relationship between the Cabinet and Congress "would be less serious than the *sub rosa* relations" which were then prevalent. Instead of dividing the President from his department heads, they believed, the question period "would probably place a premium on agreement on policy within the Executive Branch for it would be extremely embarrassing for different officials to appear before the House with different stories."

The staff noted that the need for policy coordination raised two additional implications. First, there would have to be more consultation within the administration in order to attain advance agreement on presidential programs. This suggested a more effective use of the Cabinet than was being made. In the second place, the seven correctly foresaw that any attempt by the Chief Executive to secure departmental conformity to his policy would be subjected to severe attack from those legislators who had objected to the legislative clearance procedure of the Budget Bureau.

The group also anticipated that oral questioning "might have some effect on the type of person appointed to head agencies." Presumably the effective departmental official would need to be more than the "quiet type" who was a capable administrator. The discussion brought agreement that the administration might receive better treatment before the full House membership than it did before the specialized—and often parochially interested—committees. But while there might be "less hitting below the belt" than occurred in committee, "an unpopular official could easily be crucified" on the floor.

In reporting the staff meeting's conclusions to Budget Director Smith, Stone concluded that "the effects of the proposal would probably not be profound. Both its advocates and its opponents would probably be disappointed." [36] After the summary of the discussion had been typed, Stone penned the following message to Smith: "I have given here more consideration to the favorable views of staff than to the unfavorable ones which Levi and I think outweigh the favorable." [37] Stone and Levi were the members of the group who had known Smith the longest, the former having been initially appointed by the director and the latter having been his assistant in Michigan.

There is no record of Smith's own reaction; however, three days after the staff meeting in the Administrative Management Division, Acting Director of the Budget Wayne Coy, who was substituting for Smith, agreed with the recommendation of the staff divisions and approved for clearance the agency replies which had been prepared in response to Kefauver's inquiry.[38] Within a week, the affirmative opinions of the War Production

Board, Foreign Economic Administration, and Federal Communications Commission were received and approved for return to Kefauver.[39]

One component of the Division of Administrative Management which had not been represented in Stone's staff meeting of December 18 was the International Section. This group consisted of three political scientists who were strongly in favor of the Kefauver measure. Two of the three, John A. Vieg and Walter H. C. Laves, joined George Graham, who had been at the Stone conference, and met with Representative Kefauver for a Capitol luncheon on December 28, 1943. The congressman impressed all three as "a highly intelligent, soft-spoken gentleman . . . seriously concerned both to improve working relationships between the two great political branches of the government and to raise the caliber and the prestige of the Congress." [40]

Before the luncheon, Kefauver had shown the Budget Bureau representatives a stack of correspondence from departmental officials and distinguished private citizens who endorsed his resolution. He indicated that no unfavorable replies had been received. Proof of widespread public support for the measure was found in a Gallup poll which indicated 72% approval for bringing the Cabinet before the Congress.[41]

House Speaker Sam Rayburn's hostility toward the proposal was discussed. Rayburn's "cold attitude" apparently was not based on an opinion as to the probable effects upon executive-legislative relations. Instead, the speaker had "something approaching an obsession"—as one member of the luncheon conference later described it—that the floor of the House of Representatives should be closed to all but members. Rayburn had strenuously objected to Madame Chiang Kai-shek's appearance before the House, but the demand to advance the prestige of America's struggling Asian ally had overcome his reservations.[42] He was more successful in maintaining his views when his refusal to permit further "outside" floor discussion compelled the 435 representatives to overflow the small Library of Congress auditorium in order to hear Secretary of War Henry L. Stimson and Chief of Staff George Catlett Marshall report to them on strategy and war mobilization problems. Congressional convenience would have been served more adequately if the reports from the two War Department officials had been heard in the House chamber.

The three political scientists were favorably impressed by the fact that Kefauver had "already tried to take into consideration whatever practical criticism and objections could be brought up against the plan." [43] They returned to the Budget Bureau determined to secure a more effective endorsement of the idea from the director and, ultimately, the President.

Two days prior to the New Year, a "paper barrage" was begun in the International Section. John Vieg forwarded to Budget Director Smith a summary of Graham's, Laves's, and his own impressions of the Kefauver luncheon.[44] Walter Laves and Francis Wilcox, also of the International Section, wrote separate memorandums and submitted them to their division head, Donald C. Stone.

Laves believed that the Kefauver resolution offered an excellent opportunity "for establishing more effective working relations between the Hill and the White House and the various executive agencies." As to the fear that administration representatives would be subjected to heckling, Laves doubted that this opinion was justified since "a large number of the younger Congressmen . . . [would] be ready to pitch in at any time to make certain that there is fair play and no unnecessary bickering." Stone's marginal notation revealed that he took a pessimistic view of this belief as just "topping."

Laves continued by framing the issue as "a challenge . . . to the American people to see whether the democratic form of government based upon an independent legislature and executive can be made to work." He believed that the President had been "in many respects unsuccessful" in making a contribution to better executive-legislative relations. The only time that there appeared to be cooperation was in the early New Deal "when the White House had greater political power and was able to compel Congressional concurrence." [45]

Stone scribbled his reactions to many of Laves's suggestions as he read through the memorandum. Such sardonic comments as "Just like an invitation to tea at Aunt Nellie's," "Nothing like staging a bull fight," and "Embarrassment can be applied with polish as well as with vegetables" showed that Stone's opinion remained unchanged.[46] He continued to be "very bearish."

Wilcox's entry into the channel of memoranda fared no better. The statement of this former professor of political science at the University of Louisville that the Kefauver question period "would sharpen the responsibility of the administrative branch to the Congress and to the people" brought the marginal retort from Stone that "the Constitution provided it [the administrative branch] should be independent of Congress."

Wilcox believed that the proposed procedure would make each department head more alert to public relations and each citizen more interested in governmental affairs. He urged that the Bureau of the Budget "clear its sights and take appropriate action," since House Resolution 327 was "definitely associated with better administrative management." [47]

The next day, Vieg followed up his luncheon report to Smith with an analysis of the "Kefauver Proposal in a Broader Perspective." Vieg entertained no doubts as to the constitutionality of the question and answer period. To support his position, he cited the approval of Chief Justices Taft and Hughes and such distinguished constitutional lawyers as Elihu Root and John W. Davis. The new procedure would make a "significant contribution" to better administrative management within the executive branch. General congressional knowledge of execu-

tive policies would be increased. Reciprocally, the administration would gain "both a better appreciation of legislative intent
in formulating a program and a clearer understanding of popular reaction to their own execution of it." Concerning one of
the main assignments of the Bureau of the Budget, the procedure would require the Cabinet officials "to pull together and
to coordinate their activities and programs."

Beyond the many operational advantages which he envisioned, Vieg thought there was a compelling reason to endorse
the efforts of the representative from Tennessee. The great
value of the idea was in its strengthening of American democracy:

By building into the process of popular government in the United
States such an element of drama as would be assured through face-
to-face, out-in-the-open discussion of the people's business on the
floor of Congress, this plan would contribute something now sadly
wanting in the American system. Democracy depends on vigilance
by its citizenry but that vigilance depends in turn on visibility in
the government. The Kefauver plan would guarantee more visibility
for the working of our democracy than we have ever had before.[48]

The counterattack was not long in coming. Stone asked two
of his closest associates to prepare an analysis specifying disadvantages of the question period. By January 8, 1944, the
replies of Fred Levi and Don K. Price were ready. Levi, who
headed Stone's Government Organization Section and who has
been described earlier as "very bearish" toward the Kefauver
idea, remained dubious.

Price—in Washington as a Coast Guard officer—had recently
completed an article comparing the merits of the presidential
and parliamentary systems.[49] Before his entry into the Coast
Guard in 1943, Price was an assistant director of the Public
Administration Clearing House in Chicago. One former member of the Budget Bureau has referred to Price as "part of the
Louie Brownlow crowd." Besides revealing the close attach-
ment of the members to Brownlow, the designation grouped

together those who believed that America's greatest contribution to government was the institution of the Presidency.[50] Brownlow had been Price's superior at the Clearing House.

Price found two major objections to the question hour. In the first place, there would be "a tendency to extend the week-by-week supervision of Congress over the detail of administration," and, secondly, the proposal was merely an attempt to "copy in the Presidential system a device that is an integral part of the Parliamentary system." How a feature of either system was necessarily mutually exclusive and incompatible with the other was not explained.

The main obstacle to an effective implementation of the Kefauver plan was the local basis of the representatives as opposed to the national interest represented by the President. Baiting bureaucrats was held to be "a favorite vote-getting device" to impress the folks back home. The consequences from these limitations, Price gloomily foresaw, would be "disintegrating and purposeless sniping at the Administration." [51]

Like Price, Levi failed to explain his broad generality that "the greatest theoretical objection to the proposal is that it fails to discriminate between the British and American systems of Government, and undertakes indiscriminately to transplant a practice from one to the other." Revealing something of an executive inferiority complex, Levi attacked the Kefauver resolution as having "the potentiality of becoming another link in the 150-year long chain of legislative invasion upon the Executive." He noted in detail the current infringements by Congress and the practice of the standing committees in concerning themselves with day-to-day agency operations.

While admitting with derision that the views of experts "in the structure and functions of political systems are valuable," he suggested that Budget Director Smith—before deciding as to the effectiveness of the question hour—ascertain the views of present and former members of Congress. As for Levi, the plan would "inevitably weaken the Executive over a period of time" and "merely dramatize and not solve executive-legislative disunity." [52]

Stone forwarded—without adding his usually prolific marginal comments—the two memorandums to Smith's office with this covering note: "Based upon the reports of the professors on our staff, I have come to the conclusion that the proposal of Kefauver represents the greatest discovery since the incandescent light in 1879." [53]

Early in January, before receiving the Price and Levi analyses, Smith wrote Kefauver a friendly note enclosing a reprint of Price's article, "The Parliamentary and Presidential Systems." [54] Although Smith and Kefauver met once for lunch during the next month to discuss the possibility of the President's and Budget Bureau's supporting the resolution, events were occurring in Congress which would go far toward preventing the final resolution of the issue.

MR. SABATH AND THE RULES COMMITTEE

Following his November 26th address, Kefauver was greatly encouraged by the response of congressional colleagues, influential citizens, newspapers, and the public in general. The almost unanimously favorable endorsements of the executive departments and independent establishments gave him some cause for optimism. On November 30, 1943, Secretary of the Interior Harold L. Ickes, bypassing the legislative clearance procedure, strongly endorsed the resolution.[55] Secretary of War Stimson, an advocate of the basic idea since 1910, telephoned Kefauver to offer his support. Stimson's undersecretary, Robert P. Patterson, later added his interest.[56]

Praise for Kefauver's efforts came from John W. Davis, who in 1924 might have been President and at the pinnacle of American public life—except for the few words of Calvin Coolidge and the many votes cast for that laconic candidate. One of the most distinguished constitutional lawyers of his era, Davis had "not the slightest doubt" about the constitutionality of the resolution. The question period did not "trench . . . on our doctrine of the separation of powers." Although there were three separate branches, it was still a single government dedicated to serving a common purpose; consequently, "there is no reason whatever why the right hand should not know what the left hand doeth or vice versa." [57]

Newspaper and public support was surprisingly strong. Leading journals in all sections of America editorially supported the proposal.[58] The favorable response noted by Gallup's Institute of Public Opinion also was heartening to Kefauver. Gallup offered three major reasons why almost three fourths of those sampled were in favor of the idea. Closer legislative-executive relations, a better informed public, and a needed check on bureaucracy and inefficiency were listed as major advantages by this sample. The small group (7%) in opposition feared that the question period might be used as an opportunity to harass the administration rather than to secure information for the intelligent exercise of the legislative function.[59]

The obvious enthusiasm of many people for Kefauver's plan had little effect on the attitude of the House leadership. Adolph J. Sabath, the venerable chairman of the powerful Rules Committee, had agreed to a hearing on House Resolution 327 for Tuesday, February 1, 1944. On Saturday, January 29, 1944, Sabath informed Kefauver that he was postponing the hearing and made no promise that he would reschedule it. Kefauver announced Sabath's action to the House on January 31, stating that he was exceedingly disappointed by the decision.[60]

Unknown to Kefauver, Mr. Sabath had sought the advice of President Roosevelt earlier in the month. In a letter of January 12, 1944, the Rules Committee chairman had noted that "demand" was being made for a hearing on the question period resolution and that before agreeing to a hearing he would like the President's views on the proposal. Sabath suggested that the President might wish to confer with the Cabinet and independent agency heads concerning the matter and stated that he would "be pleased to withhold hearings" until the President did so.[61]

Within a week, the Sabath letter and Kefauver resolution were considered briefly in the Cabinet. Vice President Henry A. Wallace, Attorney General Francis Biddle, and Secretary of the Interior Harold Ickes endorsed the idea. The President did not express an opinion and did not seem particularly interested one way or the other. The principal opponent within the Cabinet—as the main advocate outside—was a native of Tennessee. Secretary of State Cordell Hull, who had served almost a quarter of a century in Congress as first a representative and then a senator, argued that any legislative questioning would be on "a purely political basis and in an irresponsible way." Speaker Rayburn and other congressional leaders were known to be opposed "and that was the end of it" as far as Cabinet discussion was concerned.[62]

A few days after the Cabinet session of January 21st, the President wrote Sabath, informing him that "we have all discussed it [the Kefauver resolution] somewhat informally and we are agreed that we should like to talk this over further with you and the Speaker and John McCormack before any action is taken by the Rules Committee, as it presents many long-range problems." Roosevelt also solicited Sabath's advice as to whether or not the three Republican counterparts of the House leadership should be invited to the White House at a later date in order to discuss the proposal.[63]

Sabath phoned the President's office at once requesting an appointment for himself and the two other Democratic leaders. The chairman left word that he preferred the Speaker and majority leader to think that it was the President who wanted the conference and not to be told that he had initiated the meeting.[64]

In anticipation of the February 1st hearing, Kefauver had mimeographed a nineteen-page statement discussing advantages and meeting objections to his resolution. Noting that a representative's average length of service was slightly over four years, Kefauver concluded that most of Congress was relatively lacking in "a necessary working knowledge of the organization of the big executive departments." [65]

Although he devoted many pages of his prepared—but undelivered—testimony to reciting the favorable comments of individuals who advocated the Pendleton plan to seat the Cabinet on the floor, Kefauver desired that his report and question period be distinguished carefully from its suspected ancestors.[66] He held that "the arguments against the Pendleton-Taft plan had some merit," and that his resolution was designed to meet those objections. Instead of requiring the attendance of Cabinet members and providing them with seats on the floor, the question and report period would be voluntary. Sessions were not to be more frequent than once a week and not to exceed two hours in length. Now the Cabinet would come only to provide information, while the earlier proposals had permitted the department head to participate in any debate affecting his agency. Presumably the time of busy executives could be saved by allowing them to remain at their departments tending to administrative duties. Their infrequent appearance might also alleviate fears of "interfering" with Congress, "supplanting" the standing committees, or being "the entering wedge of the parliamentary system." [67]

Standing committees would continue to function and annual reports still would be submitted. Under the question hour procedure, broad issues of policy were to be elaborated so that members might secure a general and current understanding of departmental problems rather than relying for their information on committee hearings—which often were not printed and when published usually remained unread. The Cabinet could also secure a clearer knowledge of congressional intent in regard to the statutes which were entrusted to their care.[68]

As for any changes in the balance of power between the legislative and executive branches, Kefauver avowed that his resolution would "do nothing of the sort." With reference to the "aping England" argument which usually was bandied about by the opposition, he thought that it was impossible to "have the parliamentary system, in view of the constitutional provision which says that no member of the Congress can hold any executive position." [69]

Incorporating some of the suggestions made since he had offered his proposal in October, the Tennessee representative urged that oral questions be germane to the written questions and that, in special cases, "an under-secretary or one of the secretary's principal assistants" could appear in place of the department head if it was agreeable to both the secretary and the standing committee responsible for that policy area.[70]

On February 1, 1944—the day on which the elusive hearings were scheduled—Representative Kefauver sent an urgent letter to President Roosevelt asking him to intervene with the House leadership so that the proponents of the resolution would "at least be given an opportunity to present . . . [their] case." Kefauver believed his procedure would aid the enactment of Roosevelt's "enlightened and necessary foreign policy." [71]

Kefauver added that "the Speaker of the House, it is true, does not look upon this idea with favor," and then professing his devotion to Mr. Rayburn, the representative continued, "in candor I must say that he is against any substantial reform of Congress' methods." The congressman included a copy of the testimony which he had prepared for the Committee on Rules.

The Kefauver letter, with the exception of the paragraph concerning the Speaker's attitude, was excerpted and sent to Speaker Rayburn by the President, who asked: "Will you be good enough to let me know how I can reply?" [72] On February 15, a three-sentence "brush off" which had been prepared was sent to Kefauver by Roosevelt. While admitting that the question period had "some advantages," the President noted that it involved "many fundamentals which tend to raise the difference between Congressional government and Parliamentary government." The Chief Executive advised that "just at this moment, in an election year, I would be inclined offhand to defer the discussion until next Winter." [73]

Following the receipt of the President's letter, Kefauver telephoned the White House for an appointment to discuss his resolution. Although Major General Edwin M. Watson, one of the secretaries to the President, called the request to Roosevelt's attention on several occasions, the Chief Executive said "later" and the meeting was never arranged.[74]

Kefauver also sent a copy of his letter to the President to Harold Smith at the Budget Bureau.[75] His enthusiasm rising in direct proportion to the pressure being generated against him by the House leadership, Kefauver dispatched at the same time letters to respected publicists, influential private citizens, and prominent government officials.[76] To all, he mentioned that Chairman Sabath had unexpectedly blocked House Resolution 327. Some were invited to testify for the plan. Still others were encouraged to write directly to Sabath.

Kefauver's hope for success had partially revived during the first week in February when he received a promise of editorial support from several nationwide magazines; a favorable analysis by George B. Galloway, chairman of the Committee on Congress of the American Political Science Association;

and knowledge that further discussion would take place within the Budget Bureau. Kefauver was informed that the resolution would receive a strong endorsement by *Life* magazine later in the month.[77] Galloway believed that after the arguments had been weighed the "net balance" favored the "pros." Holding that "efforts to solve the problem of improving the channels of communication between Congress and the Executive must not be postponed until political science has been perfected," Galloway agreed that the question period was "worth a trial." With pragmatic bluntness, he suggested that "if it works reasonably well, it can be gradually perfected. If it is abused, it can be abandoned." [78]

On February 4, 1944, the Kefauver resolution had been considered at a Budget Bureau staff meeting. All the participants were sent a copy of the proposal in advance as well as a memorandum listing the possible advantages and disadvantages from the standpoint of the executive departments. The question to be decided was included with the agenda: "Do we favor adoption of the resolution, or do we prefer to sit tight?" [79] They sat tight.

Following this decision by the Budget Bureau, Director Smith lunched with Kefauver. The director promised "when the opportunity arises, I will do whatever I can to be helpful." [80] Kefauver urged that "if anything is to be done, it should be done now." [81] The opportunity apparently never arose that year.

In addition to the disappointing news from the executive branch, the heavy artillery of the House Democratic elite was unlimbered and leveled at Kefauver on March 23, 1944, when Missouri's Clarence Cannon took the floor. Cannon reigned supreme as chairman of the powerful Appropriations Committee. He was also in regular attendance at meetings of the Democratic Steering Committee. While admitting the popularity of the measure, he claimed that the question and report period was more in harmony with the English than the American system. Congress already had sufficient tools to enforce accountability upon the executive branch through resolutions of inquiry, committee investigations, regular departmental reports, and the personal contact that existed between legislators and bureaucrats.[82]

Cannon vividly portrayed the future that would ensue if Kefauver's procedure became law. There would be packed galleries, radio broadcasts of the sessions, and "loaded" questions to department heads by publicity-minded congressmen. The result would be "a political fencing match."

Attacking the ancient argument that the Chief Executive would have to select "stronger" Cabinet members if they were to survive constant congressional interrogation, Cannon decided that the House must choose between "executives or exhorters." Furthermore, since the executive power was constitutionally vested solely in the President, the response of a department head would not commit the occupant of the White House at all. The renowned authority on parliamentary law concluded that the whole scheme was "impracticable, obstructive, and unworkable." He hoped that it would be buried so permanently that critics of Congress would "never again be able to disinter its moldering bones." [83]

A week later, Representative Kefauver provided his colleagues with a detailed answer to each of Cannon's charges. Kefauver reported that over 250 daily newspapers had expressed their support. He obviously was voicing the feelings and gropings of the "newcomers" to Congress who—by both their inexperience and the inevitability of the seniority system —were effectively precluded from the channels of official information and governmental policy. Committee Chairman Cannon, Kefauver suggested, could be content with the established modes of communication since his role as head of one of the most influential committees placed him in a position to demand access to and receive information from the most independent of administrators.[84] Despite Kefauver's extremely able oratorical effort and his concentration on securing the approval of scores of freshman congressmen as well as that of the public and newspapers, the question and report period resolution went no further. The intransigence of the House leadership had prevailed.

FURTHER WHITE HOUSE CONSIDERATION

During the opening week of the next Congress, which met in January, 1945, Representative Kefauver—in response to Roosevelt's less than enthusiastic suggestion that the question period be considered after the election—again wrote the President.[85] On January 11, 1945, Roosevelt replied promising to take the matter up again with the Cabinet. He noted that "it goes without saying that I am wholly in favor of the objective, though I cannot tell you at this moment my final thought on the procedure suggested." Upon receipt of his department heads' opinions, he assured Kefauver that he would be glad to meet with him.[86]

At the same time, the President sent a memorandum as well as a copy of the Kefauver proposal and their exchange of letters to eighteen Cabinet officers and independent agency heads with the invitation: "Let me have your thought." [87] The first to respond was Secretary of War Stimson, who noted that the proposal was "one which I have studied and believed in for many years" and recalled that in 1912, at his suggestion, President Taft had recommended seating the Cabinet in Congress.[88] Donald M. Nelson, the former chairman of the War Production Board who was serving as personal representative of the President, suggested that Roosevelt appoint a subcommittee of the Cabinet to work with Congress "in finding the most workable means of attaining the objective of the Kefauver resolution." [89]

Sixteen of the eighteen agency heads finally fulfilled the President's request and furnished their opinion on the question period idea. Of the sixteen, seven were strong advocates, four were vigorously opposed, and five favored it in part but opposed certain procedures.[90]

The opposition was based on Kefauver's alleged failure to take into account the differences between the British and American systems, on the impropriety of including quasi-judicial bodies in the plan, on the lack of authority for the department head to refuse to answer improper questions, on the confusion which would arise from the "quick" answer, and finally on the belief that the question period would merely be a further duplication of committee effort.[91]

James F. Byrnes, the director of the Office of War Mobilization and Reconversion, urged that regardless of whether various Cabinet members or the President favored or opposed the question period, the administration should not comment on a matter which solely involved a change in congressional procedure not requiring legislation and consequently did not call for either the President's approval or his veto. There was also a more practical reason for proceeding cautiously in the formulation of an executive opinion on the matter and Byrnes reminded the President that "the Speaker has strong feelings against Mr. Kefauver's proposal." [92] Byrnes himself was a moderate and recent convert to the question period having "reached the conclusion it could do no harm and might do much good." [93] Not so reluctant was Attorney General Francis Biddle, who held that there was "no essential difference between the appearance and interrogation of members of the Executive Branch before Congressional committees and their similar appearance in the House itself." [94]

Failing to hear from the President for over a month and a half, Kefauver sent him an "exploratory" letter on March 6, 1945, praising the orientation program which had been carried out by the 79th Club of the House and noting how eager the representatives were to secure information concerning administration policies.[95] On the same day, Roosevelt dropped a note to Byrnes enclosing the extract of the replies from the department heads. He queried: "What do you think I should do next about it? Shall we just dry it up?"[96] Byrnes replied urging no action before talking with the congressional leadership, especially since "Sam Rayburn . . . was unusually strong in his opposition to the proposal" and the President was dependent on the Speaker in legislative matters. He suggested that Roosevelt secure Rayburn's opinion as to whether or not a recommendation should be made by the administration in response to the request of a single representative or whether a recommendation should wait until a House committee requested the Executive's views.[97]

On March 14, Justice Byrnes was asked by Roosevelt to draft a reply to Kefauver's recent letter.[98] Three weeks before his death, the President signed a letter to Kefauver which politely entombed the question period proposal from the administration's point of view. Roosevelt wrote that neither he nor his Cabinet should submit to the House any recommendations concerning changes in that body's rules. The President distinguished between his right to submit a recommendation for legislation which he then could approve or veto and interference in the internal affairs of the House. However, if the House did adopt the Kefauver proposal, Roosevelt assured the representative that the administration would "be glad to comply with the suggested procedure."[99]

The burden of enacting the reform had been returned to Capitol Hill.

Congress Looks at Itself

EARLY IN JANUARY, 1945, with the opening of the new Seventy-ninth Congress, Representative Kefauver reintroduced his basic measure as House Resolution 31. There were two modifications in this later version. The committee under whose jurisdiction the agency was placed would have authority to invite a subdivision head to appear and deliver an answer. In the case of a department, the secretary would be allowed to designate his deputy or assistant secretaries to reply for him. The second change required that the supplementary oral questions asked on the floor "be germane to the subject matter of at least one of the written questions." [1]

At almost the same time, Senator J. William Fulbright—who as a House member had expressed interest in Kefauver's endeavor to improve executive-legislative relations—offered substantially the same proposal (S. Res. 7) in the Senate. One alteration in the Fulbright version provided that the "relevancy of questions . . . when raised, shall be submitted to the Senate and be decided without debate." [2]

This passing of the initiative for determining the appropriateness of questions from the department head to the legislative body was objected to by the acting secretary of state, Joseph C. Grew.[3] Grew did favor in general, however, the question and report period as contributing "to a more thorough understanding and cooperation between the House of Representatives and the Executive Departments." [4]

Both Fulbright and Kefauver were given an opportunity to present their case before the Senate Rules Committee chaired by Harry Flood Byrd. Despite Fulbright's plea that the question and report period would be "a step" in the direction of curing the "evil of distrust" which existed between the executive and the legislature, the committee failed to act.[5]

Although the Senate Rules Committee was not moved by the spirit of reform in 1945—and was particularly antagonistic to the question period—many in Congress were anxious to reorganize. The Allied recovery from the setback in the Battle of the Bulge made it almost a certainty that peace would come again to Europe before the end of the year. With the arrival of less hectic times, Congress might reassert control over more aspects of public policy—if it first had its own house in order.

All over America, articles and books appeared offering palliatives to restore congressional prestige. Interested professional associations of planners and political scientists established committees and commissioned students of government to analyze the legislative function at the federal level in order to recommend modes of operation which would enable Congress to keep pace with the needs of a twentieth-century industrial-urban society.[6]

The subject of congressional rejuvenation intrigued members on each side of the aisle in both chambers. To evaluate the various proposals for increasing legislative effectiveness, Representative A. S. Mike Monroney revived a measure which had been passed in the final month of the last Congress. On January 11, 1945, he reintroduced a concurrent resolution authorizing a Joint Committee on the Organization of Congress.[7]

Within a month, the Monroney resolution was before the Senate, but not in the form in which it had left the House. As approved by the House, the resolution provided that the committee could recommend a proposal such as Kefauver's question period. The Senate Rules Committee under the watchful eye of Chairman Byrd decided to foreclose that avenue of study as well as to prevent any tampering by a committee of reformers with the Senate's cherished possession of unlimited debate.[8] An amendment to the Monroney measure was added in the Senate which prohibited "any recommendations with respect to the rules, parliamentary procedure, practices, and/or precedents of either House, or the consideration of any matter on the floor of either House." [9]

Despite the protests of such a forward-looking representative as John Martin Vorys, of Ohio, that the amendment was "'screwy' and insulting to the committee and . . . to the intelligence of the House itself," the House of Representatives was compelled to accept the Senate restrictions or forego any improvement at all.[10]

Senator Robert La Follette and Representative Monroney were elected co-chairmen of the new 12-member bi-partisan committee. Dr. George B. Galloway, chairman of the Committee on Congress of the American Political Science Association—who had been favorably inclined to the question hour idea—was appointed staff director.[11]

Extensive hearings were held during the spring and summer of 1945. Kefauver and Fulbright as well as several "newcomers" appeared and testified in favor of a question period. In addition Fulbright now supported not only the idea of seating the Cabinet in Congress but also the proposal for a joint cabinet made up of both department heads and congressional leaders.

The Arkansas senator's idea of a joint executive-legislative cabinet composed of the department heads appointed by the President and the chairmen of the proposed joint standing committees of both houses was not a new one.[12] Princeton Professor Edward S. Corwin, one of the nation's outstanding authorities on constitutional law, had urged a joint cabinet in lieu of the Pendleton-type proposal. He stressed that since most of Congress's work was done in committee, the Cabinet head would receive a better hearing there. On the other hand, if Congress needed information, it could be secured more efficiently by investigation than "by the wasteful and pretentious methods of parliamentary interpellation." [13]

Professor Corwin believed that the proposed joint cabinet would not require a constitutional amendment, since the individual participants remained primarily in either the legislative or the executive branch. A mere executive order by the President or a resolution of the Congress would be sufficient to establish the group. While the new creation, similar to the historic Cabinet, would have only an advisory relationship with the Chief Executive, a great advantage lay in its institutional capacity to combine the political sagacity which came from long tenure in elective public office with the administrative capacity needed to coordinate the large federal departments. Once a policy had been agreed upon, the congressional delegation, since it contained the recognized party leaders, could presumably return to Capitol Hill and mobilize legislative support for the program. Alternatively, the proposed cabinet, because of the political power it represented, provided more effective control over presidential action.[14]

A mutation of the Corwin plan had been suggested in 1943, when Senator Alexander Wiley, one of the ranking Republicans on the Foreign Relations Committee, introduced a resolution authorizing the creation of a foreign relations advisory council. The secretary of state and some of his principal assistants were to serve with the chairmen and the ranking minority members of the House and Senate committees having jurisdiction over international relations. The President, because of the Senate's constitutional function with regard to treaties and appointments, would be permitted to select additional senators for service on the council.[15]

Wiley never was able to secure a hearing for his suggestion to grant Congress a larger role in international policy formulation. Foreign Relations Chairman Tom Connally successfully evaded Wiley's demands, despite the latter's rhetorical query: "Is it the Executive's war or the people's war?"[16] The administration also was opposed, although Secretary Hull, profiting from both President Wilson's errors at Versailles and Senate unrest, did appoint a few senators and representatives from the two parties to the delegations of several international conferences.

In the upsurge of the congressional reform wave, which seemed to gain momentum as the nation neared victory and as the problems of demobilization and reconversion became nearer than the distant future, Corwin's idea of a joint cabinet was revived. Thomas K. Finletter, in a few years to become President Truman's air force secretary, performed the resuscitation rites in 1945 when he attempted to answer in the affirmative the title of his book, *Can Representative Government Do the Job?* Finletter agreed with the Corwin solution because he thought that the Pendleton-Kefauver alternatives failed to provide the needed cooperation between the two branches. Finletter correctly realized, however, that if his joint cabinet was to attain any measure of success Congress and the Presidency should be controlled by either one or the other of the major parties. To achieve this formal harmony, Finletter recommended that the Constitution be amended to grant the power of dissolution to the President.[17]

Another version of the basic Corwin idea was offered to the La Follette-Monroney Committee by William Yandell Elliott, a Harvard political scientist. Elliott, who a decade before had written *A Need for Constitutional Reform,* outlined the creation of six advisory councils on which the chairmen of standing committees and departmental officials would serve. These policy-coordinating bodies covered such broad functional areas as national defense, fiscal affairs, social security, national resources, commerce and trade, and legal and organizational questions.[18]

As in the case of the joint cabinet proposal there was a wide range of opinion as to the actual operation of the question hour. An Oregon representative, Harris Ellsworth, doubted that this aspect of English government could be grafted onto the American system. Instead, he proposed that a deputy secretary who would "sit as a Member of the House of Representatives" be appointed in each department. Ellsworth even favored voting privileges on the floor for the official! But agency heads, first- and second-term representatives, and private citizens provided verbal backing for Kefauver's plan.[19]

Over several months of hearings, four members of the Joint Committee on the Organization of Congress indicated their support for the question hour. This quartet was divided evenly with regard to partisan affiliation and included Chairman La Follette and Representative Earl C. Michener for the Republicans and Vice Chairman Monroney and Senator Claude Pepper for the Democrats. The duet on the committee which offered overt opposition made up in vocal resistance what they lacked in numerical strength. Senate Minority Leader Wallace H. White sympathized with the "poor Secretary" who might be situated in the well of the House of Representatives "and have 435 Members . . . go after him." [20] Representative E. E. Cox, of Georgia, had earlier agreed with this view.[21] Cox was also a member of the House Rules Committee and had been the "leading opponent," besides Chairman Sabath, in blocking consideration of the Kefauver resolution.[22]

On March 4, 1946, after thirty-nine public hearings, the Joint Committee on the Organization of Congress submitted its report to both houses. The committee stated that better cooperation could be obtained if the executive branch gave "Congressional leaders a part in the formulation of policy, instead of calling upon them to enact programs prepared without their participation." [23] In accordance with this belief, a legislative-executive council was recommended. The majority policy committees of the Senate and House were to meet regularly with the executive "to facilitate the formulation and carrying out of national policy, and to improve the relationships between the executive and legislative branches of the Government." [24]

The lone dissent to this suggestion was voiced by Representative Cox, who a year previously had objected to the Kefauver plan because it "would make possible the Cabinet officers or their representatives . . . lecturing the House." [25] Participation by the congressional leadership in the making of policy was no more appealing to him than was the possible intrusion of the department heads into legislative deliberation.

Although the committee placed an emphasis on prior consultation and discussion between the two branches of the government, it refused to recommend or condemn the Kefauver question and report period. While granting that there were valid arguments by both the proponents and the opponents of the measure, the committee never seriously considered them. The Senate amendment to the authorizing resolution effectively precluded such discussion.

Neither the joint cabinet nor the question period plan has been implemented, although congressional leaders have been invited to the White House with increasing regularity. During the past decade, both ideas have been scrutinized only infrequently. Such attention aptly merited the conclusion of one of the strongest advocates of the legislative-executive cabinet: "Nobody was much interested in it."

In July, 1950, the demoralizing defeats suffered by the American forces in Korea led to a fleeting revival of the question period idea on the House floor. At a time when the Communist legions from North Korea were forcing General MacArthur's beleaguered and almost nonexistent Allied troops toward the sea, Congresswoman Edith Nourse Rogers called on her colleagues to require the administration's defense officials "to appear before the Congress to talk to us and to tell us why our men were sent to Korea completely unprepared, and what can be done in the future." [26] Republican Rogers, having made her verbal assault, took a route of hasty retreat similar to the one she had taken five years before.[27]

The cry of "Communism, Korea, and Corruption" in 1952, which swept the Grand Old Party behind General Dwight D. Eisenhower to its first presidential victory in two decades, also brought with it narrow Republican control of the Congress. Since 1949, when Democrat Kefauver was promoted to the Senate by the favorable votes of Tennessee citizens, he had not attempted to revive his entombed reform. Following the change of administration and congressional control, Kefauver with the cosponsorship of Senator Fulbright resubmitted the proposal, on January 29, 1953, as Senate Resolution 58.[28]

In a statement prepared for the *Record,* Kefauver stressed that "the need of closer collaboration between Congress and the administration . . . was never more essential than now, in this confused time which is neither clearly peace nor war." [29] The Senator was not long in finding out that, although it might not be war, the various members of the administration were almost unanimous in offering paper resistance to his plan.[30]

Undoubtedly an important reason for a failure to implement the joint cabinet proposal in the postwar period has been the inability of either Democrats or Republicans to maintain control of both the executive and the legislature for any long duration. Factors other than the lack of congressional-presidential party unity are responsible for the failure of the Kefauver resolution. But there are also reasons for the continued appeal of the question period idea as well as of the various similar proposals which were made earlier.

(XII)

The Cabinet and the Reform

AS HISTORICAL ANALYSIS has shown, the idea of allowing the President's Cabinet an opportunity to appear before Congress has not arisen solely among the legislators on Capitol Hill. Since the First Congress, when Hamilton, Knox, and Jay attempted actual explanation before the Senate and House, Cabinet members have voiced varying degrees of approbation for the reform.

Although during the era of the Pendleton debates in the latter half of the last century a sprinkling of departmental officials sanctioned the enactment of the procedure, it has been in the twentieth century that the greatest support as well as the strongest objections have been found among the agents of the Chief Executive. Under both the Taft and Harding administrations, the President and various department heads approved of the plan.

As to a gain in power for either Congress or the executive if debate or questioning were permitted, the reactions of many members of the Roosevelt, Truman, and Eisenhower Cabinets were equally divided between those who believed that Congress would gain and those who maintained that neither branch would benefit.[1] No member thought that the executive would gain if the practice were inaugurated.

One Cabinet position which seems to have aroused great congressional concern and antagonism during the last three administrations has been that of the secretary of agriculture. From the early New Deal days of Henry Wallace through the era of Ezra Taft Benson this position has been a focal point of usually opposed and deeply rooted sentiments as to how the plight of the hard-pressed farmer might be alleviated. At times, each of the five heads of agriculture since 1933 has been the object of vigorous condemnation both on the floor of the two houses and within the confines of the committee rooms of the Senate and House committees on agriculture and appropriations. Yet of these five secretaries, three believed that it would have been to their advantage to appear in a question period before the full membership of the House.

One former agriculture secretary emphasized that he had "always believed in the educational advantages of the British system," and then hastily added—perhaps remembering a long series of prior legislative assaults against his knowledge, patriotism, and integrity—"Of course this assumes that Congressmen are open to reason." Although two of the favorably inclined secretaries also would favor full debate privileges for a Cabinet officer, the third believed that such a course of action "would create confusion and resentment" as well as raise a constitutional question.

Of the two secretaries who were opposed to the question and report period, one had extensive experience in both the House and Senate. While admitting that "we need a lot more frank talk between both branches," he advised that "some of the ablest administrators in Washington would be chopped down on the Senate floor." For him there was no exact equation between executive ability and the capacity of an individual to chart a polished course in the rocky crags of political debate.

This opinion that there is little correlation between the successful administration of a department and repartee on the floor was shared by Dean Acheson, secretary of state under President Truman. Acheson admitted that he once believed the question and report period had more merit. He specifically

objected to the assumption made by both Justice Story and
Senator Pendleton that the "strongest" men in departmental
management would be those most effective on the floor: "Sometimes men are gifted in both endeavors; but, as I have ob-
served government for a good many years, it is as often,
perhaps more often, not the case." [2]

Secretary Acheson believed that he had experienced a
typical question period. In May, 1950, following his return
from a session of the North Atlantic Treaty Organization, he
appeared before members of the Senate and House in the
Library of Congress auditorium. He concluded that the episode was not pleasant: "The questioning in this meeting
seemed to bear out the misgivings I have expressed." These
"misgivings" involved not so much the manner in which the
questions were asked, but the fact that many of them were
not germane to the specific developments at the NATO
Council in London. The questions asked by the legislators
ranged over all phases of America's foreign policy.[3] One of
Acheson's most loyal followers in the House thought that the
secretary's presentation "did some good even though his
aristocratic appearance and bearing was against him." [4]

The absence of "the tradition of discipline in relevance
which permits Mr. Speaker in the House of Commons to
maintain strict control" was not just a fault of the question
period, stated Acheson. Instead, it was inherent in all congressional procedure. When Acheson testified for eight days before
the two committees on armed services which were examining
the recall of General Douglas MacArthur from the Far East,
he lamented that "not more than an hour of the examination
related to the relief of General MacArthur." Perhaps Attorney
Acheson took too legalistic and literal a view of the functioning of congressional committees. The committee's thirst for
broad policy information possibly was revealed by the favorable comment of Senator Richard Russell, who presided at the

MacArthur hearings. There Russell thanked Acheson for giving the legislators "a better grasp of the many very staggering problems" which confronted him as secretary of state.[5]

Some of Mr. Acheson's colleagues in the Truman Cabinet also had misgivings about congressional committee actions, but unlike the former secretary of state their qualms concerned not so much the broad scope of questioning as the narrow circle of listeners. One of these former department heads maintained that "to have the opportunity to appear on the floor would acquaint the majority of the members . . . with the ramifications, problems, and needs" of the departments. Another regretted that "under the present scheme of things" necessary information upon which to base legislative decisions was "for the most part buried in Committee Hearings." The first official had engaged in over two decades of executive-legislative relations on behalf of his department before he became its head. He held that members of Congress "appreciated having more information about the conduct and business" of his agency.

Information has been given to legislators—other than committee members—but at a cost: a cost in both departmental resources and those of the individual Cabinet officer. Each department maintains a full-time staff, often headed by an assistant secretary who is charged with legislative liaison. These busy men deal primarily in individual contacts and relationships. When a major effort is undertaken to gather congressional support for a departmental project, additional personnel are detailed from the agency, "friendly" congressmen are recruited to visit their fellow members, and the White House legislative liaison staff is temporarily concentrated on the single area.

The unsatisfactory aspects of the departmental liaison officer's role have been well stated by one of the fraternity's more successful practitioners. In 1945, the State Department's principal congressional emissary, Assistant Secretary of State Dean Acheson, described—for the benefit of the La Follette-Monroney Committee on the Organization of Congress—the limitations inherent in his position. He confessed that experience had taught him that Congress wanted officers "who know what they are talking about" to appear before it, namely, "the officers who are charged with the responsibility of performing the task and know about it." Mere "mouthpieces" and "departmental lawyers" were not welcome. Conversely, Acheson was convinced that if agency representatives came into closer contact with the opinions of the popular representatives the "reality" with which department programs were concocted would be enhanced.

If they [the department officials] are protected by having in between them and Congress an officer who is supposed to take all of the knocks and discussion of the Congress, then they never grow up, they do not understand what has happened. . . . The inherent difficulty in a job dealing with congressional relations is [that] in order to speak with any knowledge and authority you have to have your roots in the organization and the work of the department, you have to be responsible for certain activities and you have to have people responsible to you.[6]

As much as Cabinet members might desire to establish and develop a beneficial relationship with members of Congress, some have found that the demanding nature of departmental duties and the always present "fires to put out" practically restrained them to their more administrative tasks. One newly appointed department head—before leaving the House of Representatives to assume his future responsibilities—promised his fellow legislators that he would maintain a close association with them. When he was confronted with the complexities of his new job, although he set aside a period on his weekly calendar "for maintaining contact . . . as time went on this was pushed further and further into the background."

Others in the Cabinet were restrained psychologically by their conception of "proper" legislative-executive relations. Usually these officials have been indoctrinated with a law school view of the separation of powers. They often have failed to ascertain the nuances which the politician—devoting his energies to making the system work—realizes almost intuitively. Truman's secretary of agriculture, Charles Brannan, was in the former category, according to one of his most faithful advocates in the House: "Brannan—as much as I like him —thought that all you had to do was propose the issue and the rest would take care of itself."

Further ineffectiveness in executive-congressional contact has been caused by the committee structure. Each department head is assured of at least partial supervision by not less than four committees, because of the division of Congress into a House and a Senate and of the committees into legislative and appropriations. The diverse functions that are often grouped by tradition or convenience under a departmental tent frequently enlarge a secretary's legislative commitments.

When a secretary realizes the importance of satisfactory legislative-executive relations, he seeks out the best in political and departmental talent to aid him with congressional contacts. Most Cabinet members make themselves readily accessible when Senators and Representatives call on them for an appointment. This, however, was not always the case. A former department head under Roosevelt reported that "certain members of the Cabinet looked upon any appointments coming from Congress with suspicion."

To establish the needed personal acquaintanceships—hard to acquire because of the pressures of agency business, the diffuseness of legislative committee structure, and the sheer size of the two houses—Cabinet members often make personal

expenditures for social entertainment. One of the most successful of these hosts reported that "about twice a year I entertained my Congressional friends at an informal supper at my
house, inviting fifty or sixty of them at a time." He added:
"This gave me an opportunity to get to know them well."
Not all department heads could afford such social expenses,
and Congress inserts no money in agency budgets to provide
for its own extracurricular enjoyment.

Sometimes it is forgotten that congressmen are people. As
human beings they are amenable to deference, attention, and
even flattery. Even when a representative has been of the
opposite party from that of the Cabinet officer and the
President, he usually appreciates any consideration shown him
by the executive branch. His pride and self-respect are
wounded if it seems to him that departmental largess is being
showered on all other members except himself. A freshman
Democrat in the House expressed his bitterness at the State
Department's congressional liaison when he suggested that
"if Mr. Dulles had spent a few more hours with us than
minutes—and not been constantly flying around the world,
then the President wouldn't be in the trouble he is in now
with cuts in his foreign aid bill." This congressman felt that
if Christian Herter, then undersecretary of state, instead of
spending "all of his time convincing those who were already
convinced" when he visited the House Office Building, "had
spent a few minutes with the newcomers the situation would
have been different." The representative concluded, significantly for the standpoint of the State Department: "Frankly
when I came I was for Foreign Aid, but they unsold me so
I have voted for all the cuts." [7] The question—an interesting
one—is whether the congressman was "unsold" by the lack of
rational argument or by what he regarded as a lack of personal
deference.

A prominent member of Congress—who was a "Modern

Republican" before the Eisenhower administration courted the phrase—criticized the tendency of an agency head to turn over the task of "selling" his program to Congress by hiring "New York lawyers" to head presentation teams. The committees, witnessing the apparent lack of interest, acted accordingly. This same representative offered an example of an official respected by the legislators:

Now a real effective executive head was Ed Stettinius when he was Lend Lease Administrator. He came to all the hearings before committee. When he felt a witness wasn't responsive, he would interrupt and after getting the chairman's attention he would make his own statement in answer to the question. If some congressman asked a question and no member of the executive agencies present knew the answer, the representative could be sure that the next morning there would be a letter on his desk which provided the answer. After the bill left committee, Stettinius sat in the gallery and watched the debate on the floor. The congressmen knew that he knew what he was talking about and appreciated it.[8]

Those members of the Cabinet who did not believe that a question period would have been advantageous to their congressional relations usually based their conclusion on one of three reasons: either the practice would violate the separation of powers; or because of the traditional use of committees by Congress, there would be little gain from appearances on the floor; or, finally, the responsibility of the department head to the President would be undermined.

Cabinet members who used the "separation of powers" argument usually took pains to differentiate the American from the British system, without considering the procedure on its merits or questioning whether of itself it would be compatible with a separate Congress and executive. Replying to Senator Kefauver's request for an opinion concerning the "question and answer period resolution" which he had introduced at the beginning of the Eisenhower administration, Attorney General Herbert Brownell stated:

Senate Resolution 58 is subject to an objection which, in my opinion, is fundamental. It is related to our doctrine of the separation of powers and our system of three coordinate and distinct departments of Government. The founding fathers could have adopted a system under which the executive officers would be agents of and accountable to the Congress. But they did not.[9]

The existence of the committee system with the powerful influence exerted by the chairmen caused several Cabinet members to regard floor appearances as "academic," or at least as no improvement in administrative efficiency. A former secretary of agriculture believed that "the arguments on both sides usually have been reasonably well sifted and marshaled in the committee report which accompanies the bill to the floor. Hence, a Cabinet officer could add little during the floor debate that could not be presented by the member who advocates his point of view."

While Secretary of State John Foster Dulles was interested in the question period because he believed "it essential that as many members of the Congress as possible have direct access to such information," he offered one reservation:

My concern is, however, that such appearances before the Senate, and presumably similar sessions with the House, would not reduce the number of separate meetings with the various committees of the Congress, which, as you know, require a very large share of the time of some Cabinet officers and which often need to be on an "executive" basis.[10]

Most significant was the fear that the institution of a procedure permitting the Cabinet to appear in Congress would tend to undermine presidential direction. A former occupant and current student of the Presidency stated concisely the relationship which he believed should exist between the President and his department heads:

A Cabinet member, by the way, should speak for himself only to the President. After the Chief Executive has made his decision, the Cabinet member, whether or not he personally is opposed to it, can speak only for the President. If he does speak for himself, he can and should be fired.[11]

A member of the Roosevelt Cabinet expressed the same apprehension and insisted that "to answer questions and participate in debate would eventually involve the Cabinet officer and perhaps the President in unhealthy political agreements and compromises." One of Mr. Truman's department heads believed that Congress should provide by joint resolution that Cabinet members be "responsible to the President alone for their lawful conduct and responsible to the courts alone for their unlawful conduct."

Attorney General Brownell found himself keeping company with former President Truman when it came to a matter of presidential authority. He strenuously objected to the possibility that the "presence of executive officers in the Congress . . . would create the appearance that they are responsible to two masters, the Congress and the President." [12]

President Eisenhower's first secretary of the treasury, George M. Humphrey, elaborated on the administrative objections to the Kefauver proposal. Holding that "the development of an administration's policy in any field may well be a matter of growth," Humphrey insisted that the inquisition of a single department head might delay such a policy evolution. The expression of views to Congress by one Cabinet member, whose jurisdiction frequently did not encompass the total policy area, might give undue rigidity to executive discretion.[13]

Although it is evident that the suspicion of potential legislative interference was intense, no department head advocated doing away with appearances before congressional committees! Not one Cabinet member believed that the executive would increase its power over Congress by the implementation of the question period. Consequently, it would be surprising to discover that many in Congress—although granted that they view the government from a different institutional focus—would express a fear of executive encroachment as a result of the inauguration of a question period.

(XIII)

Congress and the Reform

SINCE THE PASSAGE of any proposal to seat the Cabinet in Congress is dependent upon the action of at least one of the two houses, it becomes pertinent to inquire into the characteristics of both those who have favored and those who have opposed the measure. In order to generalize as to the reasons for the continued appeal of (and resistance to) the idea of permitting the department heads to appear in the national legislature, data were compiled from three sources: (1) historical proceedings, (2) interviews, and (3) questionnaires.[1]

HISTORICAL ATTITUDES

The historical attitude survey analyzed the ninety-three members of both the Senate and House of Representatives who, since 1789, have expressed an opinion in recorded debate on the idea of Cabinet participation in congressional proceedings. It covered five periods: (1) 1789, at time of passage of the Treasury bill; (2) 1792, during the St. Clair debate; (3) 1864–65, Pendleton's House bill; (4) 1879–81, Pendleton's Senate bill; and (5) 1943–47, the Kefauver resolution for a "report and question period" in the House.

The characteristics selected as a basis for discerning the possible motivations of the proponents and opponents were; (1) age; (2) years in Congress; (3) committee chairmanships held; (4) party affiliation; (5) educational background; (6) affiliation with legal profession; (7) region from which elected. (See Table 1.) The smallness of the sample for each

Table 1. *Profiles of the five groups for and against seating the Cabinet in Congress during the periods when the issue was active in Congress*

	1789		1792	
Characteristic	For(11)	Against(5)	For(6)	Against(6)
Age				
Median	42	45	34	47.5
Average	43.1	47	37	46.3
Years in Congress				
Median			3	3
Average			2.66	2.66
Committee chairman-ships held				
Party affiliation				
Federalist	7	4	4	3
Jeffersonian Republican	3	1	1	3
Democratic				
Unknown	1		1	
Educational background				
No higher education	1	2	1	
Attended college	2	1	2	1
Graduated from college	6	2	3	5
Additional graduate work	2			
Education abroad		1		3
Affiliation with legal profession				
Lawyers	8	2	5	3
Non-lawyers	2	3	1	3
Unknown	1			
Regional origin				
New England	5	1	2	
Atlantic Central	4	2	3	
South	2	2	1	6
Midwest				
West				

	1864–1865		1879–1881		1943–1947	
	For(7)	Against(9)	For(8)	Against(4)	For(23)	Against(14)
	42.0	44.0	52.0	58.5	46.0	61.5
	41.8	45.0	51.0	59.5	49.7	60.2
	2.0	4.0	8.5	17.0	4.0	16.0
	3.0	4.3	8.5	17.5	4.5	16.2
		3	3	4	1	5
	4	6	4	3	10	5
	3	3	4	1	13	9
		1	1	2		1
	1	4	3	2	2	
	6	4	3		5	1
			1		16	12
	1				4	
	6	8	7	3	12	13
	1	1	1	1	11	1
	2	1	2	2	3	1
	1	4		2	2	1
	1		1		7	8
	3	4	4		5	4
			1		6	

Source: The Biographical Directory of the American Congress, 1774–1949, 81 Cong., 2 sess., H.Doc. 607 (1950).

period imposed obvious statistical limitations; however, some of the results still appeared to be of interest.

(1). Age. It was evident that in each of these five periods the median and average ages of those who objected to bringing the Cabinet before Congress were relatively greater than the median and average ages of those who favored the plan. In 1789 the members of the opposition were approximately three years older than the advocates of Cabinet participation; in 1792, ten to twelve years older; in 1864–65, only two to three years older; in 1879–81, almost eight years older, and in 1943–47, about ten to fifteen years older.

(2) Years in Congress. One might expect that if the opponents' ages were greater, their length of service in Congress also would have been longer. After omitting the first two periods (1789 and 1792) when the tenure for both groups was the same owing to the newness and stability of the first few Congresses, such an expectation was met. In 1864–65, when the opponents were on the average two to three years older, their number of years in the House was also two to three years greater than that of those who supported the first Pendleton bill. This pattern was similar for 1879–81 and 1943–47, where the differences in age were almost identical with those accruing from years spent in Congress.

(3) Committee Chairmanships. The older age and longer service of the opponents would lead one to believe that seniority and its capstone, the committee chairmanship, might be factors in evoking opposition to the reform. Thus it was revealing that the opponents included a greater proportion of committee chairmen. Since there were no permanent standing committees in the First and Second Congresses, this analysis began with 1864–65. During the debate over Pendleton's bill in the House, a third of the nine representatives who were opposed occupied committee chairmanships. No one who endorsed the reform in debate held such a position.

In 1879–81, when Pendleton revived his measure and ad-

vocated it before the Senate, the number of chairmen on both
sides was almost equal: three favored the measure and four
opposed it. The latter four, however, made up the whole opposition. The three chairmen supporting Pendleton contributed
slightly over one third of the proponents' strength.

Among the twenty-three representatives who voiced approval of the Kefauver resolution, only one chaired a committee, while more than one third (five out of fourteen) of
those against the plan were committee chairmen. The sole
chairman in favor of the question period headed the committee on memorials (usually not recognized as a group of
great internal power), while the opponents were aided by
the chairmen of the committees on appropriations, military
affairs, and rules. These three committees would rank on any
list of the most influential organizations within the House of
Representatives.

(4) Party Affiliation. It might be anticipated that the anti-
administration party in Congress would take advantage of
any proposal which sought to make department heads accountable to the legislative branch. Yet there was no correlation between the congressional opposition in any one of these
five periods and a significant amount of support for the plan.
In fact, it was interesting to note that in each period the
party which had control of the executive has had more of
its members both for and against the proposal than did the
party out of power.

During the Washington administration, there were more
Federalists on both sides of the argument than there were
Jeffersonian Republicans. More Republicans supported and
opposed the bill introduced by "Peace Democrat" George H.
Pendleton during the Civil War than did members of the
Ohio representative's own party. This pattern was continued
during the Hayes and Garfield Presidencies. Although three
Republican senators disagreed with Pendleton's bill as against
one Democrat, four senators in each party supported Pendle-

ton. During the Second World War, with Franklin Roosevelt
and the Democratic party well entrenched in the executive,
more Democrats than Republicans both supported and opposed the Kefauver question period. Such behavior suggests
the thesis of Samuel Lubell that the issues of each era are
fought out within the majority party.[2] A crude psychology
could also hold that the frustration of the younger members
of the majority party—owing to the greater privileges and
easier access to the executive of their own senior members—
might be greater than that of the minority party whose members do not expect as much since their group is obviously not
in political control.

(5) Educational Background and Legal Training. No relationship was apparent with reference to the position taken on
the reform and the legislators' level of education. Considering
the constitutional questions which have been voiced consistently by the opponents, it is noteworthy that more lawyers
than non-lawyers in each period have approved bringing the
Cabinet before Congress.

Since 1864, however, a greater percentage of those opposed
have been lawyers, rather than non-lawyers. For instance, in
the 1943–47 period, there were almost as many non-lawyers
(eleven out of a total of twenty-three) as lawyers in favor of
the Kefauver resolution. But thirteen of the fourteen in opposition were members of that ancient and honorable profession.

(6) Regional Origin. Excluding the first two periods because
of the limited expanse of the United States and omitting the
third (Civil War), owing to the disaffection of the South, a
regional comparison of approval and disapproval was made
for 1879–81 and 1943–47. (See Table 2.)

Approval and disapproval within an area was balanced
fairly well in all five regions except the West, where support
has been unanimous. One might have expected the Midwest
and South to provide substantial strength for the Cabinet

measure with Midwesterners Pendleton, Garfield, Taft, Harlan, and Thom, and Southerners Montague, Maverick, Kefauver, and Fulbright as its sponsors. Both areas, however, contained an equally high amount of opposition. Much of this reaction could be attributed to the one-party dominance in each of these regions. The South cast its ballots primarily for Demo-

Table 2. Regional distribution of members of Congress for (31) and against (18) seating the Cabinet in Congress, 1879–1947

Region	For		Against		Percentage in favor by region
	Number	Percentage of total for	Number	Percentage of total against	
New England	5	16.1	3	16.7	62.5
Middle Atlantic	2	6.5	3	16.7	40.0
South	11	35.4	8	44.4	57.9
Midwest	6	19.5	4	22.2	60.0
Far West	7	22.5	0	00.0	100.0

crats and the Midwest for Republicans. As legislators from such one-party areas usually remained in office longer, this generally meant that a greater percentage of committee chairmanships would be held by either Midwest Republicans or Southern Democrats depending on which party had a majority in Congress.

THE ROLE OF THE COMMITTEE CHAIRMAN

Tentatively, some support can be found (in the historical data) for the conclusion that seniority and particularly the occupancy of a committee chairmanship were strategic factors in determining opposition to the idea of seating the Cabinet in Congress. Does contemporary data concerning the attitudes of representatives in the Eighty-fifth Congress (1957) tend to support or refute this hypothesis? [3]

There was no over-all clear distinction (as there had been

in the historical survey) with reference to age and tenure in Congress between the advocates and objectors to the procedural reform. In fact, there was seeming refutation of it when "Newcomers" and "Old-timers" in the House of Representatives were compared. (See Table 3.) [4] The preponderance of opposition among the "Newcomer" Republicans might be accounted for by the fact that the House was controlled by the Democrats and a consequent fear existed that Republican department heads would be "badgered." No evidence was gathered to support or refute this explanation.

Table 3. Opposition to the question period for the Cabinet in Congress in terms of seniority in the House

	Democrats	Republicans
Old-timers	70.2%	74.5%
	(33 out of 47)	(24 out of 35)
Newcomers [a]	68.5%	87.7%
	(38 out of 51)	(42 out of 49)

[a] Defining "Newcomer" as a member having less than nine years service in the House.

	Democrats	Republicans
Old-timers	73.3%	77.2%
	(55 out of 75)	(51 out of 66)
Newcomers [b]	69.6%	83.3%
	(16 out of 23)	(15 out of 18)

[b] Defining "Newcomer" as a member having less than two terms (four years) service in the House.

Source: Cabinet-Congressional Relations Questionnaire (85th Congress, 1957).

The higher opposition than expected (based on the historical data) among those with less seniority could conceivably be explained by the fact that there had been no prior period of "education" for the reform. Three fourths of the House had been elected since the end of the Second World War—which was the last time that the idea of bringing the Cabinet before Congress had received extensive floor debate.

An examination of the attitudes of those in both parties who were located at the extreme ends of committee service provided support for the conclusions reached in the historical profiles. (See Figure 2.) Of the nineteen House committee chairmen, eleven responded to the questionnaire. Of these respondents, ten (or 90.9%) were opposed to the idea of a question period in the House. Only one favored it. A similar situation existed among the ranking minority members (the senior Republicans on each committee who would have been chairmen if their party had had a majority in the House as a whole). Only seven of the nineteen senior committee Republicans responded. Five of the seven were opposed to the question period and two were for it.

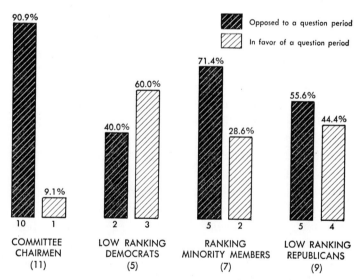

Figure 2. *The effect of committee position on the opinion of members of Congress concerning the desirability of a question period for the Cabinet in Congress*

Source: Cabinet-Congressional Relations Questionnaire (85th Congress, 1957).

More tolerance for the reform seemed to be exhibited by the members of both parties who were lowest in committee seniority. Of the nineteen low-ranking Democrats, only five responded. Two of the five were opposed while three were in favor. Of the nineteen low-ranking Republicans, almost half (or nine) answered. Five of these were opposed, while four approved. The differences—between the chairmen and ranking minority members versus the combined low-ranking Democrats and low-ranking Republicans in the sample—do seem revealing.

Two explanations might be advanced for the obvious hostility of committee chairmen and ranking minority members to permitting the Cabinet either to debate or to answer questions in the House. The first would be that these chairmen and their minority counterparts with many years of service fear a decrease in their own power and influence. If the department heads were granted privileges of the floor, the chairmen's role as the administration's spokesmen in Congress might be diminished.[5]

A distinguished political scientist has held that seekers after power tend to rationalize their private motives in terms of the public interest.[6] Thus the almost unanimous cry by those opposed to the Pendleton plan that Congress would lose prestige and the executive would gain in influence in supposed violation of the constitutionally sanctioned separation of powers can be carried one step further: It is not Congress which might lose influence but the members within both houses who maintain their positions of power through seniority.

Although none of the committee chairmen would agree that their main reason for opposition to the question hour was because its inauguration would disrupt their established relationship to a specific department, ten of the thirty-five proponents responding were convinced that this was the principal reason for the opposition within Congress. (See Table 7.) A less "personal" explanation, from the standpoint of the committee chairmen, would be that they have adjusted themselves to a workable system and that in their view the Pendleton and Kefauver plans would result in bedlam rather than in improved communication. With reference to adaptation to the system, the chairman of one of the most important Senate committees and a leader of the so-called Inner Club remarked that upon arriving in Washington a quarter century before, he thought that the question hour was a "good idea." He explained his change of position: "But the longer I'm with the committee system the more successful I think it is. We just need wisdom on both sides to make it work. I think we have the greatest form of government." The Senate has always emphasized tradition and continuity of procedure. Much concern was expressed regarding maintenance of the separation of powers doctrine. A senior Republican senator, who chaired Senate committees when the Grand Old Party was in power, stressed that "you don't want to break up the idea of coordinate branches of government by messing with the mechanism."

The ranking minority member of a House committee summarized his view of those who favor a question period by saying "they haven't been here long enough to know better." No doubt some of the past support for the reform has come from the younger members who have been frustrated, in part, by the institutionalization and status systems prevalent within both chambers. Regarded in his district or state as an important personage, the freshman legislator embarks for Washington with a heady feeling of victory behind him. As a newcomer he is considered a "tenderfoot" and rapidly learns that seniority pertains not only to his assignment and placement on committees, but also to his offices, furniture, and parking privileges, and to almost everything else which involves a choice among members. Others have become rooted in Washington long before the "tenderfoot." The Speaker, Sam Rayburn, of Bonham, Texas, has been returned biennially for almost a half century. Close behind, also a survivor of twenty-four consecutive elections, is Carl Vinson, of Georgia, who arrived in 1914, and in recent decades, when his Democratic party was in control of the House, has served as chairman of either the committee on armed services or one of its two predecessors (the committee on naval affairs) for over twenty-five years.

The committee chairman has access to the decision-making centers *of* the executive branch. At times by default, and at other times by desire, the chairman has also become a decision-making center *for* the executive branch. It is not difficult to perceive that Cabinet members are also "tenderfeet" compared to such long-serving House committee chairmen (when the Democrats have been in a majority) as Vinson of armed services (25 years), Clarence Cannon of appropriations (14 years), and Brent Spence of banking and currency (12 years). A similar situation exists in the Senate, with both Harry F. Byrd, who—off and on, depending on party control—has presided over either rules or finance for a total of nineteen years, and Richard Russell of armed services with seventeen years in the chairmanship.

A congressional staff member has described the "breaking in" process of the newcomer: "Freshmen come here with stars in their eyes. Then when they give their first speech on the floor and are lit into by some old-timer, they retire for a couple of months with their tail between their legs. Pretty soon they come out and learn to live with the system." Evidence of such an evolution was seen in the current opinions of two representatives who had been Kefauver's strongest House supporters during the question and report period debate of 1943. Both of these men were still in the House, but fourteen years had elapsed. Although one continued to be opposed to the seniority system (and on the Senate side to the filibuster), in regard to the question hour idea, he held: "As I get older, I get less imaginative about changes in the technical procedure in order to improve communication." The other, still convinced "that the British Constitution is a better one" than the American, concluded: "Our system works as it is. I would not say now some of the things that I said when I first entered Congress. I thought then that the question period was a pretty good idea."

CONTEMPORARY ATTITUDES

Although Congressmen are presumably more perceptive than most to human motivations, there was disagreement as to the principal reason some members favored and others opposed "granting the Cabinet the privilege of the floor." [7]

Of the 45 representatives out of the sample of 182 who favored a question period, 38 gave what they considered to be the main reason why some members of Congress were in favor of granting the Cabinet the privilege of the floor. (See Table 4.) Almost two thirds of these respondents founded their advocacy on the fact that "Congress needs more information upon

Table 4. Ranking of reasons for granting the Cabinet the privilege of the floor, as stated by the House proponents (38) of the question period

	Number	Percentage
Need of Congress for more information	24	63.3
Younger M.C.'s wish to overcome the influence of committee chairmen and the seniority system	4	10.5
Greater congressional control over the executive	4	10.5
To increase congressional prestige	4	10.5
Preference for British parliamentary practices	1	2.6
To harass the opposition if it controls the executive	1	2.6

Source: Cabinet-Congressional Relations Questionnaire (85th Congress, 1957).

which to base its decisions." In addition, a handful claimed that they supported the question period in order (1) to overcome the influence of the committee chairmen and the seniority system, (2) to secure more congressional control over the executive, and (3) to increase congressional prestige. Of the remaining two individuals in the sample one considered the reason to be an admiration for British parliamentary practices and the other a desire to harass the opposition party if it had control of the executive.[8]

The opponents of the question period saw the advocates' motives differently. (See Table 5.) The overwhelming claim of those in favor that they wanted more information was given only third place by the opposition, one fourth of whom believed that the major reason for support was favoritism for British parliamentary practices. One fifth believed that the proponents desired more congressional control over the executive. Twelve members of Congress stated that the main reason the proponents favored bringing the Cabinet to the floor was for the purpose of harassing the opposition party if it controlled the departments. All twelve were Republicans. They possibly lacked confidence in the motives of their fellow legislators, especially since the House was dominated by the Democratic

Table 5. Ranking of reasons of those who favor granting the Cabinet the privilege of the floor, as stated by the House opponents (74) of the question period

	Number	Percentage
Preference for British parliamentary practices	19	25.7
Greater congressional control over the executive	15	20.3
Need of Congress for more information	13	17.6
To harass the opposition if it controls the executive	12	16.2
Younger M.C.'s wish to overcome the influence of committee chairmen and the seniority system	6	8.1
To favor executive branch over Congress	6	8.1
To increase congressional prestige	3	4.0

Source: Cabinet-Congressional Relations Questionnaire (85th Congress, 1957).

opposition while their own party held the Presidency. During the reign of the Truman administration and the Eightieth Republican Congress, Democrats would probably have entertained similar reservations.

There were no committee chairmen among the six opponents who held that the question period advocates desired to short-circuit both the committee chairmen and the seniority system. In fact, all six were on the bottom one fourth of their committees in terms of seniority. Another half dozen thought that the reformers probably favored the executive branch over Congress. Three members gave the proponents the benefit of the doubt when they granted that they favored the proposal in order to increase congressional prestige.

What were the reasons for opposition to the idea of bringing the Cabinet before Congress? Basically, one third of the opponents who answered that question saw no gain in information by the adoption of the proposed procedure. (See Table 6.) A quarter of this opposition feared an increase in executive power. Another one fourth were divided equally between objection to a prolongation of daily sessions and a disruption of congressional procedure. Less than one tenth believed that the

Table 6. *Ranking of reasons for not granting the Cabinet the privilege of the floor, as stated by the House opponents (98) of the question period*

	Number	Percentage
No gain in information	33	33.7
Increased power of executive branch	25	25.5
Prolongation of congressional daily sessions	13	13.3
Disruption of congressional procedure	13	13.3
Disruption of committee chairman's relationship to specific department	8	8.2
Unconstitutionality	3	3.0
Aversion to imitation of British parliamentary practices	3	3.0

Source: Cabinet-Congressional Relations Questionnaire (85th Congress, 1957).

committee chairman's power-relationship was sufficient cause for disapproval. Again, none of these were committee chairmen, although they ranged in length of service from one to thirty-three years. Three members held that the admission of the Cabinet was unconstitutional. A similar number based their objection on the desire to avoid imitation of British parliamentary methods.

The supporters of the question period believed that the chief motivation for opposition was the possible disruption of a committee chairman's relationship to a specific department. (See Table 7.) Except for the interchange of this belief with the opponents' emphasis that the reform would fail to gain any information, the advocates' ranking of opposition motives coincided fairly accurately with that of the opponents.

The fear was noticeably great that a question period would increase the power of the executive over Congress. Both sides listed this second as their main reason for opposition to the idea. (See Tables 6 and 7.) In answer to a hypothetical question which assumed that "the Cabinet were allowed the privilege of debate or submitted to questioning in Congress," almost 45 percent of the total sample of 182 believed that the executive

Table 7. Ranking of reasons of those who oppose granting the Cabinet the privilege of the floor, as stated by House proponents (35) of the question period

	Number	Percentage
Disruption of committee chairman's relationship to specific department	10	28.6
Increased power of executive branch	8	22.9
Disruption of congressional procedure	7	20.0
No gain in information	5	14.3
Prolongation of congressional daily sessions	2	5.7
Aversion to imitation of British parliamentary practices	2	5.7
Unconstitutionality	1	2.8

Source: Cabinet-Congressional Relations Questionnaire (85th Congress, 1957).

would benefit from the change. (See Table 8.) There was a substantial difference, however, between those who actually supported the question period and those who did not. Less than one sixth of the advocates, but over half of the opponents, thought that the executive would gain at the expense of Congress. A majority of the proponents stated that neither branch would increase its power and that "relations would be the same." Slightly over a quarter of the opposition believed that this was the case. Although more than one fourth of the ques-

Table 8. *Percent distribution of congressional opinion on whether a question period for the Cabinet in Congress would result in a growth in power for Congress, the Executive, or neither*

	Benefit to Congress	Benefit to the Executive	Benefit to neither	No answer to question
Total replying to questionnaire (182)	9.3	44.6	34.6	11.5
Democrats (98)	10.2	44.9	31.6	13.3
Republicans (84)	8.4	44.0	38.0	9.6
Total replying to questionnaire in favor of question period (45)	26.7	15.5	55.6	2.2
Democrats (27)	33.3	18.5	48.2	
Republicans (18)	16.6	11.1	66.7	5.6

Source: Cabinet-Congressional Relations Questionnaire (85th Congress, 1957).

tion period followers were convinced that the benefits would accrue to Congress, less than 4 percent of those opposed to the reform agreed (five respondents out of 137).

The more discontent a congressman harbored over the supposed state of Cabinet-congressional relations, the more likely he was to advocate a question period as a possible solution to the difficulties. (See Figure 3.) Several reasons were given for dissatisfaction: among them, a general lack of responsiveness by the Cabinet when they appeared before committee, an unawareness of departmental affairs by some administrators and, on occasion, executive arrogance and discourtesy.

The group which believed that Cabinet-congressional relations were unsatisfactory consisted of two distinct types: one

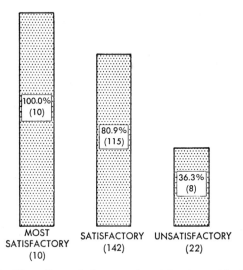

MOST SATISFACTORY (10)   SATISFACTORY (142)   UNSATISFACTORY (22)

Figure 3. The effect of degree of satisfaction with Cabinet-congressional relations on opposition to a question period for the Cabinet in Congress

Note: The more satisfied a representative was with the state of Cabinet-congressional relations, the more likely he was to oppose the question period.

Numbers at bottom of columns indicate total number of respondents in each category. Numbers within the columns indicate the total respondents who were opposed to the question period.

Source: Cabinet-Congressional Relations Questionnaire (85th Congress, 1957).

subgroup contained the young and what could be loosely labeled as the more "liberal" representatives, and the second incorporated both some nationally prominent congressional investigators and some older members who were active critics of Roosevelt, Truman, and Eisenhower administration policies.[9]

A Midwestern Republican who entered Congress during the Truman administration accused the executive of "a lack of understanding—and respect—for Congress." He related that in the summer of 1957 the Treasury had determined that a rise in the debt limit would be needed. Yet nothing was said to the staff of the Joint Committee on Internal Revenue Taxation, the chief of whom had been with the committee since 1928. This lack of communication was not appreciated by Congress. Even more disturbing to this representative were: "the cases where civil servants and military leaders give committees misleading information on which the members base their decision and then give the accurate information to a friendly committee member for leakage to the press or do it directly."

A Midwestern Democrat thought that there was "a feeling of natural competition" with the department heads who frequently "come down to the Hill on the defensive." In the Senate, this opinion was echoed in the objection that "Cabinet members come before our committees with long prepared statements that use up time and thus cut down on the opportunity to question them." Many members of both houses were worried over the constant tendency by agents of the executive branch "to slip around legislative intent" when implementing the statutes. One senator claimed that in one case the trouble was not so much innocent bypassing of congressional intent as that the agency head was a "man of deceit." It is fair to say that the senator was a Democrat and the agency head was a Republican. The situation by which one party is elected to responsibility for the executive and the other controls the committees of Congress which seek to enforce accountability makes for tension and "politics" which one member "suspected everywhere."

A congressman's opinion as to Cabinet responsiveness often was related to his particular policy orientation and his personal experience with a department head. A member who was unhappy over the advocacy of reciprocal trade by both parties when they were in control of the Presidency believed that the Cabinet was very unresponsive. This congressman's charge of "unresponsiveness," however, could be attributed more to the fact that none of the three previous administrations had supported his views than to the fact that the department head did not answer his questions while appearing before committee.

Sixteen of the twenty-two respondents who thought that Cabinet-congressional relations were "unsatisfactory" were Democrats. In interviews, several of these members claimed that their objection was motivated not so much by partisanship as by resentment against "the system." Agreeing with this disclaimer of party antagonism, a third-term Republican expressed some of his peers' feelings when he concluded: "A lot of us Republicans have often felt that the Cabinet was maybe even more responsive to the Democratic Congressmen, so there is no difference at present with reference to party, especially with the Democrats controlling Congress." The predominant attitude of the House toward Cabinet responsiveness was summed up adequately by one of the most distinguished Democratic committee chairmen: "We think the Cabinet is very responsive before our committee—especially when they agree with our position."

EQUAL BUT NOT SEPARATE

Satisfaction with the committee system in the Senate and House provided the reason for much of the opposition to a question and report period. The very existence of the system also offered hope for some who favored bringing the Cabinet before Congress.

Ideological support for a "separation of powers" between legislative and executive branches weighed heavily with many members in both chambers. One typical reaction aptly stated the dogma and revealed the dilemma:

Cabinet officers belong to the executive branch. The Congressional committees give the executive branch an opportunity to express their opinions. The floor is for the deliberation of the legislative branch. The three branches will function best if they are kept separated as they now are.

Few opponents of the reform recognized the fact that "separation" is virtually nonexistent as a result of the committee system. One senator punctured the dogma when, after stating that the committees were "the agents of Congress," he queried: "Why can't the principal do what its agents do?" The strong feeling that the floor was sacrosanct against the intrusion of "outsiders" belied the accepted fact that, since most of the legislative work was done in committee, the votes usually were decided prior to any deliberation on the floor. A Republican senator who did not favor the question hour ably summarized this latter practice:

Testimony is given in committee and that is where it should be provided. No matter how high the intellectual qualities of a senator, he can't know everything about pending legislation—it is just an impossibility. I found that I had to make a number of presumptions. With agricultural legislation, I follow George Aiken [the ranking minority member of the Senate committee on agriculture] . . . he is sound.

There was no disagreement on the fact that the important deliberations took place in committee—in the same committee where members of the Cabinet were permitted to testify. A senator who inquired as to the activities of the principal's agent might well express dissatisfaction with an answer based on a dated and inaccurate mythology.

None of the supporters of the Cabinet reform expressed a desire to do away with the committee system. They recognized the necessity for detailed examination of the complicated legislation which was a product of the modern industrial and regulatory state. Most held that the ability to question effectively a department head grew with the accumulation of committee experience in considering agency affairs. They did, however, desire to alleviate what they thought were evils of the committee system. Among these "evils" was the almost "life and death" power of some committee chairmen to determine both agenda and frequency of meetings.[10] Even if a measure received consideration, it was sometimes "buried" or delayed until the end of the session when floor action became impossible. At times, a vacillating presiding officer has allowed the discussion to wander or has overlooked the desire of the minority to contribute to interrogation. But even more important than these long-recognized abuses of the committee system were some of the members' own anxieties concerning the danger of specialization to their role as a congressman. Legislators tend to become so absorbed in the time-consuming work of their committees that little time remains in a day filled with constituent demands for enlightenment on broader aspects of national policy. Similar to Kefauver and his supporters in 1943, several representatives argued that the committees' failure to disseminate their hearings rapidly—if at all—was a major factor in the information gap. Even with efficient distribution, busy congressmen and their already overworked staffs still would be confronted with the problem of finding time to extract significant policy statements from the pounds of verbiage.

A strong advocate of the Eisenhower administration's policies, while opposed to the proposition allowing the Cabinet the right of free debate, was convinced that departmental officials should appear in order to provide information:

Frankly, the administration's policy statements are pretty vague. And when debate is taking place on some legislative proposal, the question invariably arises as to how the administration feels about it. The Republican leadership will give us some view supposedly based on their attendance at the President's Tuesday leadership conference. However, most of us often suspect that the Republican leadership has either added something or is as vague on the policy as we are.

Many members of Congress remained unimpressed as to the validity of this opinion. They claimed that the testimony was available and the executive's position easily ascertainable.

A WEAKENED PRESIDENCY?

A few individuals in both houses were disturbed over any institutionalization of the Cabinet in its relations with Congress, since they felt the result would be a demise of the Chief Executive's power. A feminine member of the House of Representatives pilloried the Eisenhower administration for displaying a tendency in this direction:

I feel that this administration has been enabled to disguise many of the most reprehensible policies of the President by camouflaging them as [Secretary of Agriculture Ezra Taft] Benson's policies or [Secretary of the Treasury George M.] Humphrey's policies, or [Secretary of the Interior Douglas] McKay's policies, when in our constitutional system, they are and must be the President's policies. To recognize the Cabinet as distinct from the President would further the dangerous trend toward political irresponsibility which this administration has so greatly encouraged.

A freshman Democratic senator also condemned "the general tendency to disassociate the President from the actions of the undefined organism known as 'the administration.'" To allow the Cabinet a place on the Senate floor would "weaken the Presidency, and make it much more difficult for the Congress to fix responsibility."

Advocates of a question period heartily differed with the senator's belief in congressional inability to fix responsibility under their procedure. Agreeing with the Kefauver backers who were in the Bureau of the Budget during the 1943–44 debates, some proponents contended that a public response to legislative questions would promote uniformity in policy. In fact, it would strengthen the President's position since the statements of his department heads would be witnessed by all. One senator claimed that the procedure would eliminate much of the "double-dealing" which was rife: "For example, from my state we have two senators, each from a different party. When one of us phones the Department of the Interior we get one story; when the other phones he gets a different version. This leads to confusion."

In addition to the practical satisfaction with the committee system and a theoretical concern for the nature of the Presidency, more human considerations have prevented the enactment of the reform. A committee chairman described the House as "a place of prima-donnas." A senator viewed his colleagues in less flattering terms: "We have a lot of jackasses and damn fools around here." Still others were convinced that there would be "grandstanding," "haranguing," and "badgering." Whether braying or nagging, these members felt that it all added up to one thing for the Cabinet: an unpleasant experience. And for the country: more partisanship.[11]

Given this intensity of feeling, it was even more surprising that almost one fourth of the House sample and a quarter of the Senate sample favored a question period. Were these hopes realizable in the future? Or would they continue to be portents of present frustrations?

(XIV)

The Future for Reform

THE GREEK PHILOSOPHER PLATO once asserted that if only philosophers were kings and kings were philosophers all might be well with the world. This statement may come to the mind of the student and practitioner of government who analyzes the relationships between the American Presidency and Congress —divided as they are by a constitutionally sanctioned separation of powers—and finds himself face to face with a labyrinth of proposals as to how both branches might be brought into greater harmony and cooperation without sacrificing their essential functions.

Almost eighty years have elapsed since the young Mr. Wilson stirred reformers' imaginations with a Utopia of Cabinet government that combined parts of the British model with the American concept of a separate executive chosen by all the people. Opponents saw in such a scheme the disorder and futility that were associated with the Third Republic of France, where the president had become a ceremonial figurehead in the formulation of public policy. While Wilson and his disciples, such as Corwin and Finletter, were talking about a Cabinet *from* Congress, the opposition aroused by them was also detrimental to the plans of those who advocated the Cabinet *in* Congress. Even this latter group experienced an evolution in its thinking. Pendleton's plea that the whole Cabinet be granted seats in Congress—enabling them to enter into any debate which concerned their departments—was far different from Kefauver's more limited plan that some of the Cabinet merely submit to questioning at least once every two weeks under specified procedures.

A new breed of reformer, however, is weary of hoping that Congress will impose a sense of responsibility on itself. They would urge that a remedy of legislative-executive deadlocks which prevent majority opinion from being translated into needed public policy lies in the invigoration of American political parties. Although only recently oriented to "the group basis of politics"—a scholarly realism upon which the politician has long acted in order to survive—these diagnosticians regard procedural changes within Congress and the executive as quite hopeless and visionary without a more fundamental reform of the party structure.[1] It is often implied that those favoring an innovation such as the question period—whose inauguration would depend on the sanction of either house—are somewhat utopian, if not naive. But, sadly, the quest for basic party reform often leads into the same utopian maze.[2]

At the root of the difficulty in reconciling thought and action is the climate for reform created by the nature of the American political system and the political base upon which candidates for the Presidency and Congress contest. To be elected, both must balance group against group and consolidate sufficient opinion to provide a majority. A President who attains a winning potpourri of urban and rural, business and labor, racial and religious elements (as well as their related subcategories), among others, has a combination which differs not merely in degree but in kind from that gathered by the aspirant for the national legislature who faces a similar task on a smaller and narrower scale.

For the congressman, the base of his power is the constituency ranging in area from a small segment of a large metropolis to a whole state in the less populated regions of the country. Here the citizens who ultimately return or reject the incumbent are located. Depending on the intra- and inter-party competition, the incumbent's record may at any moment be exposed and charged with "diverging" from local feeling. "They [the voters] remember the one time you were against them rather than all the times you were for them" is an old axiom of Capitol Hill which frequently conditions legislative behavior.

Once in Washington, the legislator finds himself forgetting the defense of his locality and its interests only at his peril. And he did not come to sacrifice himself. Yet the expensive nature of present-day campaigning may cause him to ponder ways of reconciling the aims of various national groups with those of his constituency. If he is successful, he may enlist the resources—both human and financial—of either the electric utilities, the farm machinery manufacturers, the building and construction trades, or even the Committee for an Effective Congress, not to mention such larger conglomerations of power as the Chamber of Commerce and the American Federation of Labor–Congress of Industrial Organizations.

In the House, the new member is confronted with a diffusion of satrapies which would give pause to the most unifying of Caesars. These pockets of leadership include a vast number of committees and subcommittees which are "little legislatures" in power but not in breadth of membership. The reward for a newcomer's effectiveness is his potential return to office. To be effective is often to sit either on a committee which will be of benefit to one's constituency or on one which is powerful enough so that colleagues on other committees will take cognizance of one's desires. An agricultural committee composed mostly of rural-oriented representatives cannot be expected to appear overly deferential to the needs of metropolitan areas when they seem to conflict with those of their farm and small-town supporters. In conjunction with the legislative and appropriations committees and their numerous subgroups, equally powerful forces exist in the House which further condition behavior. Majority and minority leaders, whips, the Speaker, and the Rules Committee: all stand ready to hinder the unco-operative and reward those "who understand the way things work."

To overcome the seeming vastness of the House, a congress-man seeks associations and relationships with his colleagues from his own state and party, members who arrived when he did, and fellow committeemen with whom he is sure to be shar-ing legislative problems in the sessions ahead. As a result of the desire to establish friendships and exchange information with those on other committees, more formal affiliations occur. Usually all who are elected at the same time will organize a group such as the "86th Club" which includes representatives from both parties who were elected to the Eighty-Sixth Con-gress in November, 1958. Such a bipartisan body is of little "political" value and serves primarily as a focal point for social and orientation activities. More valuable from the standpoint of legislative tactics are the smaller bodies similar to the "S.O.S.," whose dozen or so Republican members meet twice weekly during the session, once on Tuesday afternoon in one of the participants' offices for a brief business and social gather-ing and then for a Wednesday morning breakfast where the guest speaker may vary from the President of the United States to a foreign ambassador. In addition, there are still other groups organized on a state basis and also by party within the state.

Based on his committee assignment and the paths to the ex-ecutive branch often constructed as a result of the desire to serve constituent demand, each legislator, in time, builds his own net of associations with the departments and the interest groups affected by their policies. As the years pass, the member who is returned to office in election after election and who has automatically ascended the committee hierarchy by seniority is likely to have a keener grasp of the relationships and effects of a departmental action than many Cabinet appointees. Cer-tainly those legislators who sit on the appropriations committees in each house are accorded a special deference by both political and career administrator alike.

Even if the department head has acquired a previous understanding of public affairs through periodic assignments to Washington during times of national emergency, he has much to learn and—once he arrives—little time in which to do it. The cost of his education is likely to be great and the returns to the government are frequently in arrears when he leaves his post to reenter private life. A distinguished Senate committee chairman estimated that it cost the taxpayers "billions of dollars" to educate one Cabinet executive to his responsibilities. "Wrong" decisions which are later rectified account for a secretary's high tuition in the school of practical politics. When at last he has acquired a fundamental understanding of the complexities of his department and its constituency, too frequently it is time to retire to the life from which he came. A new man then begins the long process of education.

Similarly to representatives and senators, Cabinet officers arrive in Washington with varying degrees of commitment to both their localities and an assortment of interest groups and causes. They acquire and drop other commitments during their stay. Although ultimately responsible to the President, each department head is constantly pushed and pulled by the "vertical" (hierarchically within the executive branch) and "horizontal" (between agencies, Congress, and the public) forces which impinge on his department and its functions. His success often will be judged as much by the groups which he can keep pacified as by the administrative skill with which he guides his department toward its goals. His retention or dismissal is largely based on his relationship with the President. Chief Executives have kept Cabinet members despite their unpopularity with some factions of Congress and dismissed them regardless of any following they might have. Thus President Eisenhower backed Secretary of State John Foster Dulles and Secretary of

Agriculture Ezra Taft Benson in the face of severe criticism from some quarters of Congress. On the other hand, Jesse H. Jones, secretary of commerce from 1940 to 1945, was dismissed by Franklin D. Roosevelt after the 1944 election because the President believed that the secretary had opposed his fourth term nomination and was behind a conservative revolt against him. Notwithstanding Jones's great strength in Congress and his influence in the business community resulting from work as reconstruction finance administrator, he had proved expendable.[3]

The not-so-expendable career servant, following a "legislative" version of Jefferson's maxim that "few die and none resign," frequently finds it more advantageous to cater to the whims of the strategically located legislator and pressure group than to those of the seemingly ever rotating series of political appointees layered above him. The inexperience of the political executive is also a reason why Congress depends on the civil service for reliable information as to departmental policy and operations. One representative revealed his trade secret for effective committee performance when he reported: "Whenever a secretary or an assistant secretary testifies, I always look to see who is sitting beside him. After I find out that man's name, I phone him up and talk over the agency's problems with him—for he is the one who really knows." Congressional anxiety about a Cabinet officer's grasp of departmental affairs can be great. A senator with several decades of seniority and knowledge illustrated the deeply felt antagonism which can arise when, referring to Eisenhower's second defense secretary, Neil H. McElroy (who had come to his post from the presidency of the Procter and Gamble Soap Company), he asked: "How can a soap salesman advise thirty-year Members of Congress on the defense policy of the United States?"

Some Cabinet members realize the environmental limitations within which they operate; others never do and thus become increasingly frustrated throughout their tenure. Secretary of Agriculture Benson, in an address to departmental employees, recognized an awareness of agency pressures on the politically designated executive, as follows:

Part of our job in the front office is to direct in an over-all way, as we can, the vast array of talent, education, technical and professional "know how" that is assembled in this branch of the government. And to do even that effectively, we must rely heavily upon your advice and assistance. It is humbling, but it is also wholesome, for us to realize that we need the Department far more than the Department needs us.[4]

By their very nature, the constituencies of department heads and committee members are more homogeneous than that of the President. Both executive and legislator serve as focal points and integrators of ideas within their realms. Each must choose among the alternatives when he casts his vote or recommends a course of action. Although the attempt has been made to use the Cabinet as a discussion center where the participants could elevate themselves above the parochial interests of their agencies and consider public policy in its broadest sense, this effort has not been wholly successful.[5] Most Cabinet officers and their staffs resent the opinions of "outsiders" whom they regard as "less knowledgeable." Perhaps such provincialism is to be expected from the long history of President-Cabinet relations where department heads have striven to gain the Presidential ear. Such behavior is only a reflection of the American system in which the executive power is vested in a President and not in one's Cabinet colleagues. But to rest content with this *status quo* would not be enough in a society which places value in "politics." For politics is conflict, and conflict enhances the presentation of alternatives for resolution—the essence of responsible democracy.

One of the most perceptive and realistic of the present-day political scientists, Professor David Truman, of Columbia University, has aptly commented concerning the various proposals for reform which are offered to rectify the alleged ills of our present governmental system:

As intellectual exercises the more sweeping reform designs are instructive. As symptoms of dissatisfaction with existing arrangements they are significant and may accelerate the possibility of change even when their specific suggestions are fruitless. As concrete programs of political development, however, they are visionary. Like all utopias, they sketch a most inviting destination, but they do not indicate how we can get from here to there. An examination of the route is at least as important as a tempting description of the journey's end.[6]

He has stated that "the proposal for the appearance of cabinet officers on the floor of the House or Senate" is one of those schemes which do "not reach the heart of the problem of integrated access and coordinated policy because they are not based upon the concrete facts of political relationships in the United States." [7]

Any answer must first differentiate between the Cabinet in Congress with full debating privileges as envisioned by Pendleton and the question and answer period offered by Kefauver. It is reasonable to expect that the former proposal, if enacted, might have a greater impact than the latter on the relationships currently existing under the separation of powers. A Cabinet in Congress with all but the right to vote would mean an opportunity for constant entanglement in the legislative process which takes place on the floor of both chambers. The question and report period provides for more limited access with an emphasis on the provision of information rather than a "free for all" where administrative badgering would face continuous congressional heckling. Although this does not mean that the question period would necessarily be free of the pitfalls which seem to be inherent in the first alternative, it would appear to offer less possibility of petty and unproductive controversy.

Specifically, Professor Truman asks two questions concerning the reform. The first is "What would such an appearance do to an executive branch already split by agency rivalries and by strong 'horizontal' relationships between subordinate administrators and legislative committees?" [8] Limiting our discussion to the question period and examining the first query, we find two problems: (1) the effect of the question period on agency rivalries, and (2) the effect of the question period on the "horizontal" relationships between subordinate officials (usually career civil servants) and the legislative committees which oversee their activities.

With regard to agency rivalries, the question period, while obviously not completely eliminating them, might well require a procedure by which conflicts could be forwarded to the White House for reconciliation and decision. Doubtless, this innovation would not guarantee contentment within those departments which believed themselves to be on the "losing" side. But it would guarantee the opportunity for responsible democracy to operate. The President and his staff could act if they considered it desirable to do so. Evasion by the executive branch would still be possible, but it would be more noticeable under a system where supplementary oral questions might follow up the original written one and where similar queries could be posed repeatedly. The question period process envisions a focal point in Congress on which the interested citizen might fix his attention.

Concerning the horizontal relationships between career officials and legislative committees, a question period would not eradicate them and probably should not, even from the "policy-coordinating" standpoint of a President and his appointees. Bonds of friendship between the Hill and career bureaucracy can be a useful tool in the hands of a skilled political administrator. If the relationships between the lower departmental levels and the membership of a particular congressional committee were of aid to the department's programs, then the question period should solidify and supplement them. On the other hand, if an administration's policies were being undermined by such relationships, it would be advantageous for the agency head to be able to "set the record straight" for the other members of Congress and maybe even for some of the committee.

The opportunity to appear in the chamber instead of just the committee room would bring the Cabinet and Congress into more frequent contact than is presently possible. Although secretaries do appear before various committees on the Hill (and this would continue under the question period), the present procedures are not conducive to informal exchange. The Cabinet officer arrives shortly before he is to testify and is seated at a table below his inquisitors who form a semicircle on a raised dais above him. The chairman and several committee members assemble at the scheduled hour and perhaps wave or shake hands. Other legislators will wander in throughout the testimony. In fairness to the senators or representatives, who frequently are supposed to be in two meetings at the same time, attendance elsewhere is encouraged by the long statements which many secretaries feel compelled to read. In brief, there is little chance for the inhabitants of both domains to sit and chat. While meetings could take place in each other's offices, reticence and questions of status prohibit such meetings for any reasons beneath the most pressing.

Professor Truman next inquires how the question period would "operate in the context of diffused leadership, group 'membership,' and localism that characterizes legislative behavior." Again, while we cannot predict the outcome, we can speculate upon it. The problems of leadership, allegiances, and narrow area interest would not be eliminated. But by providing a focal area in which members of the majority and the minority parties—administration and Congress—could explore public policy, the question period might well aid in the formulation of party alternatives. This would not necessarily submerge those intransigent islands of leadership lying in the sea that must be traveled by a legislative bill. However, the consciousness aroused by such explorations might through a gathering public opinion overcome a member's deference to the more articulate local sentiments.

The aim of the question period is not that of eliminating alleged evils, but rather that of placing in their proper perspective those forces with which government inevitably contends. Responsible democracy would be aided by broadening the comprehension of the people's elected representatives and by alerting agency administrators to emerging problems.

Within the executive branch, the question period would be a useful administrative tool and stimulus to compel action that otherwise might not be taken. Its potential could well lie in breaking through the ever-growing log jam of reports, data, letters, and aides which is the hallmark of the administrative state. An example of the responsiveness which can be secured when the Cabinet officer is confronted with a problem for the first time can be found in almost all congressional committee hearings. In May, 1957, for instance, following the testimony of Secretary Benson before the committee on agriculture and forestry, Senator Edward Thye (Republican, Minnesota) raised a question about the delays resulting from the procedural excesses of the dairy inspectors located along the Mexican border. After numerous inquiries and attempts to remedy the situation with lower departmental officials, Thye related his story to Benson. The secretary admitted that it was "the first time this has come to my attention," and stated that he would "be very glad to check into it immediately." [9]

Some have argued that both the congressional committee and the press conference are adequate substitutes for the question period.[10] While it is true that communication can be improved as a result of questions posed and answered in both forums, it is usually also true that the interrogators do not wholly represent all the interests at stake. Although a member of the Senate agriculture committee might be satisfied with a secretary's answer, it is possible that a legislator who represented a more urban constituency might desire more or different information.

Both the press conference and the committee interrogation have been beneficial in promoting critical evaluation of public policy and in acquainting Cabinet members with situations which otherwise might not have received their attention. The process of preparing for these meetings by anticipating questions is educational in that it acquaints department heads with the affairs committed to them and requires the coordination of departmental thought on certain subjects. With a question period, committees still would be active, and necessarily so, because of the great complexity in the legislation required to govern a modern industrial society.

From the journalists' standpoint a question period would overcome two major weaknesses which now exist. First, the Cabinet member currently can schedule press conferences to suit his convenience and not that of his interrogators. Thus the timing and interval between conferences are not controlled by the "demands" of an evolving situation which might be in the interest of the public to understand but rather by the whims of the official as to what he believes the public ought to be permitted to understand—which can mean nothing at all. In a crisis, the Cabinet officer can hide his head as does the proverbial ostrich.

Second, there is a basic difference between "parrying" a question from a reporter and answering a member of Congress who will vote periodically on the agency's appropriations and functions. On the floor of either house, the recognition of those who could ask supplementary questions would not rest with the department head as it does in the press conference.

In addition, there is a more substantive issue which involves the caliber of the interrogation. Several Cabinet members have publicly expressed their concern over the lack of intelligent questioning in which many reporters engage. This results partly from most reporters' diversity of activities and their consequent superficial knowledge of the subject matter covered. Only the wire services and a few metropolitan papers can afford a staff large enough to permit much specialization. Usually, the farther away one gets from Washington, the poorer the questioning becomes as the police-beat reporter is called in to cover the visiting celebrity.

Another dissimilarity between the press conference and an institution such as the question period of the British House of Commons has been noted by a participant-observer of the Washington press corps. From a first-hand knowledge of both systems, Douglass Cater has concluded that the political background of the questioner in Commons who is aware that he may someday have to answer similar queries makes for a sense of responsibility amid partisanship. With the reporter, however, the quest for news may easily overcome any sense of responsibility.[11]

The present backdoor and sidedoor methods of operation in the committees of Congress, while notable feats in political maneuvering, are not conducive to political responsibility. Without political responsibility, there is always the danger of unnoticed usurpation, drift, or rule by the legions of experts— called "bureaucrats" by some. "Bureaucracy"—an arrangement of decision-making centers to formulate, evaluate, and implement, but not ultimately to decide public policy—in itself is not the evil. Large organizations, whether in industry, labor, education, or government, require the systematized gradation of authority. It is "bureaucracy" in the sense of "unresponsiveness" which is abhorrent to a democratic society.

For responsible democracy to grow and flourish, both a

strong Congress and a strong executive are required. In the case of either branch's abdication, the forces of public and private bureaucracies will enter the policy vacuum. The Cabinet in Congress would provide the opportunity for a fuller revelation of national policy. With such revelation would come the essentials for accountability.

A hint has been given of the goal of the reform. But what of Professor Truman's basic indictment which is applicable to most reformers and not just those who favor the question period? He has charged that the advocates have not outlined "how we can get from here to there." Many of the proponents have rested their case merely on a plea for senators and representatives to enact their proposal. This is not enough. Although the reformers may have lacked articulation as to the pluralism of American politics and the "criss-crossing relationships" among President, Congress, Cabinet, and private groups, among others, there is no indication that most of them did not instinctively understand their environment.[12] On the contrary, they were reacting to it and were a part of that pluralism. Of course, a few no doubt have been intrigued by the thought that if only the question period were adopted, all would be well. As one author has stated, "the American people . . . are strongly addicted to the belief that political mechanics chiefly determine political dynamics and that governmental efficiency is largely the result of logically integrated, streamlined governmental structures." [13]

Despite possible advantages in the question period for Congress, the executive, and interested citizens, its inauguration would almost of necessity require a "rebellion" by many of the younger legislators, chafing at the restrictions imposed on them by the entrenched in both parties who maintain their power through seniority. The principal congressional agitation over the reform has occurred in times of national emergency: the Civil War and the Second World War. A domineering President or a major disaster which required rapid action and great administrative discretion by the administration could spark further demands for this type of information and legislative review.

Congress has changed its internal procedures only with reluctance, although the "revolt" against the power of Speaker Joseph Cannon at the end of the first decade of this century is evidence that it can be done. More likely, as James MacGregor Burns suggests, when reform does come it "will doubtless be part of a great popular movement to achieve certain social ends, rather than an isolated effort to improve Congress." [14]

Certainly an era of divided government during which Congress is controlled by one party and the Presidency by the other might lead to an attempt to secure the type of legislative oversight which is inherent in the question period. Interestingly, President Eisenhower has alluded to "a more vocal support for some change" in the direction of the parliamentary system as a result of the electorate's propensity to split their tickets when choosing the President and Congress.[15]

Additional support might originate with members from districts of intense two-party competition, whose stimulus would be the continued frustration resulting from the "bottling up" by their more senior colleagues of legislation which the former believed necessary for reelection. The adoption of the question period should be considered as a supplement, perhaps even a prerequisite, to what some regard as more basic party reform. Party responsibility will be achieved only when inroads are made on the rigidities of the seniority system and when more consistent policies are advocated by each party's legislators and executives.

The innovation of a question period would probably not be as overwhelming as its advocates allege nor as chaotic as its opponents predict. Lacking the tradition of British debating, the intimate chamber of the House of Commons (smaller in size although not in membership), and the neutrality of Mr. Speaker of the Commons as opposed to his counterpart in the American Congress (where the leader of the majority is also Speaker of the House), a question period might be only as successful as its participants wanted it to be. But given the advantages of the question period which could accrue to those involved regardless of their particular identification and association, even a limited degree of success is sufficient to justify the attempt.

Chronology of Recorded Visits by Members of Cabinet to Sessions of First Congress, 1789–1790

Senate in Executive session	Cabinet member	Reason for visit	Source
First Session			
May 25, 1789	Secretary of War Henry Knox	To deliver Presidential message	*Senate Executive Journal*, I, 3.
June 11, 1789	Secretary of Foreign Affairs John Jay	To deliver Presidential message	*Ibid.*, p. 5.
June 16, 1789	Jay	To present papers relevant to the nomination of William Short	*Ibid.*, p. 6.
June 17, 1789	Jay	To present papers relevant to the nomination of William Short	*Ibid.*
July 22, 1789	Jay	To discuss the consular convention with France	*Ibid.*, p. 7.
August 22, 1789	The President and Knox	To secure approval of an Indian treaty	*Ibid.*, p. 20.
August 24, 1789	The President and Knox	To secure approval of an Indian treaty	*Ibid.*, p. 23.
September 17, 1789	Knox	To deliver Presidential message	*Ibid.*, p. 26.
September 29, 1789	Knox	To deliver Presidential message	*Ibid.*, p. 34.
Second Session			
January 11, 1790	Knox	To deliver Presidential message	*Ibid.*, p. 36.
August 7, 1790	Knox	To deliver Presidential message	*Ibid.*, p. 58.

Senate in Legislative session	*Cabinet member*	*Reason for visit*	*Source*
First Session			
August 7, 1789	Knox	To deliver Presidential message	*Annals,* I, 58.
August 10, 1789	Knox	To deliver Presidential message	*Ibid.,* p. 61.
September 16, 1789	Knox	To deliver Presidential message	*Ibid.,* p. 80
September 26, 1789	Jay	To deliver Presidential message	*Ibid.,* p. 88.
September 29, 1789	Jay	To deliver Presidential message	*Ibid.,* p. 92.
Second Session			
January 12, 1790	Knox	To deliver Presidential message	*Ibid.,* p. 936.
January 21, 1790	Knox	To deliver Presidential message	*Ibid.,* p. 938.
House of Representatives			
First Session			
August 7, 1789	Knox	To deliver Presidential message	*Annals,* I, 684.
August 10, 1789	Knox	To deliver Presidential message	*Ibid.,* p. 689.
September 16, 1789	Knox	To deliver Presidential message	*Ibid.,* p. 893.
Second Session			
January 12, 1790	Knox	To deliver Presidential message	*Ibid.,* p. 1055.
January 21, 1790	Knox	To deliver Presidential message	*Ibid.,* p. 1076.
January 22, 1790	Secretary of the Treasury Alexander Hamilton	To deliver report of Postmaster General	*Ibid.,* p. 1076.
March 1, 1790	Knox	To deliver Presidential message	*House Journal,* 1 Cong., 2 sess., p. 43.
March 12, 1790	Knox	To deliver Presidential message	*Ibid.,* p. 56.

Sources: Annals of Congress, 1 Cong., 1 & 2 sess., I, 1789–90.
Journal of the Executive Proceedings of the Senate, I, 1789–90.
Journal of the House of Representatives, I, 1789–90.

APPENDIX II

Representative Proposals to Change the Relationship of the Cabinet to Congress

PENDLETON'S PROPOSAL OF 1864

1. The bill (H.R. 214)

Be it enacted by the Senate and House of Representatives of the United States of America in Congress assembled, That the Secretary of State, the Secretary of the Treasury, the Secretary of the Navy, the Secretary of the Interior, the Attorney General, and the Postmaster General, shall be entitled to occupy seats on the floor of the House of Representatives, with the right to participate in debate upon matters relating to the business of their respective departments, under such rules as may be prescribed by the House.

Sec. 2. *And be it further enacted,* That the said Secretaries, the Attorney General, and the Postmaster General, shall attend the sessions of the House of Representatives, immediately on the opening of the sittings on Mondays and Thursdays of each week, to give information in reply to questions which may be propounded to them under the rules of the House.

2. Amendments to the Rules of the House to implement H.R. 214

That the Clerk of the House of Representatives shall keep a notice-book, in which he shall enter, on request of any member, any resolution requiring information from any of the executive departments, or any question intended to be propounded to any of the Secretaries, or the Postmaster General, or Attorney General, relating to public affairs or to the business pending before the House, together with the name of the member and the day when the same will be called up.

The member giving notice of such resolution or question shall, at the same time, give notice that the same shall be called up on Monday or Thursday of the succeeding week: *Provided,* That no such resolution or question shall be called up, except by unanimous consent, within less than three days after notice shall have been given.

The Clerk shall, on the same day on which notice is entered, transmit to the chief officer of the proper department a copy of the resolution or question, together with the name of the member proposing the same, and of the day when it will come before the House for action.

On Monday and Thursday of each week, before any other business shall be taken up, except by unanimous consent, the resolutions and questions shall be taken up in the order in which they have been entered upon the notice-book for that day.

The member offering a resolution may state succinctly the object and scope of his resolution and the reasons for desiring the information, and the Secretary of the proper department may reply, giving the information or the reasons why the same should be withheld, and then, without further debate, the House shall vote on the resolution, unless it shall be withdrawn or postponed.

In putting any question to the Secretaries, or the Attorney General, or Postmaster General, no argument or opinion is to be offered, nor any fact stated, except so far as may be necessary to explain such question. And in answering such question, the Secretary, the Attorney General, or Postmaster General, shall not debate the matter to which the same refers, nor state facts or opinions other than those necessary to explain the answer.

KEFAUVER'S REPORT AND QUESTION PERIOD RESOLUTION OF 1943
(H.Res. 327)

Resolved, That rule XXXIII of the Rules of the House of Representatives be amended by adding at the end thereof the following new paragraph:

"3. There shall be held in the House immediately following the reading of the Journal on at least 1 day in each period of 2 calendar weeks, but not oftener than 1 day in any 1 calendar week, a 'question period,' which shall not consume more than 2 hours, during which heads of departments and independent agencies are requested to answer orally written and oral questions propounded by Members of the House. Each written question shall be submitted in triplicate to the committee having jurisdiction of the subject matter of such question, and, if approved by such committee, one copy shall be transmitted to the head of the department or independent agency concerned, with an invitation to appear before the House, and one copy to the Committee on Rules with a request for allotment of time in a question period to answer such a question. Subject to the limitations prescribed in this paragraph, the Committee on Rules shall determine the date for, and the length of time of, each question period, and shall allot the time in each question period to the head of a department or independent agency who has indicated to the committee his readiness to deliver oral answers to the questions transmitted to him. All written questions propounded in any one question period shall be approved by one committee. The latter half of each question period shall be reserved for oral questions by Members of the House, one-half of such time to be controlled by the chairman of the committee which has approved the written questions propounded in such question-period and one-half by the ranking minority member of such committee. The time of each question period and the written questions to be answered in such period shall be printed in two daily editions of the *Record* appearing before the day on which such question period is to be held, and the proceedings during the question period shall be printed in the *Record* for such day."

Sources: A. *House Reports*, 38 Cong., 1 sess., No. 43, 8.
B. *Congressional Record*, 78 Cong., 1 sess., 89:7 (November 12, 1943), 9458.

APPENDIX III

Chronological Listing of Legislation Introduced in Congress, 1864–1953, Proposing a Change in the Relationship between Congress and the Cabinet

No.	Date	Sponsor	Bill No.	Source
1.	February 8, 1864	George H. Pendleton	H.R. 214	Cong. Globe, 38 Cong., 1 sess., part 1, 526.
2.	March 26, 1879	Pendleton	S. 227	Cong. Record, 46 Cong., 1 sess., 9:1, 72.
3.	December 8, 1881	Pendleton	S. 307	Ibid., 47 Cong., 1 sess., 13:1, 53.
4.	January 5, 1886	John D. Long	H.R. 1081	Ibid., 49 Cong., 1 sess., 17:1, 416.
5.	February 18, 1913	Henry S. DeForest	H.Res. 846	Ibid., 62 Cong., 3 sess., 49:4, 3364.
6.	April 7, 1913	Andrew J. Montague	H.R. 1938	Ibid., 63 Cong., 1 sess., 50:1, 91.
7.	December 6, 1915	Montague	H.R. 4	Ibid., 64 Cong., 1 sess., 53:1, 14.
8.	April 2, 1917	Montague	H.R. 38	Ibid., 65 Cong., 1 sess., 55:1, 122.
9.	June 18, 1917	George P. McLean	S. 2468	Ibid., 65 Cong., 1 sess., 55:4, 3755.
10.	July 31, 1917	Philip L. Campbell	H.R. 5614	Ibid., 65 Cong., 1 sess., 55:6, 5635.
11.	May 19, 1919	Montague	H.R. 557	Ibid., 66 Cong., 1 sess., 58:1, 24.
12.	May 20, 1919	McLean	S. 509	Ibid., p. 61.
13.	January 27, 1920	Charles A. Mooney	H.R. 12,104	Ibid., 66 Cong., 2 sess., 59:2, 2134.
14.	April 11, 1921	Montague	H.R. 2211	Ibid., 67 Cong., 1 sess., 61:1, 94.
15.	April 12, 1921	McLean	S. 59	Ibid., p. 143.
16.	August 20, 1921	Clyde Kelly	H.R. 8345	Ibid., 61:5, 5377.
17.	April 22, 1924	William Upshaw	H.R. 8838	Ibid., 68 Cong., 1 sess., 65:7, 6930.
18.	January 6, 1925	Meyer Jacobstein	H.R. 11,364	Ibid., 68 Cong., 2 sess., 66:2, 1360.

No.	Date	Sponsor	Bill No.	Source
19.	January 22, 1925	Mooney	H.R. 11,855	Ibid., 66:3, 2338.
20.	December 7, 1925	Mooney	H.R. 199	Ibid., 69 Cong., 1 sess., 67:1, 399.
21.	December 7, 1925	Kelly	H.R. 3873	Ibid., p. 450.
22.	December 7, 1925	Montague	H.R. 3908	Ibid.
23.	December 14, 1925	McLean	S. 1543	Ibid., p. 768.
24.	February 9, 1926	Loring Black	H.R. 9100	Ibid., 67:4, 3660.
25.	March 4, 1926	James Couzens	S. 3406	Ibid., 67:5, 4959.
26.	December 5, 1927	Kelly	H.R. 91	Ibid., 70 Cong., 1 sess., 69:1, 20.
27.	December 5, 1927	Montague	H.R. 5625	Ibid., p. 94.
28.	December 5, 1927	Mooney	H.R. 5627	Ibid.
29.	April 15, 1929	Montague	H.R. 17	Ibid., 71 Cong., 1 sess., 71:1, 27.
30.	April 15, 1929	Kelly	H.R. 99	Ibid., p. 29.
31.	April 29, 1929	Mooney	H.R. 2162	Ibid., p. 659.
32.	December 8, 1931	Kelly	H.R. 4603	Ibid., 72 Cong., 1 sess., 75:1, 161.
33.	December 8, 1931	Montague	H.R. 4625	Ibid.
34.	March 11, 1933	Kelly	H.R. 3074	Ibid., 73 Cong., 1 sess., 77:1, 239.
35.	March 29, 1933	Montague	H.R. 4338	Ibid., p. 1007.
36.	January 3, 1935	Byron B. Harlan	H.R. 1410	Ibid., 74 Cong., 1 sess., 79:1, 48.
37.	February 6, 1935	Harlan	H.R. 5493	Ibid., 79:2, 1625.
38.	March 9, 1937	William R. Thom	H.R. 5476	Ibid., 75 Cong., 1 sess., 81:2, 2068.
39.	July 15, 1937	Maury Maverick	H.R. 7875	Ibid., 75 Cong., 1 sess., 81:7, 7200.
40.	December 10, 1937	Thom	H.Res. 377	Ibid., 2 sess., 82:2, 1310.
41.	December 3, 1942	Estes Kefauver	H.R. 7842	Ibid., 77 Cong., 2 sess., 88:7, 9317.
42.	January 25, 1943	Kefauver	H.R. 1479	Ibid., 78 Cong., 1 sess., 89:1, 378.
43.	October 19, 1943	Kefauver	H.Res. 327	Ibid., part 6, 8544.
44.	January 4, 1945	J. W. Fulbright	H.Res. 31	Ibid., 79 Cong., 1 sess., 91:1, 31.
45.	January 6, 1945	Kefauver	S.Res. 7	Ibid., p. 81.
46.	January 3, 1947	Kefauver	H.Res. 17	Ibid., 80 Cong., 1 sess., 93:2, 49.
47.	January 29, 1953	Kefauver and Fulbright	S.Res. 58	Ibid., 83 Cong., 1 sess., 99:1, 615.

Cabinet-Congressional Relations Questionnaire

Name   Age
District   No. yrs. in Congress
Com. chairmanships held   Party ( ) Dem. ( ) Rep. ( ) Other
                                 Occupation prior to election:———

1. a. On the whole, Cabinet relations with Congress have been (*check one*)
   - ( ) most satisfactory.
   - ( ) satisfactory.
   - ( ) unsatisfactory.

   b. Would you favor a proposal to seat Cabinet officers on the floor of either the House or Senate (or both) with the privilege to *participate in debate,* but not vote?
   - ( ) Yes
   - ( ) No

   c. Would you favor a proposal to have Cabinet officers appear at specified times on the floor of either/or both Houses of Congress *to answer questions* which are asked by the legislators?
   - ( ) Yes
   - ( ) No

   d. Do you favor any modifications of these proposals? If so, what are they?

2. If the Cabinet were allowed the privilege of debate or submitted to questioning in Congress, such a change would favor the growth in power of (*check one*)
   - ( ) the Congress.
   - ( ) the Executive Branch.
   - ( ) neither, relations would be the same.

3. What is the *main* reason, in your opinion, why some members of Congress *have favored* granting the Cabinet the privilege of the floor? (Check one answer only. If that reason agrees with your own personal reason, both check and circle it. If your personal reason is different, circle another answer.)
   - a. ( ) want more Congressional control over the Executive (make Cabinet accountable to Congress, etc.).

b. (   ) younger members of Congress want to overcome the influence of committee chairmen and the seniority system.

c. (   ) favor the Executive Branch gaining more control over Congress.

d. (   ) favor the practices of the British parliamentary system.

e. (   ) Congress needs more information upon which to base its decisions.

f. (   ) want to harass the opposite party, if it controls the Executive.

g. (   ) increase the prestige of Congress since the Cabinet would announce administrative decisions on the floor instead of in press conferences at their departments.

h. (   ) conservatives in Congress want to harass liberals in the Executive.

i. (   ) Other: _____

4. What is the *main* reason, in your opinion, why some members of Congress *have opposed* granting the Cabinet the privilege of the floor? (Check one answer only. If that reason agrees with your own personal reason, both check and circle it. If your personal reason is different, circle another answer.)

a. (   ) would not be any gain in information already available to Congress.

b. (   ) would disrupt committee chairman's relationship to specific department.

c. (   ) would increase power of the Executive branch over Congress.

d. (   ) is unconstitutional.

e. (   ) would prolong Congressional daily sessions with no particular gain.

f. (   ) would lead to disruption in Congressional procedure.

g. (   ) do not want to imitate British parliamentary methods.

h. (   ) Other: _____

5. Are there any *other reforms* that you believe would be advisable in improving Congressional-Cabinet relations than the ones suggested by the previous questions? Please specify.

6. If you have any additional comments you feel would be helpful in an analysis of Congressional-Cabinet relations, please write

☐ them on the back of this page. Check the box on the left if you wish to receive a brief complimentary summary of the findings.

Anonymity will be preserved and your answers will be seen only by the author. Thank you very much for finding time in a busy day to cooperate with us.

Please sign here ─────────────────────────

The Attitude Survey: Methods and Results

METHODS

In August, 1957, the questionnaire reproduced in Appendix IV was sent to all members of the Senate and House of Representatives. The author was concerned not so much with the predictability of results as with the insights that could be gleaned from individual responses. Certain limitations made extremely difficult a complete or representative response. Many members of both houses are well guarded by efficient secretaries. Although individually typed cover letters went with the questionnaires, it was doubtful in many cases whether the survey ever got past the front desk, especially since the postmark and return address were not from the particular legislator's geographical constituency.

In addition to their employment of protective secretaries, many of the people's representatives have established strict policies of refraining from answering all questionnaires, except perhaps their annual revision for *Who's Who in America*. Although one of the ranking House committee chairmen broke his rule in this case, he did not start a trend.

August was the close of the session and thus congressmen were more rushed than usual. Under the circumstances the quantity of the responses was amazingly large.

When one attempts to survey all units in a universe, he leaves his response to individual whim and caprice. Three fourths of the representatives were not in Congress when the Kefauver debates took place in 1943. For many, it was a new idea that they were considering, and they had undergone no prior "education" period as to the measure's "pros and cons." A wide variety of motives could determine a legislator's decision to answer: perhaps he believed in the reform and wanted to assure it of at least one vote. Or perhaps he thought it was utterly useless and hoped to bury it once and for all. One must assume that such individual motivations canceled each other out.

A word remains to be said about questions 3 and 4 on the questionnaire (see Appendix IV). The forced choice reasons listed in questions 3 and 4 were selected because they have recurred historically as stated reasons for support or opposition to the proposal to seat the Cabinet in Congress. The member was asked to distinguish, if necessary, between those motivations he attributed to others and his own personal convictions. Only thirteen representatives and three senators admitted to holding different personal motives than those which they attributed to their colleagues as to support or rejection of the idea of granting the Cabinet the privilege of the floor. The differences were scattered and of no importance.

When the questionnaires were returned, the answers to the various questions were added to such biographical data for the individual member as party, age, committee assignment, region from which elected, years in Senate or House, occupation prior to election, political experience, formal education, and seniority ranking both within the party and the committee on which he served.

How adequate then was the sample in terms of the House of Representatives? At the time the questionnaire was mailed, there were 433 members of the House, since two vacancies existed. The following replied:

		Members	
By party	*Total number*	*Number replying*	*Percentage replying*
Democrats	233	98	42.1
Republicans	200	84	42.0
	433	182	

	The House		The Sample	
By region	*Total number*	*Allocation among regions*	*Total replies*	*Allocation among regions*
New England	28	6.4%	7	3.8%
Atlantic Central	100	23.1	33	18.2
South	120	27.7	56	30.8
Midwest	131	30.3	57	31.3
West	54	12.5	29	15.9
	433	100.0%	182	100.0%

By age	*The House*	*The Sample*
High	83	82
Median	54	54
Low	31	31
Average	53.9	53.9

By years of service	The House	The Sample
High	45	45
Median	9	9
Low	1	1
Average	10.8	9.8

Proportion of lawyers	246 out of 433	106 out of 182
	56.8%	58.2%

Percentage of response by committee (in decreasing order)

Education and Labor	63.3
Interstate and Foreign Commerce	57.6
Ways and Means	52.0
District of Columbia	52.0
Interior and Insular Affairs	51.6
Agriculture	50.0
House Administration	44.0
Post Office and Civil Service	44.0
Armed Services	43.2
Veterans Affairs	40.9
Foreign Affairs	40.6
Judiciary	37.5
Government Operations	36.6
Rules	33.3
Un-American Activities	33.3
Appropriations	32.0
Banking and Currency	26.7
Public Works	26.5
Merchant Marine	19.4

Since the Senate replies were not used quantitatively in the text, comments as to the representativeness of the sample are reserved for the section on discussion of the "Senate Results."

RESULTS

The House of Representatives

1. Of the 182 replies in the sample, 45 favored the question period proposal (see Appendix IV, 1c) usually associated with the Kefauver resolution.

		Percentage
Total in sample	182	
In favor of question period	45	24.7
Opposed to question period	137	75.3

		Percentage
Division by party		
In favor of question period	45	
Democrats	27	60.0
Republicans	18	40.0
Opposed to question period	137	
Democrats	71	51.8
Republicans	66	48.2

2. The proposal to grant the Cabinet the privilege to participate in debate (see Appendix IV, 1b), usually associated with the name of Senator Pendleton, was opposed consistently by the 137 who had objected to the question period. In addition, 26 of the 45 or 57.7% who had favored the Kefauver proposal withdrew their support when it came to a matter of allowing Cabinet participation in debate.

The Senate

Complete compilations of Senate data were not included in the text because of the size of the response (36 out of 95 [one vacancy], or 36.3%), the overrepresentation of Republicans (58.3% of the total replying compared to an actual strength of 48.4% within the Senate), a large regional differential, and a median age discrepancy larger than that of the House sample.

Despite these limitations, the Senate proponents and opponents agreed with the House finding as to the major motivation of the advocates (Tables 4 and 5, Chapter XIII). While agreement also was found with the opponents' main reason for opposition ("No gain in information"), the House and Senate proponents differed in their interpretation of opposition motives.

Ten members of the House or 28.6% of those replying (Table 7, Chapter XIII) had believed that the major reason for opposition was the fear of disruption of the committee chairman's relationship to a specific department. The Senate proponents believed that the primary reasons for opposition were fears that congressional procedure would be disrupted or that there would be no gain in information. Since there were only two senators in each category (out of a total of seven answering that bloc of questions), these answers are relatively insignificant. One of the seven thought that the committee chairman's relationship was the main factor for opposition.

With regard to support for the privilege of the Cabinet to be questioned, the Senate revealed the same tendency as the House (Figure 3, Chapter XIII). The more discontented a senator felt concerning Cabinet-congressional relations, the more support he gave to the proposal. Only one senator believed relationships were "most satisfactory," and he opposed the measure; 31 senators thought them "satisfactory," and of these 8 or 25.8% supported the question period; 3 held that conditions were "unsatisfactory," and of these 1 or 33.3% favored the question period.

All 36 senators answered the hypothetical power change question (see Appendix IV, 2). They agreed with the House ranking of the component factors:

	Senate		House	
	Number replying	*Percentage replying*	*Number replying*	*Percentage replying*
Power change would benefit:				
The Executive	13	36.2	81	44.6
The Congress	8	22.2	17	9.3
Neither	12	33.3	63	34.6
No answer	3	8.3	21	11.5
Total	36	100.0	182	100.0

As in the House, those who stated that Congress would gain in power derived half of their support (4 out of 8) from senators who had favored the question period (see Table 8, Chapter XIII).

1. For those interested in the strength and weakness of the question period proposal, the box score of the Senate sample's reaction is included:

Of 36 in sample:	10 favored question period	27.8%
	26 opposed question period	72.2
		100.0%

By party:	10 favored	
	4 Democrats	40.0%
	6 Republicans	60.0
		100.0%

	26 opposed	
	11 Democrats	42.3%
	15 Republicans	57.7
		100.0%

The ratio of Republicans to Democrats must be kept in mind when these percentages are considered.

2. A tendency similar to that shown in the House was seen in the withdrawal of support from full Cabinet privileges of debate by those who favored the question period plan (see Appendix IV, 1b and 1c).

Only one of the four Democrats who favored the question period also supported free debate; only one of the six Republicans did likewise. The Pendleton suggestion had hardly any support compared to that given the question period.

3. As in the House data, no significant correlation was noted between educational level, previous political experience, occupation prior to election, or committee assignment and support for the question period.

Notes

I: INTRODUCTION

1. Louis Brownlow, former chairman of the President's Committee on Administrative Management, to the author (January 13, 1958).

2. Art. II, sec. 1.

II: THE HERITAGE OF THE FEDERALISTS

1. The Constitution provided no guidelines as to the number of departments to be established. The clause that authorized the President to require reports and opinions in writing from "Heads of Departments" implied that there were to be departments. On August 20, 1787, Charles Pinckney submitted to the Constitutional Convention his plan for a council of state which would include the heads of the departments of domestic affairs, commerce and finance, foreign affairs, war, marine, and state, among other members. The convention failed to sanction the proposal. See Max Farrand, ed., *The Records of the Federal Convention of 1787*, II, 335–37.

Pennsylvania Senator William Maclay, on the other hand, thought that the establishment of executive departments by legislation was "putting into the hands of—[the President's]—officers the duties required of him by the Constitution." *Journal of William Maclay*, ed. by Edgar S. Maclay, p. 103. Maclay believed that if the President saw a function which should be performed he should signify to the Senate his desire to create a particular position and nominate a man to fill it. If the Senate concurred, both the position and the man would be approved. The House, according to Maclay, "would get the business before them when salaries came to be appointed, and could thus give their opinion by providing for the officers or not." *Ibid.*, p. 104.

2. *Annals of Congress*, 1 Cong., 1 sess., I (May 19, 1789), 369.
3. *Ibid.*   4. *Ibid.*, p. 370.   5. *Ibid.*   6. *Ibid.*, p. 372.
7. *Ibid.*, p. 380.   8. *Ibid.*, p. 383.
9. *Ibid.*, I (May 21, 1789), 396.

10. *Ibid.*, I (June 16, 1789), 456.   11. *Ibid.*, p. 462.

12. Madison to Edmund Randolph (May 31, 1789), in Madison, *Writings*, ed. by Gaillard Hunt, V, 373.

13. *Annals of Congress*, 1 Cong., 1 sess., I (June 17, 1789), 500.

14. *Ibid.* (June 18, 1789), p. 530.   15. *Ibid.*, p. 543.

16. *Ibid.*, I (June 19, 1789), 576.

17. *Ibid.*, I (June 22, 1789), 585.

18. *Ibid.* In the Senate, however, a removal clause was kept in the foreign affairs bill by the deciding vote of Vice President Adams who broke a 10 to 10 tie on July 16, 1789. Maclay, *Journal*, p. 116. Senator Maclay had argued that impeachment was the only removal of an officer authorized by the Constitution. To leave the removal power in the hands of the President would mean that no man of "independent spirit" could accept office since he would be of little service to the community "if afraid of the nod or beck of a superior." *Ibid.*, p. 111. Disagreeing, Connecticut's Oliver Ellsworth held that the President was the executive officer and that the Constitution interfered only with his appointment power, and did not take his removal power from him. *Ibid.*, p. 112.

William Maclay's journal is one of the most colorful documents of our political history. He was an ardent advocate of the Revolution and denounced all whom he suspected of tending toward aristocracy. Because the Senate proceedings in the early years were not recorded verbatim, his journal provides an essential—though prejudiced—source concerning Senate activity in the First Congress. Unfortunately, there are significant gaps in Maclay's record because sickness kept him away from the Capitol for as long as three weeks at a time.

19. Madison to Edmund Randolph (May 31, 1789), in *Writings*, ed. by Hunt, V, 373.

20. Ames to George Richards Minot (May 31, 1789), in Ames, *Works*, ed. by Seth Ames, I, 52.

21. *Annals of Congress*, 1 Cong., 1 sess., I (June 24, 1789), 592.

22. *Ibid.*, I (June 25, 1789), 592.   23. *Ibid.*, pp. 592–93.

24. *Ibid.*, p. 593.   25. *Ibid.*, p. 594.   26. *Ibid.*

27. *Ibid.*, pp. 594–95.   28. *Ibid.*, pp. 596–97.

29. Samuel E. Morison, "Fisher Ames," in *Dictionary of American Biography* (hereafter cited as *D.A.B.*), I, 244–46.

30. The statute replacing a three-man treasury board with a superintendent of finance was approved by the Continental Con-

gress on February 7, 1781. It provided, in part, that the superintendent "digest and report plans for improving and regulating the finances." Gaillard Hunt, ed., *Journals of the Continental Congress: 1774–1789*, XIX, 126. Secretaries did "attend" Congress during the Confederation but usually not for the purpose of oral explanation. Most of the interchange between Congress and the departmental officials was by correspondence. On February 22, 1782, an attempt to provide the secretary of foreign affairs with a seat in Congress failed; however, Congress did approve a clause leaving the option with the secretary as to the mode of communication. *Ibid.*, XXII, 90.

31. *Annals of Congress*, 1 Cong., 1 sess., I (June 25, 1789), 600–2.

32. *Ibid.*, p. 604.   33. *Ibid.*, p. 607.

34. Ames to George Richards Minot (June 25, 1789), in Ames, *Works*, I, 56.

35. *Annals of Congress*, 1 Cong., 1 sess., I (May 14, 1789), 35–36. When he learned of the original recommendation by the Senate committee, Thomas Jefferson aptly wrote from France that it was "the most superlatively ridiculous thing I ever heard of." Jefferson to James Madison (July 29, 1789), Madison Papers.

The concern of at least some of the Senate with "form" was not merely a passing fancy, if the account of an admittedly antifederalist participant is to be credited. In his diary entry for August 20, 1789, Maclay notes the argument between Senator Ralph Izard, of South Carolina, and Vice President Adams over the fact that President Washington's chief assistant was "introduced quite up to the Vice-President's table to deliver messages." Maclay reports that the Senate had already discussed the matter and he thought the consensus was for heads of departments to be admitted to the table but a private secretary to be received only to the bar. The senator concludes his version with "our Vice-President, however, never seems pleased but when he is concerned in some trifling affair of etiquette or ceremony. Trifles seem his favorite object. . . ." Maclay, *Journal*, p. 127.

36. *Executive Journal of the Senate*, I (June 16, 1789), 6. Although the Department of Foreign Affairs had been created by an act of July 27, 1789 (1 *U.S. Statutes at Large*, 28), it was soon found that there was need for an agency to maintain records, keep the Great Seal, publish certain enactments, and perform other functions pertaining to internal affairs. Therefore, by an act of

September 15, 1789, the name of the department became the Department of State and the title of the secretary changed accordingly (1 *U.S. Statutes at Large,* 68).

37. *Executive Journal of the Senate,* I (June 17, 1789), 7; Maclay, *Journal,* p. 78.

38. Madison to Edmund Pendleton (July 5, 1789), Madison Papers.

39. *Annals of Congress,* 1 Cong., 1 sess., I (July 21, 1789), 51.

40. *Ibid.,* I (July 22, 1789), 51–52.   41. *Ibid.*

42. *Ibid.,* I (July 27, 1789), 52–54. On July 29, 1789, the Senate accepted Jay's recommendation concerning the convention to define and establish the privileges and functions of the consuls and vice-consuls between France and the United States and unanimously resolved that "the Senate do consent to the said convention, and advise the President of the United States to ratify the same." *Ibid.,* I (July 29, 1789), 54. The principal stumbling block had been the wish of the Congress under the Confederation to place a time limit on the agreement. A twelve-year period was agreed upon. For the Continental Congress's instructions of 1787 to Jefferson, who was handling the negotiations in Paris, see *Secret Journals of the Congress of the Confederation—Foreign Affairs,* IV, 377–81.

43. *Ibid.,* I (August 7, 1789), 58–59.

44. *Ibid.,* I (August 10, 1789), 61.

45. Washington, *Writings,* ed. by John C. Fitzpatrick, XXX, 373–74, 377–79.

46. *Annals of Congress,* 1 Cong., 1 sess., I (August 21–22, 1789), 65–69.

47. Maclay, *Journal,* p. 128.   48. *Ibid.,* pp. 130–31.

49. Washington, *Writings,* ed. by Fitzpatrick, XXX, 374.

50. Maclay, *Journal,* p. 132. *Annals of Congress,* 1 Cong., 1 sess., I (August 24, 1789), 69–71. Washington's decision not to return to consult with the Senate did not mean that he believed it improper for his Cabinet to appear. On August 4, 1790, almost a year after the initial episode with the Senate over the Creek Indian treaty, he forwarded the final version. He concluded his message: "If the Senate should require any further explanation, the Secretary of War will attend them for that purpose." *Ibid.,* 2 sess., I (August 4, 1790), 1024–25.

51. Art. I, sec. 7, cl. 1.

52. *Annals of Congress,* 1 Cong., 1 sess., I (September 11, 1789), 78.

53. See Leonard D. White, *The Federalists,* p. 118, for the mustering of evidence as to Hamilton's role in drawing up the Treasury Act.

54. Hamilton to James Duane (September 3, 1780), in Hamilton, *Works,* ed. by Henry Cabot Lodge, I, 213–39.

55. Madison, *Journal of the Federal Convention,* ed. by Erastus Scott, I, 175–87. In the Constitutional Convention, Hamilton had expressed great admiration for the British monarchy (p. 182); he favored an absolute veto for the President (p. 102), who would hold office for life (p. 183), and would appoint department heads without Senate approval (p. 185).

56. *Annals of Congress,* 1 Cong., 2 sess., I (January 9, 1790), 1043.

57. *Ibid.,* pp. 1043–44.   58. *Ibid.,* p. 1044.

59. *Ibid.,* p. 1045.

60. *Ibid.,* I (January 22, 1790), pp. 1076–77.

61. Jefferson objected to Hamilton's tactics as "mischief." White, *The Federalists,* p. 69. Representative John F. Mercer remarked that the legislators "do not come here to go to school, or hear lectures from the Secretaries on finance or any other subject." *Annals of Congress,* 2 Cong., 2 sess., III (November 20, 1792), 707. Pennsylvania's William Findley still later described Hamilton's relationship with the House as that of a "despotic Prince" and not a "dependent Secretary." *Ibid.* (March 1, 1793), pp. 922–23.

62. Washington to Jefferson, Hamilton, and Knox (April 4, 1791), in *Writings,* ed. by Fitzpatrick, XXXI, 272–73. Washington stated that he would have asked the vice president to attend the sessions, but he assumed that Adams had already left for Boston.

63. Washington to Jefferson, Hamilton, and Knox (June 16, 1794), in *ibid.,* XXXIII, 403. Washington specifically authorized his cabinet to "carry any unanimous decision into effect."

64. Randolph C. Downer, "Arthur St. Clair," in *D.A.B.,* XVI, 294.

65. *Annals of Congress,* 2 Cong., 1 sess., III (March 27, 1792), 490.

66. *Ibid.,* p. 491.   67. *Ibid.*   68. *Ibid.,* p. 493.

69. "The Anas" (March 31, 1792), in Jefferson, *Writings,* ed. by Andrew A. Lipscomb and Albert Ellery Bergh, I, 303.

70. "The Anas" (April 2, 1792), in *ibid.*, p. 304.
71. *Ibid.*, p. 305.   72. *Ibid.*
73. "The Anas" (January 2, 1792), in *ibid.*, p. 292.
74. "The Anas" (March 7, 1792), in *ibid.*, p. 293. (See also *Annals of Congress*, 2 Cong., 1 sess., III [March 8, 1792], 452.)
75. "The Anas" (March 12, 1792), in *ibid.*, p. 301.
76. *Annals of Congress*, 2 Cong., 2 sess., III (November 13, 1792), 679.
77. *Ibid.*, pp. 679–80.   78. *Ibid.*   79. *Ibid.*
80. *Ibid.*, pp. 680–81.   81. *Ibid.*, p. 681.
82. *Ibid.*, p. 683.   83. *Ibid.*
84. Samuel E. Morison, "Elbridge Gerry," in *D.A.B.*, VII, 224.
85. *Annals of Congress*, 2 Cong., 2 sess., III (November 13, 1792), 683–84.
86. Jefferson to T. M. Randolph, Jr. (November 16, 1792), in *Writings*, ed. by Lipscomb and Bergh, VIII, 439.
87. *Annals of Congress*, 2 Cong., 2 sess., III (November 14, 1792), 685.
88. *Ibid.*, p. 686.   89. *Ibid.*, pp. 686–87.
90. *Ibid.*, pp. 688–89.
91. Jefferson to Thomas Pinckney (December 3, 1792), in *Writings*, ed. by Lipscomb and Bergh, VIII, 443.
92. The only possible exception to this statement is revealed in a debate on July 6, 1797, over the impeachment of William Blount. Samuel W. Dana said: "When this subject was under debate with closed doors, the Secretary of State [Colonel Timothy Pickering] was present, and when it was doubted whether the publication of these papers might impede the prosecution of an inquiry into the business, they were informed by him that such steps were taken as that the publication of the papers could not have a bad effect." *Annals of Congress*, 5 Cong., 1 sess., VII (July 6, 1797), 458. Hinds has cited this case as a "possible" example of a Cabinet member discussing an issue in Congress. See Ascher C. Hinds, comp., *Hinds' Precedents of the House of Representatives of the United States*, Vol. II, sec. 1587. There is no conclusive proof—because of the inadequacy of records—that this incident occurred before the full House and not in a special committee.
93. On November 17, 1794, William Smith stated that if the House thought it expedient it could admit the Secretary of State; Jonathan Dayton agreed, adding: "The House had a right to call

Heads of Departments to give their opinions on any particular subject if they thought proper." *Annals of Congress,* 3 Cong., 2 sess., IV (November 17, 1794), 885–86. The growing attitude of legislative independence was better represented by Virginian John Nicholas, who on January 12, 1795, in an attempt to reject a message to Congress from the secretary of war (Colonel Timothy Pickering), objected to "too much deference to the Heads of Departments." *Ibid.* (January 12, 1795), p. 1072.

III: FROM UNION TO DISUNION

1. On November 9, 1804, Gaylord Griswold had offered a House resolution calling on the Secretary of the Navy to communicate the names of the officers and men who had been led by Captain Stephen Decatur against the Tripoli pirates, as well as the details of that famous adventure, so that the House might grant them their just honors. John Randolph insisted, and Griswold agreed, that the resolution be amended to read "that the President of the United States be requested to cause to be laid before this House. . . ." *Annals of Congress,* 8 Cong., 2 sess., XIV (November 9, 1804), 683. In the next session, however, the irascible John Randolph, in an attack on Jefferson's foreign policy, lamented that the heads of departments did not have seats on the floor. *Ibid.,* 9 Cong., 1 sess., XV (April 7, 1806), 984.

At the height of one-party Republican domination, on the eve of the misnamed "era of good feeling," resolutions were being issued to individual secretaries. See the resolution offered in the House on February 21, 1816, requesting the secretary of war to furnish a statement of the militia expenses incurred in the War of 1812. *Annals of Congress,* 14 Cong., 1 sess., XXIX (February 21, 1816), 1047. Randolph was gone and possibly the Republicans had more faith in the discretion of their own department heads than the antagonistic Anti-Federalists had in Alexander Hamilton.

2. Entry for March 1, 1807. *Memorandum of Proceedings in the United States Senate: 1803–1807,* ed. by Everett Somerville Brown, p. 634.

3. For the thesis that Jackson's Kitchen Cabinet was not really a cabinet in the institutional sense since it lacked continuity and regular membership, see Richard P. Longaker, "Was Jackson's

Kitchen Cabinet a Cabinet?," *The Mississippi Valley Historical Review,* XLIV (June, 1957), 94–108.

4. *Register of Debates,* 23 Cong., 1 sess., 10:1 (December 11, 1833), 30.

5. *Ibid.,* pp. 31–36.   6. *Ibid.* (December 12, 1833), p. 37.

7. *Ibid.* (December 26, 1833), p. 65.   8. *Ibid.,* p. 70.

9. *Ibid.* (December 30, 1833), p. 77.

10. *Ibid.* (January 17, 1834), pp. 286–87.

11. Joseph Story, *Commentaries on the Constitution of the United States,* II, 333, section 866.

12. *Ibid.,* p. 334, section 866.

13. Elizabeth Kelley Bauer, *Commentaries on the Constitution, 1790–1860,* p. 159.

14. William Rawle, *A View of the Constitution of the United States of America,* 2d ed., p. 184.

15. *Ibid.*   16. *Ibid.,* p. 187.   17. *Ibid.,* p. 188.

18. *Ibid.*

19. Joseph Story, *Commentaries on the Constitution of the United States,* II, 335, section 867.

20. A President who was not "policy-less" in this interim period was James K. Polk, one of the few Presidents in history to fulfill the platform on which he ran: lower tariffs, an independent treasury, the acquisition of California, and the termination of the Oregon dispute with Britain. See Thomas A. Bailey, *American Pageant,* pp. 290–91. Polk realized that to attain his policy goals he must improve presidential liaison with the Hill. To implement this belief, the President appointed as his postmaster general, Cave Johnson, who had spent seven terms in the House. Johnson kept Polk "informed as to the status of measures, their possible rejection, and gossip as to the attitudes of other Cabinet members on them. . . . He arranged compromises . . . visited Congressmen and told them how the President would like them to vote." Those that opposed were warned that they would be "marked by the administration." See Dorothy Ganfield Fowler, *The Cabinet Politician,* pp. 60–61.

21. *Congressional Globe,* 30 Cong., 2 sess., XVIII (March 3, 1849), 676.

22. Representative Richard H. Stanton moved the proposal in the House, but it was ruled out of order. *Ibid.,* 32 Cong., 2 sess., XXVI (February 17, 1853), 665. The proposal met a similar fate in the Senate. *Ibid.* (February 28, 1853), p. 903.

IV: THE CONFEDERATE EXPERIMENT

1. "Constitution for the Provisional Government," Art. II, sec. 2, cl. 1, in James D. Richardson, comp., *A Compilation of the Messages and Papers of the Confederacy*, I, 3–13.

2. "Constitution of the Confederate States of America," Art. I, sec. 6, cl. 2, in *ibid.*, pp. 37–54. The actual motion was made by Edward Sparrow. Thomas R. R. Cobb failed in his attempt to insert a clause in the preamble declaring that "the Legislative, Executive and Judicial Departments shall be distinct." Augustus Longstreet Hull, "The Making of the Confederate Constitution," *Publications of the Southern History Association*, IX (September, 1905), 287, 291.

3. Stephens, *A Constitutional View*, II, 338–39.

4. "Second Session of Provisional Congress of Confederate States of America—May 4, 1861," in *Journal of the Congress of the Confederate States of America*, I, 182.

5. This remark was made by Senator Benjamin H. Hill, who because of his loyal support of President Davis failed to endorse the measure under the permanent constitution. See Coulter, *Confederate States*, p. 383.

6. "Proceedings of First Confederate Congress—First Session," *Southern Historical Society Papers*, XLIV (June, 1923), 3–206. *Daily Dispatch* (Richmond), May 20, 1862, pp. 2–3; May 21, 1862, p. 2.

7. *Daily Richmond Examiner* (March 24, 1862), p. 1.

8. Robert G. Cleland, "Jefferson Davis and the Confederate Congress," *The Southern Historical Quarterly*, XIX (January, 1916), 215–16.

9. R. M. T. Hunter to the Reverend J. Williams Jones, Secretary, Southern Historical Society (approx. November, 1877), *Southern Historical Society Papers*, IV (December, 1877), 311.

10. Thomas R. R. Cobb to his wife (April 30, 1861), "Cobb Correspondence," *Publications of the Southern History Association*, XI (September–November, 1907), 312.

11. C. W. Lord, "Louis Trezevant Wigfall," in *D.A.B.*, XX, 187–88. Dunbar Rowland, ed., *Jefferson Davis, Constitutionalist*, V., 102–3.

12. General James Longstreet to Wigfall (November 7, 1862),

Correspondence of Senator Louis Trezevant Wigfall, 1858–1862, Wigfall Family Papers.

13. *Journal of the Congress of the Confederate States of America, 1861–1865* (Senate, January 20, 1863), III, 24.

14. Ulrich B. Phillips, "Alexander Hamilton Stephens," in *D.A.B.*, XVII, 569–75.

15. *Ibid.*, pp. 573–75. Rudolph von Abele, *Alexander H. Stephens*, pp. 224–27.

16. Hayward J. Pearce, "Benjamin Harvey Hill," in *D.A.B.*, IX, 25–27.

17. *Journal of the Congress of the Confederate States of America, 1861–1865* (Senate, February 2, March 11, 1863), III, 44, 153.

18. *Ibid.* (Senate, March 11, 1863), III, 153. *Daily Richmond Enquirer* (March 12, 1863), pp. 1–2.

19. Whether a senator was considered as anti-administration or pro-administration depended on a series of votes cast in 1865 on such questions as making General Robert E. Lee commander in chief of the Confederate forces, requiring that the commander in chief be subject to the authority of President Davis, assigning General Joseph E. Johnston to the Army of the Tennessee, and overriding two presidential vetoes. *Journal of the Congress of the Confederate States of America, 1861–1865* (Senate, January 16, 25, 28, 1865), IV, 454–58, 490, 502.

20. *Ibid.* (Senate: March 18, 1862), II, 73–74.

21. Jefferson Davis, *The Rise and Fall of the Confederate Government*, I, 259–60.

22. Senator Robert W. Johnson, of Arkansas, secured approval of his resolution in the Senate, February 2, 1863. See *Journal of the Congress of the Confederate States of America, 1861–1865* (Senate: February 2, 1863), III, 44.

23. Edward Younger, ed., *Inside the Confederate Government: The Diary of Robert Garlick Hill Kean, Head of the Bureau of War*, p. 126.

24. *Journal of the Congress of the Confederate States of America, 1861–1865* (Senate: December 10, 1863), III, 454–55.

25. Edward Younger, ed., *Inside the Confederate Government*, p. 126 (diary entry for December 14, 1863).

26. *Journal of the Congress of the Confederate States of America, 1861–1865* (Senate: December 17, 1863), III, 477.

27. Edward Younger, ed., *Inside the Confederate Government*, p. 130 (diary entry for January 5, 1864).

28. *Report of the Committee on the Judiciary on Senate Bill, No. 150* (January 14, 1864), C.S.A., Senate Report, No. 16, p. 1.

29. *Ibid.,* p. 2.   30. *Ibid.,* p. 5.   31. *Ibid.*

32. *Ibid.,* p. 8.   33. *Ibid.,* p. 9.   34. *Ibid.,* p. 11.

35. *Report of the Minority of the Committee on the Judiciary on the Senate Bill No. 150* (January 14, 1864), C.S.A., p. 1.

36. *Ibid.,* p. 2.   37. *Ibid.,* p. 3.   38. *Ibid.*

39. *Journal of the Congress of the Confederate States of America, 1861–1865* (Senate: January 21, 22, 27; February 9, 13, 15, 1864), III, 603, 606–7, 623, 689–90, 732, 744–45.

40. Wigfall's solution to the impending military debacle was to proclaim: "Make Joe Johnston dictator and all will be well." Mary Boykin Chesnut noted this comment of the Texas senator in her diary for December 29, 1864. *A Diary from Dixie,* p. 467.

41. Edward Younger, ed., *Inside the Confederate Government,* p. 189 (entry for January 21, 1865).

42. Thomas S. Bocock to President Davis (January 21, 1865), in *War of the Rebellion: Records of the Union and Confederate Armies,* Series I, Vol. XLVI, Part II—Correspondence, p. 1118.

43. Jefferson Davis to Hon. James A. Seddon (February 1, 1865), in Dunbar Rowland, ed., *Jefferson Davis, Constitutionalist,* VI, 458–61.

44. *Richmond Examiner* (February 9, 1865), p. 1.

45. *Journal of the Congress of the Confederate States of America, 1861–1865* (Senate: February 8, 1865), XIV, 533.

46. J. L. M. Curry states that "the restricted privilege worked well while it lasted, and the occasional appearance of Cabinet officers on the floor of Congress and participation in debates worked beneficially and showed the importance of enlarging the privilege." See Curry's *Civil History of the Government of the Confederate States,* pp. 82–83.

V: THE FIRST PENDLETON BILL

1. James G. Randall, *Constitutional Problems Under Lincoln,* p. 36.

2. Hilary A. Herbert, "Cleveland and His Cabinet at Work," *Century,* LXXXV (March, 1913), 742.

3. Carl Sandburg, *Abraham Lincoln, The Prairie Years and the War Years,* p. 216.

4. *Congressional Globe,* 38 Cong., 1 sess., part 1 (February 3, 1864), p. 467.

5. Reginald C. McGrane, "George Hunt Pendleton," *D.A.B.* XIV, 419.

6. *Congressional Globe,* 38 Cong., 1 sess., part 1 (February 8, 1864), p. 526.

7. *Ibid.* (February 9, 1864), p. 552. *Biographical Directory of the American Congress, 1774–1949,* 81 Cong., 2 sess., H. Doc. 607, *passim.*

8. The New York *Times,* though first to give editorial support, was not the first newspaper to reflect favorable consideration of the Pendleton proposal. That honor belongs to Pendleton's hometown newspaper, the Cincinnati *Daily Commercial,* whose Washington correspondent, "Mack," reported in his "Letter from Washington" of January 30, 1864 (over a week before the bill was actually introduced), that the idea already had "its zealous advocates and its enthusiastic opponents." The reporter claimed that the latter based their views "upon the fear of an abuse of the privilege of questioning Cabinet officers, rather than on opposition to the legitimate use of it." After a further elaboration of the tentative arguments by both sides, he concluded that the proposition was "certainly an important one, and worthy of serious and attentive consideration." Cincinnati *Daily Commercial* (February 3, 1864), p. 1.

9. New York *Times* (March 23, 1864), p. 4.

10. Art. I, sec. 6, cl. 2.

11. New York *Times* (March 29, 1864), p. 4.

12. Art. II, sec. 3.

13. New York *Times* (March 29, 1864), p. 4.

14. *Congressional Globe,* 38 Cong., 1 sess., part 2 (April 6, 1864), p. 1448.

15. *Heads of Executive Departments* (to accompany bill H.R. No. 214), in *Reports of Committees: 1863–1864,* 38 Cong., 1 sess., House Report No. 43.

16. For the text of H.R. 214 and the amendments to the Rules, see Appendix II ("Representative Proposals to Change the Relationship of the Cabinet to Congress"), section A ("Pendleton's Proposal of 1864").

17. *Ibid.,* p. 4.   18. *Ibid.,* p. 2.   19. *Ibid.,* Appendix 3.
20. *Ibid.,* pp. 4–5.   21. *Ibid.,* p. 3.

22. For July 22, 1789, the Pendleton report cited the example of the secretary of foreign affairs attending agreeably to order and making the necessary explanations. The crediting of Thomas Jefferson with the occupancy of the position must be excused as poor historical research. Mr. Jefferson had not yet been appointed and was still in France as American minister. The important facts are: first, that the legislation providing for a Department of Foreign Affairs under the new Constitution had not been approved as of July 22, 1789, and, second, that John Jay, the Confederation's foreign secretary, was being continued on an "acting" basis. The lack of emphasis on the separation of powers under the Articles was well known, whereas there was a keener awareness of the separation under the Constitution.

23. *Congressional Globe,* 38 Cong., 1 sess., part 3 (May 30, 1864), p. 2575.

24. Union Congressional Committee, "Congressional Record of George H. Pendleton, Candidate for Vice President," p. 2.

25. *Congressional Globe,* 38 Cong., 2 sess., part 1 (January 13, 1865), p. 266. See also Ralph Korngold, *Thaddeus Stevens,* pp. 230–31. "Mack," the Washington correspondent of the Cincinnati *Daily Commercial,* reported that "Pendleton seems to have killed himself as dead as a door nail, by that last speech of his." The journalist predicted that Pendleton's enemies would have "to save him from the blows of his former friends" (the Democrats). Democratic newspapers were repudiating him. "People may talk about his being a clever gentleman, . . . but when they speak of him as a politician, he must be accorded the credit of being the worst used up man that ever figured in public life." Cincinnati *Daily Commercial* (January 25, 1865), p. 1.

26. *Congressional Globe,* 38 Cong., 2 sess., part 1 (January 25, 1865), p. 420.

27. *Ibid.,* p. 421.   28. *Ibid.,* p. 422.   29. *Ibid.,* p. 423.
30. *Ibid.,* p. 424.

31. Art. II, sec. 4: "The President, Vice President and all civil Officers of the United States, shall be removed from Office on Impeachment for, and Conviction of, Treason, Bribery, or other high Crimes and Misdemeanors."

32. *Congressional Globe,* 38 Cong., 2 sess., part 1 (January 25, 1865), p. 424.

33. *Ibid.* (January 26, 1865), p. 437.   34. *Ibid.,* p. 439.

35. *Ibid.*, p. 442.   36. *Ibid.*   37. *Ibid.*, p. 444.

38. *Ibid.*, p. 445.   39. *Ibid.*   40. *Ibid.*

41. *Ibid.*, p. 446.   42. *Ibid.*   43. *Ibid.*   44. *Ibid.*

45. *Ibid.*, p. 447.   46. *Ibid.*, p. 448.

47. New York *Times* (January 30, 1865), p. 4.

48. *Congressional Globe*, 38 Cong., 2 sess., part 2 (March 2, 1865), p. 1335. A Washington correspondent, "Ayate," for the Cincinnati *Daily Gazette* wrote that the vote of the House to allow Pendleton to give his speech during the most favorable hour in the afternoon was the result of "a general feeling that it would be pleasant to show the ablest man on the Democratic side, on the occasion of his retirement from long service in the House, some evidence of the regard his uniform courtesy and fairness had inspired." Interestingly enough, the motion to accord this honor on Pendleton "came from his most persistent political and even personal opponent in the House, Mr. Elihu B. Washburne." Cincinnati *Daily Gazette* (March 8, 1865), p. 1.

49. *Congressional Globe*, 38 Cong., 2 sess., part 2, "Appendix" (March 3, 1865), p. 103.

50. *Ibid.*   51. *Ibid.*, p. 105.   52. *Ibid.*

53. *Ibid.*, p. 108. Representative Wilson unknowingly slid over a link between Pendleton and the Federalists. Pendleton's paternal grandfather, Nathaniel Pendleton, a Revolutionary soldier and Georgia federal judge, was a friend and supporter of Alexander Hamilton, whose name was linked with the idea of seating the Cabinet in Congress. Grandfather Pendleton was the second to Hamilton at the fatal duel with Burr. C. B. Galbreath, "Ohio's Contribution to National Civil Service Reform," *Ohio Archaeological and Historical Quarterly*, XXXIII (April, 1924), 178.

54. *Congressional Globe*, 38 Cong., 2 sess., part 2, "Appendix" (March 3, 1865), p. 108.

VI: THE TENURE OF OFFICE ACT

1. *Congressional Globe*, 39 Cong., 2 sess., part 1 (December 3, 1866), p. 5.

2. Evidence that Johnson had many reasons for ridding himself of Stanton—as he finally did—has been supplied by Gideon Welles, who continued under Johnson as secretary of the navy. In his diary for July 12, 1867, Welles described a Cabinet meeting in which

Stanton notified the group that he was planning to send two letters to the Speaker requesting additional appropriations for both the Indian wars and Reconstruction. Welles, in Johnson's presence, said he thought such communications with Congress should be transmitted through the President, especially when the legislative branch was degrading the President to such an extent. Johnson, with a mildness not shown in his famous swing around the country, told Stanton to do what he thought best. " 'Then,' said Stanton, 'I will send both communications to the Speaker.' 'Very well,' said the President." "Pshaw!" said Welles in the privacy of his diary. Gideon Welles, *Diary*, III, 131–32.

3. *Congressional Globe*, 39 Cong., 2 sess., part 1 (January 10, 1867), p. 383.

4. *Ibid.*, p. 386.   5. *Ibid.*

6. *Ibid.* (January 16, 1867), p. 488.

7. *Ibid.*, p. 497.

8. Reginald C. McGraine, "George Hunt Pendleton," in *D.A.B.*, XIV, 420.

9. Gamaliel Bradford to Hayes (February 18, 1878), Rutherford B. Hayes Papers.

10. *Ibid.* (March 1, 1878).

11. Hayes, *Diary and Letters*, ed. by Charles Richard Williams, III, 473–74.

12. Geo. H. Pendleton to Hayes (April 2, 1878), Rutherford B. Hayes Papers.

13. Excerpt from letter of Pendleton to Perry Belmont (April 29, 1878) in Perry Belmont, *An American Democrat*, p. 590.

14. Cincinnati *Daily Gazette* (May 23, 1878), p. 2; New York *Times* (May 22, 23, 1878), pp. 5, 5; *Nation*, XXVI (June 6, 1878), 372–73.

15. Cincinnati *Enquirer* (May 23, 1878), p. 2.

16. Cincinnati *Daily Gazette* (May 23, 1878), p. 2.

17. *Ibid.*

VII: THE SECOND PENDLETON BILL

1. *Congressional Record*, 46 Cong., 1 sess., 9:1 (March 26, 1879), p. 72.

2. *Ibid.* (April 1, 1879), p. 141.

3. *Ibid.* (April 9, 1879), p. 312.

4. *Ibid.* (April 28, 1879), p. 967.

5. Cincinnati *Daily Gazette* (April 29, 1879), p. 1; Washington *Post* (April 29, 1879), p. 1.

6. *Congressional Record,* 46 Cong., 1 sess., 9:1 (April 28, 1879), p. 967.

7. *Ibid.*　　8. *Ibid.,* p. 968.　　9. *Ibid.*　　10. *Ibid.*

11. *Ibid.,* p. 969.　　12. *Ibid.,* p. 970.　　13. *Ibid.*

14. Claude M. Fuess and Alan Rogers Blackmer, "Justin Smith Morrill," in *D.A.B.,* XIII, 198–99.

15. *Congressional Record,* 46 Cong., 1 sess., 9:1 (April 28, 1879), p. 974.

16. Cincinnati *Daily Gazette* (April 29, 1879), p. 1.

17. *Congressional Record,* 46 Cong., 1 sess., 9:1 (April 28, 1879), p. 971.

18. *Ibid.,* p. 972.

19. *Ibid.* The Constitution provided that "no Person holding any Office under the United States, shall be a Member of either House during his Continuance in Office." *U.S. Const.,* Art. I, sec. 6, cl. 2.

20. *Congressional Record,* 46 Cong., 1 sess., 9:1 (April 28, 1879), p. 973.

21. Cincinnati *Daily Gazette* (March 28, 1879), p. 4.

22. Cincinnati *Commercial* (March 29, 1879), p. 6.

23. Washington *Post* (April 1, 1879), p. 2. A few days previously, the *Post* described President Hayes as "a fraud and hypocrite that we never expect to see duplicated." The editor doubted the sincerity of the administration's promise that no civil servant would be called upon for contributions to the Republican campaign fund. *Ibid.* (March 27, 1879), p. 2.

24. Horace White, "Cabinet Officers in Congress," *Nation,* XXVIII (April 10, 1879), 243–44.

25. New York *Times* (April 24, 1879), p. 4.

26. *Ibid.* (April 29, 30, 1879), pp. 7, 4.

27. New York *Herald* (April 29, 1879), p. 8.

28. Boston *Daily Advertiser* (April 30, 1879), p. 2.

29. Sacramento *Daily Record-Union* (April 30, 1879), p. 1.

30. *Congressional Record,* 46 Cong., 1 sess., 9:2 (May 28, 1879), p. 1659.

31. *Ibid.* (May 29, 1879), p. 1683.

32. New York *Times* (May 30, 1879), p. 3; *Biographical Di-*

rectory of the American Congress, 1774–1949, 81 Cong., 2 sess., H. Doc. 607 (1950), *passim.*

33. Frederic Logan Paxson, "James Abram Garfield," in *D.A.B.,* VII, 147.

34. *Congressional Record,* 46 Cong., 3 sess., 11:2 (February 4, 1881), p. 1201.

35. Cincinnati *Daily Enquirer* (February 5, 1881), p. 4.

36. *Senate Reports: 1880–1881,* 46 Cong., 3 sess., I, S. Rept. 837, p. 8.

37. Cincinnati *Commercial* (February 9, 1881), p. 4.

38. Washington *Post* (April 29, 1879), p. 1.

39. E. L. Godkin, "Cabinet Officers in Congress," *Nation,* XXXII (February 17, 1881), 107–9.

40. *Ibid.,* p. 109.

41. *Ibid.,* p. 110.

42. *Ibid.* (March 3, 1881), p. 149.

43. *Harper's Weekly,* XXV (February 26, 1881), 130.

44. *Congressional Record,* 47 Cong., 1 sess., 13:1 (December 8, 1881), p. 53.

45. *Ibid.* (December 13, 1881), p. 75.

46. *Journal of the Senate of the United States,* 47 Cong., 1 sess. (December 13, 1881), p. 100. Evidence that the bill still retained some life at least a year later was furnished by Gamaliel Bradford, who wrote on November 30, 1882, that the bill would "fall just as flat as last year." He objected to Pendleton's "somewhat perfunctory argument of its legality and propriety as shown from the experience of other countries, in place of a vigorous demonstration of its absolute necessity to prevent the Government from coming to a deadlock; and secondly, because the reasons which make the measure desirable for the country are precisely those which make it an object of horror to Congressmen." Bradford urged Pendleton to take to the stump and inform the people. *Nation,* XXXV (November 30, 1882), 462–63.

47. Leonard D. White, *Introduction to the Study of Public Administration,* p. 318.

48. Reginald C. McGraine, "George Hunt Pendleton," in *D.A.B.,* XIV, 420.

VIII: THE EFFORTS OF BRADFORD AND BELMONT

1. George H. Genzmer, "Gamaliel Bradford," in *D.A.B.*, II, 556–57.

2. Gamaliel Bradford, Biography, p. 10 (typewritten), in vol. 1, Political Writings (1869–1897), Bradford Papers.

3. *National Cyclopaedia of American Biography*, XIX, 29.

4. Gamaliel Bradford, Biography, p. 12, in Bradford Papers.

5. *Ibid.*, p. 11.

6. E. L. Godkin, "Something More About Our 'Case,'" *Nation*, XIV (March 21, 1872), 181–82. Bradford's letter of March 25, 1872, in reply, *ibid.* (April 4, 1872), pp. 216–17.

7. *Nation*, XVI (April 3, 1873), 234.   8. *Ibid.*   9. *Ibid.*

10. It is not surprising that one famous Speaker (1889–91; 1895–99), Thomas B. Reed, viewed Bradford's ideas with little favor. Reed believed that the desire to secure the responsible ministry of the British system could not be fulfilled by seating the Cabinet in Congress. The relationship between the Cabinet and the President, and therefore between the Cabinet and Congress, precluded a responsible ministry which might exist where the department heads were dependent upon the legislative body for their tenure. "They [the American Cabinet officers] cannot be reached for any wrong advice they might give the house or the senate. They would share in great adventures without undergoing their perils. If they won, it would be well; if they lost, it would not be ill." Perhaps the basic difference, Reed argued, was that "in this country more than anywhere else a member represents his district. His chance for a public career is just there. If he fails to suit his district he cannot go elsewhere, no matter how great and famous he is." See Thomas B. Reed, "Should the Cabinet Officers Have Seats in Congress?" *The Illustrated American*, XXII (July 31, 1897), 137–38.

11. *Nation*, XXVI (April 11, 1878), 239–40.

12. *Ibid.* (June 6, 1878), pp. 372–73. New York *Times* (May 22, 23, 1878), pp. 5, 5.

13. *Biographical Directory of the American Congress, 1774–1949*, 81 Cong., 2 sess., H. Doc. 607 (1950), pp. 837–38.

14. *Nation*, L (January 23, 1890), 72.

15. *Ibid.*, XLI (August 27, 1885), 171–72.

16. *Ibid.*, LII (February 19, 1891), 158.

17. *Ibid.* (March 5, 1891), p. 197.

18. *Ibid.*, XXXVIII (February 21, 1884), 167–68.

19. *Ibid.* (January 10, 1884), p. 34.

20. *Ibid.*, XL (May 14, 1885), 399.

21. Woodrow Wilson, "Cabinet Government in the United States," *The International Review*, VII (August, 1879), 146–63.

22. *Ibid.*, p. 151.   23. *Ibid.*, pp. 151–52.

24. *Ibid.*, p. 153.   25. *Ibid.*, p. 155.   26. *Ibid.*, p. 160.

27. *Ibid.*, p. 161.   28. *Ibid.*, pp. 162–63.

29. Woodrow Wilson, "Committee or Cabinet Government," *The Overland Monthly*, 2nd series, III (January, 1884), 25.

30. *Ibid.*, p. 26.   31. *Ibid.*, p. 28.   32. *Ibid.*, p. 29.

33. *Ibid.*, p. 30.   34. *Ibid.*, p. 33.

35. Woodrow Wilson, *Congressional Government*. In his *Constitutional Government in the United States*, published five years before he entered the White House, Wilson pictured the President as the leader of his party, who has a responsibility to all the people.

36. *Nation*, XL (February 12, 1885), 142–43.

37. Walter Bagehot, a brilliant late nineteenth-century analyst of English government, had a great effect on Woodrow Wilson and most other American political scientists. His work, *The English Constitution and Other Political Essays*, first appeared in the United States in 1877.

38. James Bryce, *The American Commonwealth*, I, 279.

39. *Nation*, L (January 16, 1890), 50.

40. *Ibid.* (January 23, 1890), p. 72.

41. Freeman Snow, "Cabinet Government in the United States," in *Annals of the American Academy of Political and Social Science*, III (July, 1892), 1–13; written in reply to Bradford's "Congress and the Cabinet," in *ibid.*, II (November, 1891), 289–99.

42. Gamaliel Bradford, "Congress and the Cabinet—II," in *ibid.*, IV (November, 1893), 421.

43. *Ibid.*, p. 420.

44. Gamaliel Bradford, *The Lesson of Popular Government*. See especially chapters 30 and 31 entitled "Executive Responsibility" in vol. 2.

45. New York *Sun* (May 29, 1899), in Bradford Papers, vol. 3 (1899–1900), p. 1.

46. Boston *Herald* (September 23, 1901), p. 1.

47. *Ibid.* (June 23, 1906), p. 1.

48. Charles F. Adams to Gamaliel Bradford (February 1, 1909), in Bradford Papers, 6:51–54.

49. Gamaliel Bradford to Woodrow Wilson (December 6, 1910), in Bradford Papers, 6:113, and Perry Belmont to Gamaliel Bradford (July 9, 1911), in *ibid.*, 6:129.

50. New York *Times* (June 24, 1922), p. 1.

51. Henry L. Stimson to Gamaliel Bradford (February 4, 1911), in Bradford Papers, 6:107; Henry Jones Ford to Bradford (January 7, 1911), in *ibid.*, 6:122; Augustus E. Willson to Bradford (autumn, 1910), in *ibid.*, 6:117.

52. George H. Genzmer, "Gamaliel Bradford," in *D.A.B.*, II, 557.

53. Perry Belmont, "Cabinet Officers in Congress," *North American Review*, CXCVII (January, 1913), 22–30.

54. Perry Belmont, "Personal Government, or Executive Officers Before Congress" (address delivered before the American Club of Paris, July 2, 1914), in his *Survival of the Democratic Principle*, pp. 293–309.

55. Perry Belmont, *An American Democrat*, esp. ch. 31, "Personal Government," pp. 581–604.

56. *Congressional Record*, 64 Cong., 1 sess., 53:5 (March 25, 1916), pp. 4820–21.

57. *Ibid.*, 69 Cong., 1 sess., 67:1 (March 11, 1925), pp. 109–10.

58. Perry Belmont, *An American Democrat*, pp. 600–3.

IX: GROWING CONGRESSIONAL INTEREST

1. Boston *Daily Advertiser* (January 7, 1881), p. 4.

2. *Ibid.*, p. 2.   3. *Ibid.* (January 6, 1882), p. 2.

4. Gamaliel Bradford to John D. Long (November 30, 1885), in Long Papers, Box 20.

5. *Congressional Record*, 49 Cong., 1 sess., 17:1 (December 17, 1885), p. 280.

6. Gamaliel Bradford to John D. Long (December 23, 1885), in Long Papers, Box 20.

7. *Congressional Record*, 49 Cong., 1 sess., 17:1 (January 5, 1886), p. 416.

8. Gamaliel Bradford to John D. Long (January 6, 1886), in Long Papers, Box 21.

9. While secretary of the navy, Long corresponded about the

Pendleton proposal with his former college classmate, Horace N. Fisher, who had written an article for a Boston newspaper in which he condemned "Rule by Parliament." Fisher's reply reveals that the essay had "raised new questions" in the secretary's mind, presumably questions more negative to the idea. Horace N. Fisher to Long (November 9, 1901), in Long, *Papers, 1897–1904*, ed. by Gardner Weld Allen, p. 402.

10. Harold Laski, the English political scientist, claimed that he had heard Theodore Roosevelt insist that seating the Cabinet in Congress would produce a wiser selection of department heads. Harold J. Laski, *The American Presidency,* p. 107.

11. *Congressional Record,* 60 Cong., 2 sess., 43:4 (March 1, 1909), p. 3458; *ibid.* (March 2, 1909, pp. 3613–19; *ibid.,* March 3, 1909), pp. 3724–27.

12. *Ibid.,* 62 Cong., 1 sess., 47:2 (May 16, 1911), p. 1229.

13. Henry Jones Ford, "The Cause of Political Corruption," *Scribner's Magazine,* XLIX (January, 1911), 60. Ford wrote Gamaliel Bradford the same month this article appeared predicting that the granting to the Cabinet of seats in Congress would eventually "be compulsory to escape from national ruin." Henry Jones Ford to Gamaliel Bradford (January 7, 1911) in Bradford Papers, vol. 6.

14. W. S. U'Ren, "State and County Government in Oregon and Proposed Changes," *Annals of the American Academy of Political and Social Science,* XLVII (May, 1913), 271–73.

15. Henry Jones Ford, *The Rise and Growth of American Politics,* pp. 369–70. It is interesting to note that Ford reproduced Pendleton's 1881 report and related excerpts from Story's *Commentaries on the Constitution of the United States. Ibid.,* pp. 383–96.

16. Henry L. Stimson and McGeorge Bundy, *On Active Service in Peace and War,* p. 61.

17. Henry L. Stimson to Gamaliel Bradford (February 4, 1911), in Bradford Papers, 6:107.

18. New York *Daily Tribune* (January 19, 1910), p. 4.

19. William Howard Taft to Henry Cabot Lodge (August 18, 1912), Taft Letterbook, in Taft Papers, 41:395. Within a year Lodge gave his support to the proposal, especially with reference to having the Cabinet members explain their departmental budgets. Henry Cabot Lodge to Henry L. Stimson (June 21, 1913), in Stimson Papers.

20. Henry L. Stimson to William Howard Taft (November 11, 1912), Semi-Official Letters of the Secretary of War, in Stimson Papers, 3:497.

21. Henry L. Stimson to Walter L. Fisher (November 11, 1912), Personal Letters of the Secretary of War, in *ibid.*, 3:280, and Henry L. Stimson to George W. Wickersham, in *ibid.*, p. 281.

22. *Congressional Record*, 62 Cong., 3 sess., 49:1 (December 12, 1912), p. 895.

23. William Howard Taft, *Our Chief Magistrate and His Powers*, p. 31.

24. *Congressional Record*, 62 Cong., 3 sess., 49:4 (February 18, 1913), p. 3364.

25. Charles McCarthy, *The Wisconsin Idea*, p. 181.

26. "Interpellation of State Officers in Wisconsin," Wisconsin Legislative Reference Library (duplicate typewritten statement in possession of author), February, 1946, p. 1.

27. *Ibid.*, pp. 1–2. Wis. Stats. (1955), secs. 13.23–13.24.

28. "Interpellation of Hon. Mark S. Catlin, Sr., Senate Chamber, March 12, 1941," Wisconsin Legislative Reference Library (duplicate transcript in possession of author).

29. M. G. Toepel, chief, Wisconsin Legislative Reference Library, to author (March 12, 1958).

30. Stimson served as secretary of war in the Cabinets of Presidents Taft, Franklin D. Roosevelt, and Harry S. Truman, and as secretary of state under Herbert Hoover.

31. Henry L. Stimson, "Initiative and Responsibility of the Executive: A Remedy for Inefficient Legislation" (address before the Law Academy of Philadelphia), May 27, 1913, p. 3, in Speeches and Writings of Henry L. Stimson, 1886–1914, Stimson Papers, Book No. 1.

32. *Ibid.*, p. 14.   33. *Ibid.*, p. 20.   34. *Ibid.*, p. 24a.

35. *Ibid.*, p. 29.

36. Henry L. Stimson to Joseph H. Choate (July 29, 1914), in Stimson Papers.

37. Ogden L. Mills, "Participation of the Executive in Legislation," *Proceedings of the Academy of Political Science*, V (October, 1914), 135.

38. N.Y. State Constitutional Convention Commission, *The Constitution and Government of the State of New York: An Appraisal*, p. 75.

39. N.Y. State Constitutional Convention Commission, *Documents of the Constitutional Convention of the State of New York,* "Meeting of the Committee on State Finances with Hon. John J. Fitzgerald" (May 26, 1915), Document No. 15, p. 49.

40. *Ibid.,* "Joint Meeting of the Committees on Governor and Other State Officers and State Finances with Hon. William Howard Taft, ex-President of the United States" (June 10, 1915), Document No. 11, p. 16.

41. *Ibid.,* "Report of the Committee on State Finances, Revenues and Expenditures, Relative to a Budget System for the State" (August 4, 1915), Document No. 32, p. 18.

42. In preparation for the 1938 New York Constitutional Convention a study committee devoted a chapter to answer affirmatively the question "Should Cabinet Members Be Subject to Questioning upon the Floor of the Legislature?" N.Y. State Constitutional Convention, *Problems Relating to Legislative Organization and Powers,* ch. 14. Meyer Jacobstein, who had introduced a Pendleton-type bill in the House in 1925, was a member of the committee which produced the report. On April 27, 1938, Delegate Arthur E. Sutherland proposed an amendment to allow department heads to participate in debate. It met a fate similar to its Stimson predecessor in 1915. N.Y. State Constitutional Convention, *Revised Records of the Constitutional Convention of the State of New York: April 5 to August 26, 1938,* pp. 105–6.

43. " 'Make Democracy Safe for the World' Says Governor McCall of Massachusetts," New York *Times Magazine* (July 22, 1917), p. 1.

44. *Debates in the Massachusetts Constitutional Convention, 1917–1918,* III, 888–89.

45. *Ibid.,* p. 902.   46. *Ibid.,* pp. 908, 910.

47. Augustus Peabody Loring, "A Short Account of the Massachusetts Constitutional Convention, 1917–1919," *New England Quarterly,* VI, Supplement (January, 1933), pp. 15, 19–20.

48. If an individual was classified as a conservative he supported John L. Bates rather than Sherman L. Whipple for convention president. He would also have voted against the initiative and referendum. *Journal of the Constitutional Convention of the Commonwealth of Massachusetts,* pp. 16–19, 600–2.

49. *Ibid.,* pp. 706–7.

50. See *A Model State Constitution* prepared by the Committee

on State Government of the National Municipal League, 5th edition. Section 502 of "Legislative Powers" entitled "Executive-Legislative Relations" provided that "the governor, the administrative manager, and heads of administrative departments shall be entitled to seats in the legislature, may introduce bills therein, and take part in the discussion of measures, but shall have no vote." With the exception of the addition of "administrative manager" and the denomination of "administrative" rather than "executive" departments, this clause has remained essentially the same since it was first published in 1921. One of the principal articles recommending this prior to 1921 was written by Richard S. Childs, an early member of the Committee on State Government. See his "A State Manager Plan," *National Municipal Review*, VI (November, 1917), 659–63.

51. *Congressional Record*, 63 Cong., 1 sess., 50:1 (April 7, 1913), p. 91.

52. Andrew J. Montague, "A More Effective Cabinet" (address before the Pennsylvania Bar Association, June 27, 1911), in *Report of the Seventeenth Annual Meeting of the Pennsylvania Bar Association*, p. 250.

53. *Ibid.*, p. 251.   54. *Ibid.*, p. 254.   55. *Ibid.*, p. 254.

56. *Ibid.*, p. 255.   57. *Ibid.*, p. 253.

58. Andrew J. Montague, "The Cabinet Before Congress," *World's Work*, XLIX (February, 1925), 358. Joseph Story, who had served in Congress as a member of the Jeffersonian Republicans, was the earliest (1833) scholarly advocate of seating the Cabinet in Congress (sec. 869). His views on the "separation of powers" doctrine are found at sections 528–32 of his work, *Commentaries on the Constitution of the United States*, I, secs. 528–32, 869.

59. *Congressional Record*, 65 Cong., 1 sess., 55:4 (June 18, 1917), p. 3755.

60. *Ibid.*, p. 3756.

61. *Ibid.*, 55:8 (May 4, 1917), Appendix, pp. 150–51.

62. *Ibid.*, 55:6 (July 31, 1917), p. 5635.

63. New York *Times* (June 24, 1922), p. 1.

64. *Literary Digest*, LXXIV (July 8, 1922), 10. *The World's Work*, XLIX (December, 1924), 121–23.

65. Nicholas Murray Butler, *Across the Busy Years*, II, 355–57. Butler remarked in these "recollections and reflections" written in

1940 that he had been interested in the Pendleton plan for over fifty years and that about a half-dozen times in that period he had persuaded some member of Congress to have the 1881 report published in the *Congressional Record. Ibid.*, p. 357.

66. William Hard, "One Immediate Reform," *Nation*, CXVIII (April 9, 1924), 397–98.

67. *Congressional Record*, 66 Cong., 2 sess., 59:2 (January 27, 1920), p. 2134.

68. *Ibid.*, 67 Cong., 1 sess., 61:5 (August 20, 1921), p. 5377.

69. New York *Times* (June 24, 1922), p. 1. President Harding wrote Kelly on June 23, 1922, that his bill was "one of the most constructive steps that can be taken in furthering the development of our governmental machinery. . . . There are in my mind overwhelming arguments that can be introduced in favor of this change in our traditions." Quoted in N.Y. State Constitutional Convention, *Problems Relating to Legislative Organization and Powers*, p. 414.

70. New York *Times* (June 24, 1922), p. 5.

71. Meyer Jacobstein to author (January 10, 1958).

72. *Congressional Record*, 68 Cong., 2 sess., 66:2 (January 6, 1925), p. 1341.

73. *Ibid.*, 69 Cong., 1 sess., 67:5 (March 4, 1926), p. 4959.

74. Upshaw's three personally selected labels are taken from a lecture leaflet which he sent to the late Secretary of the Interior Harold Ickes. "Interviews—September 3, 1941," Box 58, Ickes Papers.

75. *Congressional Record*, 68 Cong., 1 sess., 65:7 (April 22, 1924), p. 6909.

76. *Ibid.*

77. *Ibid.*, 69 Cong., 1 sess., 67:4 (February 9, 1926), p. 3660.

78. *Ibid.* (February 10, 1926), p. 3731.

79. *Ibid.*, 70 Cong., 1 sess., 69:5 (March 15, 1928), p. 4855.

80. Former President Taft related to a committee of the 1915 New York Constitutional Convention how as secretary of war he had gone to the Senate floor to attempt a rescue of what he considered some vital legislation dealing with the Philippine Islands. He cornered a senator on the committee that had waylaid his measure and asked him to get the bill out of committee and before the Senate. The senator, after denouncing the whole Philippine policy but proclaiming his friendship for Taft, accused him of lobbying. The following dialogue then ensued, according to Taft. Said

the senator: " 'I am a friend of yours, but I want to tell you that your being on the floor is noticed. It is working against you.' He said, 'I am in favor of separating the legislative from the executive.' 'Well,' I said, 'look here, Senator, what do you come down to my department for and intervene with reference to what I am to do in the Secretary of War's position?' 'Oh,' he said, 'that's different; that's personal.' " N.Y. State Constitutional Convention, *Documents of the Constitutional Convention of New York,* "Joint Meeting of the Committees on Governor and Other State Officers and State Finances with Hon. William Howard Taft, ex-President of the United States" (June 10, 1915), Document No. 11, p. 18.

81. *Congressional Record,* 70 Cong., 1 sess., 69:5 (March 15, 1928), p. 4856.

82. *Ibid.,* 74 Cong., 1 sess., 79:2 (February 6, 1935), p. 1625.

83. *Ibid.* (February 14, 1935), p. 1964.   84. *Ibid.*

85. *Ibid.,* p. 1965.   86. *Ibid.* (February 20, 1935), p. 2309.

87. Perry Belmont, *An American Democrat,* pp. 600–1.

88. *Congressional Record,* 75 Cong., 1 sess., 81:7 (July 15, 1937), p. 7200.

89. *Ibid.,* 2 sess., 82:2 (December 10, 1937), p. 1310. See also Maury Maverick, *In Blood and Ink,* pp. 187–88.

X: THE KEFAUVER QUESTION PERIOD

1. *Congressional Record,* 77 Cong., 2 sess., 88:7 (December 3, 1942), p. 9317.

2. *Ibid.,* pp. 9310–11.

3. William R. Thom to author (March 27, 1958).

4. *Congressional Record,* 78 Cong., 1 sess., 89:1 (January 25, 1943), p. 378.

5. *Ibid.,* 89:6 (October 19, 1943), p. 8544. For the full text of H. Res. 327, see Appendix II, "Representative Proposals to Change the Relationship of the Cabinet to Congress," part B, "Kefauver's Report and Question Period Resolution of 1943 (H. Res. 327)."

6. New York *Times* (January 26, 1943), p. 4.

7. *Ibid.* (October 14, 1943), p. 11.

8. *Congressional Record,* 78 Cong., 1 sess., 89:7 (November 12, 1943), pp. 9459–60.

9. *Ibid.,* p. 9460.   10. *Ibid.*   11. *Ibid.,* p. 9462.

12. *Ibid.,* p. 9463.

13. Hull's appearance was the first time since the eighteenth century that a Cabinet officer had appeared before Congress. His favorable reception was probably owing in part to prior membership in both houses of Congress. *Ibid.* (November 18, 1943), pp. 9677–79.

14. New York *Times* (November 18, 1943), p. 9; *ibid.* (November 21, 1943), IV, 3.

15. *Ibid.*

16. *Congressional Record,* 78 Cong., 1 sess., 89:8 (November 26, 1943), p. 10,038.

17. *Ibid.,* p. 10,040.

18. Estes Kefauver to John H. Fahey, Commissioner, Federal Home Loan Bank Administration (similar letter to all other cabinet and agency heads), November 26, 1943, Kefauver Papers.

19. In 1939 the Bureau of the Budget was moved to the newly created Executive Office of the President from the Treasury Department where it had been placed by the Budget and Accounting Act of 1921. Executive Order 8248 issued by President Roosevelt on September 8, 1939, outlined its functions. Among them were "to assist the President by clearing and coordinating departmental advice on proposed legislation and by making recommendations as to Presidential action on legislative enactments, in accordance with past practice." Fed. Reg., 4:3864. For a concise description of Legislative Reference's function by one of its former heads see Roger W. Jones, "The Role of the Bureau of the Budget in the Federal Legislative Process," *American Bar Association Journal,* XL (November, 1954), 995–98. For a favorable description of Roger W. Jones and an insight into the personnel involved in Legislative Reference, see Katharine Hamill, "This Is a Bureaucrat," *Fortune,* XLVIII (November, 1953), 156–58, 181–88. For a negative view of Legislative Reference's work, see Arthur Maass, "In Accord with the Program of the President? An Essay on Staffing the Presidency," *Public Policy,* III, 77–93.

20. The President's Committee on Administrative Management, *Administrative Management in the Government of the United States,* p. 2.

21. F. J. Bailey, assistant director of the Budget for Legislative Reference, to Harold D. Smith, director of the Budget (December 2, 1943), in Budget Bureau Records. For the organizational location of the Bureau of the Budget participants in the decision to

clear Kefauver's Question and Report Period Resolution (H. Res. 327) of 1943, see Figure 1, p. 142.

22. Kefauver to Smith (December 1, 1943), *ibid.*

23. V. L. Almond, chief legislative analyst, to Donald C. Stone, assistant director in charge of administrative management; L. C. Martin, assistant director in charge of estimates; and J. Weldon Jones, assistant director in charge of fiscal division (December 7, 1943), *ibid.* Actually the first reply received by the Budget Bureau was from Walter M. W. Splawn, chairman of the Legislative Committee, Interstate Commerce Commission. It was favorable; however, the letter was sent to the director's office and not to Legislative Reference. Thus, even though it was received on the afternoon of December 3, it apparently had not arrived at Bailey and Almond's office by the morning of December 7, over three days later.

24. H. A. Millis, chairman, National Labor Relations Board, to F. J. Bailey (December 3, 1943), *ibid.*

25. John F. Willmott, Budgetary Control Section, to Herman C. Loeffler, assistant chief, Fiscal Division (December 9, 1943), *ibid.*

26. Herman C. Loeffler to J. Weldon Jones (December 10, 1943), *ibid.*

27. *Ibid.*

28. R. D. Vining, assistant chief, Estimates Division, to Leo C. Martin (December 13, 1943), *ibid.*

29. *Ibid.*

30. Philip B. Fleming, administrator, Federal Works Agency, to Kefauver (December 23, 1943), *ibid.*

31. Emory S. Land, chairman, United States Maritime Commission, to Kefauver (November 30, 1943), *ibid.*

32. Frances Perkins, secretary of labor, to Kefauver (December 11, 1943), *ibid.*

33. Virgil L. Almond to Harold D. Smith (December 16, 1943), *ibid.*

34. Franklin L. Burdette, ed., *Directory of the American Political Science Association: 1945* (Evanston, Illinois, American Political Science Association, 1945), *passim.*

35. George A. Graham, chief, War Supply Section, Division of Administrative Management to V. O. Key, Jr. (December 14, 1943), Budget Bureau Records.

36. Donald C. Stone to Harold D. Smith (December 20, 1943), *ibid.*

37. *Ibid.*

38. Wayne Coy, acting director of the Budget, to Emory S. Land, Frances Perkins, H. A. Millis, and David E. Lilienthal, chairman of the Tennessee Valley Authority (December 23, 1943), *ibid.*

39. Virgil L. Almond to James Lawrence Fly, chairman, Federal Communications Commission (December 30, 1943); Donald M. Nelson, chairman, War Production Board (December 31, 1943); Leo T. Crowley, administrator, Foreign Economic Administration (December 31, 1943), *ibid.*

40. John A. Vieg, International Section staff, Division of Administrative Management, to Harold D. Smith (December 30, 1943), Budget Bureau Records.

41. George Gallup, the director of the American Institute of Public Opinion, Princeton, New Jersey, sampled the public on the following question: "A member of Congress has suggested that heads of government departments and agencies appear before Congress, when requested, to answer questions about what their departments are doing. Do you approve or disapprove of this idea?" The results which were announced shortly before Christmas, 1943, indicated that 72% approved, 7% disapproved, and 21% had no opinion on the issue. No significant geographical differences were noticed. Of the Republicans questioned 75% favored the plan; of the Democrats, 68% were in favor. New York *Times* (December 22, 1943), p. 22.

42. On February 18, 1943, Madame Chiang Kai-shek spoke separately before both the Senate and the House. This practice is not infrequent, although usually a distinguished visitor—such as the President delivering his annual State of the Union message or Prime Minister Winston Churchill or General of the Army Douglas MacArthur—addresses a joint session of the two houses. In either case, the chambers are in recess and the reporting of the guest's speech is placed in the *Record* only by unanimous consent when the houses reconvene. *Congressional Record,* 78 Cong., 1 sess., 89:1 (February 18, 1943), pp. 1108–9. In 1915, Speaker Champ Clark stated that a member could ask a question of the President when he appeared before a joint session. The inquiry would be directed at the President and he would have the right to refuse to be interrogated. Clark concluded that while it would be proper to query the Chief Executive—as the Speaker agreed had been the practice during the administrations of George Washington and John Adams—

"it would be exercising wretched taste." *Ibid.*, 63 Cong., 3 sess., 52:2 (January 13, 1915), p. 1514.

43. John A. Vieg, International Section staff, Division of Administrative Management, to Harold D. Smith (December 30, 1943), Budget Bureau Records.

44. *Ibid.*

45. Walter H. C. Laves, International Section staff, Division of Administrative Management, to Donald C. Stone (December 30, 1943), *ibid.*

46. *Ibid.*

47. Francis O. Wilcox, International Section staff, Division of Administrative Management, to Donald C. Stone (December 30, 1943), *ibid.*

48. John A. Vieg to Harold D. Smith (December 31, 1943), *ibid.*

49. Don K. Price, "The Parliamentary and Presidential Systems," *Public Administration Review*, III (Autumn, 1943), 317–34.

50. Louis Brownlow, *The President and the Presidency*, p. 18.

51. Don K. Price to Harold D. Smith (January 8, 1944), Budget Bureau Records.

52. Fred E. Levi, chief, Government Organization Section, Division of Administrative Management, to Harold D. Smith (January 8, 1944), *ibid.*

53. *Ibid.*

54. Harold D. Smith to Estes Kefauver (January 6, 1944), *ibid.*

55. Harold L. Ickes, secretary of the interior, to Estes Kefauver (November 30, 1943), "Miscellaneous: October, 1940–October, 1944," Box 86, Secretary of the Interior Files, 1933–46, Ickes Papers. Ickes enclosed a copy of his answer to United Press's Washington manager, Lyle C. Wilson, who had written on November 24, 1943, asking for an opinion on whether or not the type of appearance made by Secretary of State Hull should be regularized. Ickes informed Wilson: "I have long been of the opinion that our Government would work more understandingly, and therefore, smoothly, if members of the Cabinet, on appropriate occasions, appeared before the Congress to be questioned, or even to make voluntary statements, although the right to do the latter would have to be circumscribed carefully in order to avoid its abuse." (November 26, 1943, *ibid.*)

56. Robert P. Patterson, under secretary of war, to Ferdinand Eberstadt (January 27, 1944), Kefauver Papers.

57. John W. Davis to Estes Kefauver (December 6, 1943), Kefauver Papers.

58. For a representative sample of newspaper editorials, see *Congressional Record,* 78 Cong., 2 sess., 90:8 (January 24, 1944), pp. A382–83.

59. New York *Times* (December 22, 1943), p. 22.

60. *Congressional Record,* 78 Cong., 2 sess., 90:1 (January 31, 1944), pp. 934–35.

61. Adolph J. Sabath to Franklin D. Roosevelt (January 12, 1944), Roosevelt Papers.

62. Letters from Henry A. Wallace, Vice President of the United States, 1941 to 1945 (August 20, 1957), and Francis Biddle, attorney general of the United States, 1941 to 1945 (August 29, 1957), to author.

63. Franklin D. Roosevelt to Adolph J. Sabath (January 24, 1944), Roosevelt Papers.

64. *Ibid.,* telephone notation attached.

65. "Statement of Estes Kefauver, M.C., before the Rules Committee, in support of House Resolution 327, . . ." [January, 1944] (mimeograph), p. 2, Kefauver Papers.

66. *Ibid.,* p. 4.

67. *Ibid.,* p. 12.   68. *Ibid.,* pp. 12–13.

69. *Ibid.,* p. 17. The constitutional clause (Art. I, Sec. 6, Cl. 2) referred to declares that "No Senator or Representative shall, during the Time for which he was elected, be appointed to any civil Office under the Authority of the United States, which shall have been created, or the Emoluments whereof shall have been encreased during such time; and no Person holding any Office under the United States, shall be a Member of either House during his Continuance in Office."

70. *Ibid.,* p. 19.

71. Estes Kefauver to Franklin D. Roosevelt, President of the United States (February 1, 1944), Kefauver Papers.

72. Memorandum from Franklin D. Roosevelt to the Speaker of the House (February 7, 1944), Roosevelt Papers.

73. Franklin D. Roosevelt to Estes Kefauver (February 15, 1944), Roosevelt Papers.

74. Memorandum for General Watson to take up with the President, Wednesday, March 8 [1944], Roosevelt Papers.

75. Estes Kefauver to Harold D. Smith (February 1, 1944), *ibid.*

76. See, for example, Kefauver's letters to Francis Biddle, attorney general (February 1, 1944); Ernest K. Lindley, journalist and commentator (February 2, 1944); Associate Justice Felix Frankfurter (February 2, 1944); New York banker Ferdinand Eberstadt (February 4, 1944); and *Life* publisher Roy E. Larsen (February 4, 1944), among many others, Kefauver Papers.

77. John K. Jessup, Board of Editors, *Fortune,* to Kefauver (February 4, 1944), Kefauver Papers. The editorial referred to appeared in *Life,* XVI (February 21, 1944), 38. *Fortune,* in its November, 1943, issue, had included a thirteen-page supplement entitled "Our Form of Government." Among the changes advocated was the admittance of the Cabinet to Congress.

78. George B. Galloway, chairman, Committee on Congress, American Political Science Association, to Kefauver (February 1, 1944), Budget Bureau Records.

79. "The 'Kefauver Resolution,' H.R. 327" (Budget Bureau Staff Meeting Memorandum for February 4, 1944), *ibid.*

80. Harold D. Smith to Estes Kefauver (February 9, 1944), *ibid.*

81. Estes Kefauver to Harold D. Smith (February 11, 1944), *ibid.*

82. *Congressional Record,* 78 Cong., 2 sess., 90:3 (March 23, 1944), p. 2976.

83. *Ibid.,* p. 2978.

84. *Ibid.* (March 29, 1944), pp. 3271–74.

85. Estes Kefauver to Franklin D. Roosevelt (January 6, 1945), Roosevelt Papers.

86. Franklin D. Roosevelt to Estes Kefauver (January 11, 1945), Roosevelt Papers.

87. Memorandum from Franklin D. Roosevelt to the secretary of state (and seventeen others) (January 11, 1945), Roosevelt Papers.

88. Henry L. Stimson to Franklin D. Roosevelt (January 13, 1945), Roosevelt Papers.

89. Donald M. Nelson to Franklin D. Roosevelt (January 15, 1945), Roosevelt Papers.

90. See Brief Digest of Responses to the President's Memoran-

dum of January Eleventh [1945] Regarding H. Res. 31. Roosevelt Papers.

91. See Jesse H. Jones (January 17, 1945), Claude R. Wickard (January 18, 1945), Fred M. Vinson (January 19, 1945), Paul V. McNutt (February 5, 1945), Frank C. Walker (February 8, 1945), and Joseph C. Grew (February 27, 1945) to Franklin D. Roosevelt, Roosevelt Papers.

92. James F. Byrnes to Franklin D. Roosevelt (January 15, 1945), Roosevelt Papers.

93. James F. Byrnes to Estes Kefauver (January 15, 1945), Roosevelt Papers. The February issue of *American Magazine* carried an article by Byrnes entitled "Streamlining Congress" in which he endorsed the question period. It had been written at a time when Byrnes thought he would be no longer with the administration when it was published. Roosevelt prevailed on Byrnes to continue in his position. Although Byrnes felt that it was improper for him to comment while he was a member of the executive branch on a proposal which was solely within the province of the legislature, the issue containing the article had already gone to press.

94. Francis Biddle to Franklin D. Roosevelt (February 26, 1945), Roosevelt Papers.

95. Estes Kefauver to Franklin D. Roosevelt (March 6, 1945), Roosevelt Papers.

96. Franklin D. Roosevelt to James F. Byrnes (March 6, 1945), Roosevelt Papers.

97. James F. Byrnes to Franklin D. Roosevelt (March 7, 1945), Roosevelt Papers.

98. Franklin D. Roosevelt to James F. Byrnes (March 14, 1945), Roosevelt Papers.

99. Franklin D. Roosevelt to Estes Kefauver (March 24, 1945), Roosevelt Papers.

XI: CONGRESS LOOKS AT ITSELF

1. *Congressional Record,* 79 Cong., 1 sess., 91:1 (January 4, 1945), p. 36.

2. *Ibid.* (January 6, 1945), p. 81.

3. On November 27, 1944, Hull had left the State Department after presiding over its destinies since the advent of the New Deal

in 1933. In the spring of 1945, his successor, Edward R. Stettinius, Jr., was in San Francisco assisting in the birth of the permanent United Nations Organization. Grew as under secretary automatically became acting secretary.

4. Joseph C. Grew, acting secretary of state, to Estes Kefauver (May 22, 1945), Budget Bureau Records.

5. J. William Fulbright, "Statement on Kefauver Resolution for Senate Rules Committee" [May, 1945], in Fulbright Papers. Estes Kefauver to Harry F. Byrd, chairman, Senate Committee on Rules (May 29, 1945), Kefauver Papers.

6. On November 28, 1944, a letter from Dr. George B. Galloway, chairman of the American Political Science Association's Committee on Congress, was published in the *Record*. Galloway summarized succinctly the results of interviews held over a four-year period by 10 political scientists with members of the Senate and House. *Congressional Record,* 78 Cong., 2 sess., 90:11 (November 28, 1944), A4557–58. Two distinguished teachers of public administration, John Gaus and Leonard D. White, discussed congressional reform with George Fort Milton, editorial writer for the St. Louis *Post-Dispatch,* on the University of Chicago Round Table on January 14, 1945. Praise was voiced for Hull's appearance before Congress and for the idea of a question period. The University of Chicago Round Table, *Streamlining Congress,* Number 356, January 14, 1945, pp. 13–16. One of the first reports to appear was the widely acclaimed work of Robert Heller, *Strengthening the Congress.* Heller listed as Recommendation Ten: "Congress should experiment with periods for questioning executive department heads before each of the whole houses." For other proposals made during the Second World War which sought to bring together some legislators and department heads see *The Reorganization of Congress, A Report of the Committee on Congress of the American Political Science Association,* p. 50.

7. *Congressional Record,* 79 Cong., 1 sess., 91:1 (January 11, 1945), p. 230.

8. Representative Monroney revealed in subsequent House debate that Senate Rules Committee members "specifically objected to the proposal offered by the gentleman from Tennessee [Kefauver]." *Ibid.* (February 19, 1945), p. 1273.

9. *Ibid.* (February 12, 1945), p. 1009.

10. *Ibid.* (February 19, 1945), p. 1272.

11. The combined congressional service of all twelve members totaled 173 years, for an average of almost fourteen and a half years per man. La Follette had served 21 years, while Monroney had been in the House only seven years.

12. Testimony of Senator J. William Fulbright before the Joint Committee on the Organization of Congress, *Hearings,* 79 Cong., 1 sess., part 1 (March 22, 1945), p. 125. Hereafter cited as *Organization of Congress Hearings.*

13. Edward S. Corwin, *The President: Office and Powers, 1789–1948,* p. 361.

14. *Ibid.,* p. 362.

15. *Congressional Record,* 78 Cong., 1 sess., 89:1 (January 7, 1943), p. 41.

16. *Ibid.,* 89:2 (February 25, 1943), pp. 1296–97.

17. Thomas K. Finletter, *Can Representative Government Do the Job?* pp. 88, 98–105, 110.

18. *The Organization of Congress,* Summary of Hearings before the Joint Committee on the Organization of Congress, March 13–June 29, 1945; 79 Cong., 1 sess. (Washington, G.P.O., 1945), p. 38. A decade previously Elliott had favored giving the Cabinet seats "in the Senate with the right to appear or to speak by proxy in the lower House." William Yandell Elliott, *The Need for Constitutional Reform,* p. 204.

19. *Organization of Congress Hearings,* part 3 (May 21, 1945), p. 610.

20. *Ibid.* (May 29, 1945), p. 705.

21. *Ibid.,* part 1 (March 22, 1945), p. 123.

22. When no source is given for a quotation the information was provided on an off-the-record basis to the author.

23. *House Reports,* 79 Cong., 2 sess., No. 1675.

24. *Ibid.,* pp. 13–14.

25. *Congressional Record,* 79 Cong., 1 sess., 91:1 (January 4, 1945), p. 37.

26. *Congressional Record,* 81 Cong., 2 sess., 96:8 (July 13, 1950), pp. 10, 112.

27. On January 9, 1945, in anticipation of General George C. Marshall's and Admiral Ernest King's meeting on January 24 with senators and representatives, Mrs. Rogers inquired of Speaker Rayburn if she could "ask questions concerning the transportation of supplies." Speaker Rayburn, "speaking as an individual," advised

the gentlewoman from Massachusetts that it would be better to allow General Marshall and Admiral King "to go along without interruption and decide that question later." *Ibid.*, 79 Cong., 1 sess., 91:1 (January 9, 1945), p. 147.

28. *Ibid.*, 83 Cong., 1 sess., 99:1 (January 29, 1953), p. 615.

29. *Ibid.*

30. See Chapter XII, "The Cabinet and the Reform," *infra.*

XII: THE CABINET AND THE REFORM

1. This information is based on correspondence with 17 of the 41 present and former Cabinet officers alive in 1958. The question asked was similar to that sent to members of Congress. (See Appendix IV, question 2, p. 234.)

2. Dean Acheson, *A Citizen Looks at Congress,* pp. 79–80.

3. *Ibid.*, p. 80.

4. Interview with Democratic member of Congress.

5. Acheson, *A Citizen Looks at Congress,* p. 82.

6. Testimony of Dean Acheson, assistant secretary of state for congressional relations and international conferences, before La Follette-Monroney Committee, *Organization of Congress Hearings,* part 3 (May 14, 1945), pp. 510–11.

7. Interview with Democratic member of Congress.

8. Interview with Republican member of Congress.

9. Herbert Brownell, attorney general, to Estes Kefauver [March, 1953], Kefauver Papers.

10. John Foster Dulles, secretary of state, to Estes Kefauver (March 14, 1953), Kefauver Papers.

11. Harry S. Truman, President of the United States, 1945–53, to author (August 12, 1957).

12. Herbert Brownell to Estes Kefauver [March, 1953], Kefauver Papers.

13. George M. Humphrey, secretary of the treasury, to Estes Kefauver (February 24, 1953), Kefauver Papers.

XIII: CONGRESS AND THE REFORM

1. After the historical data had been acquired, tentative conclusions were further tested by writing to and interviewing members of the Eighty-fifth Congress. A questionnaire was prepared

which sought to elicit a reason for the senators' or representatives' support of or opposition to the Pendleton-Kefauver ideas. The results of the House survey are being used not for their statistical exactitude but for the "common sense" insights which they reveal about the congressional motivations in regard to these proposals. Collaborating data were compiled in interviews (lasting from 20 minutes to over an hour each) with fourteen senators and eighteen representatives.

2. Samuel Lubell, *The Future of American Politics,* p. 200.

3. In August, 1957, a two-page questionnaire (see Appendix IV) was mailed to all members of the House and Senate. The purpose of the survey was to gain an insight into the motivations of those who responded rather than to assure precise statistical results. Only the House survey has been reported in detail.

Of the 433 members of the House (two seats were vacant) who were sent the questionnaires, 182 (or 42.0%) responded. The data proved interesting in connection with the attempt at a historical insight into the motivations of the opponents and proponents of the proposal to seat the Cabinet in Congress and its modern modification, the question period. For further observations as to the purposes, methods, limitations, and additional results of the attitude survey, see Appendix V, "The Attitude Survey: Methods and Results."

4. Two different groupings of these categories were made. In one group, the "Newcomers" were those who had been in the House for less than two terms. The "Old-timers" were the remainder. In another grouping, the median length of service for both Congress and the sample (which is 9 years) was used to separate the two categories.

5. In the situation prevalent in the 84th and 85th Congresses, where the Democrats controlled the legislature while the Republicans dominated the executive, the point still remains valid. Although a Democratic committee chairman was obviously not an "administration spokesman," his possible loss in status owing to the presence of department heads might be just as severe as if the Cabinet officer was of his own party.

6. Harold Dwight Lasswell, *Power and Personality,* p. 38.

7. For a precise statement of the questions asked see Appendix IV. The questions have been shortened for adaptation to tabular form.

8. The latter gentleman was a Republican who had been in Congress for thirteen years. Although he believed that most others favored the reform for the opportunity it provided for party harassment, he personally supported the proposal on the grounds that it would increase congressional prestige. See Appendix V for an explanation of the difference between personal motives for support or opposition and the reasons attributed to other members.

9. The degrees of satisfaction with Cabinet-congressional relations varied significantly with the median age of each category in Figure 3. The more unsatisfactory the relationship was perceived to be, the lower the median age of the group. Thus, among Democrats those who thought relations with the Cabinet were "most satisfactory" had a median age of 61 years; those who believed them "satisfactory" had a median age of 51; while those who marked "unsatisfactory" had a median age of 41. Among Republicans the median ages were 57, 55, and 51, respectively.

10. For a recent account of the vagaries of a committee chairman's power within his domain, see Howard E. Shuman, "Senate Rules and the Civil Rights Bill: A Case Study," *The American Political Science Review,* LI (December, 1957), 962.

11. One senator was convinced that the presence of the Cabinet in Congress "would tend to weaken a much needed nonpartisan approach to legislative issues that involve the welfare of all the people of the country, irrespective of party." He decried the practice of the President's party during his tenure in the Senate (since 1945) to feel compelled to back up the Chief Executive's speech uttered in a joint session, especially when some "have been very second rate." The senator held that less partisanship was exhibited in the committee room.

XIV: THE FUTURE FOR REFORM

1. A recent advocate of this position is Princeton professor Stephen K. Bailey, who wrote an Occasional Paper published by The Fund for the Republic entitled "The Condition of Our National Parties" (New York, 1959), 24 pp., in which he urged that the "real problem is political." Bailey believes that "If our *political* institutions can be modernized by certain changes in statutory law and in political party rules, the old problems associated with separation of powers, checks and balances, and federalism would, it seems

probable, largely disappear." For him the "root of the weakness is that while the two national parties for years have genuinely competed for the Presidency they have not made a similar effort in the election of United States Senators and Members of the House of Representatives" (p. 4). The great "redirector" to the group basis of politics is Professor David B. Truman of Columbia University, who in 1951 published *The Governmental Process*, which drew in part upon Arthur F. Bentley's *The Process of Government* (Chicago, University of Chicago Press, 1908).

2. Thus Professor Bailey seeks "nine political reforms" including extending the terms of representatives to four years and senators to eight years, introducing a mathematical formula into the seniority system to recognize those members who survive two-party competition, and repealing the 22nd Amendment which limits a President to two terms. "The Condition of Our National Parties," pp. 15–16.

3. Richard F. Fenno, Jr., *The President's Cabinet: An Analysis in the Period from Wilson to Eisenhower*, pp. 234–47.

4. Ezra Taft Benson, "Legislative-Executive Relationships in the Administration of Programs as Viewed by the Executive," in *Legislative-Executive Relationships in the Government of the United States*, ed. by O. B. Conaway, Jr., p. 30.

5. Fenno, *The President's Cabinet*, pp. 139–40.

6. *The Governmental Process*, p. 530.

7. *Ibid.*, p. 531.

8. *Ibid.*

9. *Farm Program*, Hearing before the Senate Committee on Agriculture and Forestry, May 15, 1957, 85 Cong., 1 sess., p. 30.

10. Douglass Cater has credited Woodrow Wilson with inaugurating the regular Presidential press conference and has noted that Wilson's ideal "was to make it an interpellative device much like the question period in the British House of Commons." Others who have drawn this analogy are Erwin Canham, editor of *The Christian Science Monitor*, and former President Harry S. Truman. Douglass Cater, *The Fourth Branch of Government*, pp. 32, 90, 142.

11. *Ibid.*, p. 148.

12. The concept of "criss-crossing relationships" is Pendleton Herring's, in "Executive-Legislative Responsibilities," *The American Political Science Review*, XXXVIII (December, 1944), 1159.

13. Arnold J. Zurcher, "The Presidency, Congress and Separa-

tion of Powers: A Reappraisal," *The Western Political Quarterly,* III (March, 1950), 95.

14. James MacGregor Burns, *Congress on Trial,* p. 140.

15. President Eisenhower at his Press Conference on June 3, 1959:

Q. Edward P. Morgan of the American Broadcasting Company —Mr. President, the political experts have been wrong before, but some of them are speculating that there is a very real possibility that the Republicans can take the Presidency again in 1960 and again lose the Congress. Would you have any counsel to your successor or either party in dealing with a Congress of the opposition, and what do you think about this apparently increasing American political phenomenon of splitting tickets?

A. Well, Mr. Morgan, I would be glad to discuss that question sometime when we have got about two hours by ourselves [laughter] because it is very serious. And, personally, I detect a more vocal support for some change, even in basic constitutional change, so that we could incorporate into our system some of the features of the parliamentary system. But, as I say, this is a very long thing and we will have to do it a little more at our leisure, I think.

Bibliography

UNPUBLISHED MATERIALS

The inclusive dates refer to the periods for which the papers were examined.

Newton D. Baker Papers, 1918–1937. Library of Congress. Washington, D.C.

Gamaliel Bradford Papers. Massachusetts Historical Society. Boston, Massachusetts.

Bureau of the Budget Records. "Legislative Reference Division File on H.Res. 327, 78 Cong., 1 sess.," in Records of the Legislative Reference Division, Bureau of the Budget, case files on Executive coordination and clearance concerning proposed and enacted private laws, 1939–1946. Series 39.1. Folder Q 4(1). National Archives. Washington, D.C.

J. William Fulbright Papers, 1945. Office of Senator Fulbright. Washington, D.C.

Rutherford B. Hayes Papers, 1878. Hayes Library. Fremont, Ohio.

Harold L. Ickes Papers, 1933–1946. Library of Congress. Washington, D.C.

Estes Kefauver Papers, 1943–1953. Office of Senator Kefauver. Washington, D.C.

John D. Long Papers, 1886. Massachusetts Historical Society. Boston, Massachusetts.

James Madison Papers, 1789–1790. Library of Congress. Washington, D.C.

Franklin D. Roosevelt Papers, 1944–1945. Roosevelt Library. Hyde Park, New York.

Henry L. Stimson Papers, 1910–1915. Yale University Library. New Haven, Connecticut.

William Howard Taft Papers, 1908–1913. Library of Congress. Washington, D.C.

Wigfall Family Papers, 1860–1865. Library of Congress. Washington, D.C.

Woodrow Wilson Papers, 1879–1920. Library of Congress. Washington, D.C.

GOVERNMENT DOCUMENTS

Annals of Congress, 1st to 18th Congresses, 1789–1824. Washington, 1834–1856.

Biographical Directory of the American Congress, 1774–1949. 81 Cong., 2 sess., H.Doc. 607. Washington, 1950.

Congressional Directory, 85 Cong., 1 sess. Washington, 1957.

Congressional Globe, 23rd to 42nd Congresses, 1833–1873. Washington, 1833–1873.

Congressional Record, 43rd to 85th Congresses, 1873–1957. Washington, 1873–1957.

Corwin, Edward S., ed. The Constitution of the United States of America: Analysis and Interpretation. 82 Cong., 2 sess., S. Doc. 170. Washington, 1953.

Executive Journal of the Senate, 1st to 19th Congresses. Washington, 1828.

Farm Program. Hearing before the Senate Committee on Agriculture and Forestry, May 15, 1957. 85 Cong., 1 sess. Washington, 1957.

Finer, Herman. "Questions to the Cabinet in the British House of Commons: Their Applicability to the United States Congress," in The Organization of Congress: Suggestions for Strengthening Congress by Members of Congress and Others. 79 Cong., 2 sess. Washington, 1946, pp. 49–58.

Hinds, Asher C., comp. Hinds' Precedents of the House of Representatives of the United States. 8 vols. Washington, 1907.

House Reports. 38 Cong., 1 sess. No. 43. Washington, 1864.

House Reports. 79 Cong., 2 sess. No. 1675. Washington, 1946.

Hunt, Gaillard, ed. Journals of the Continental Congress: 1774–1789. Volume XIX. Washington, 1912.

Journal of the Congress of the Confederate States of America, 1861–1865. 58 Cong., 2 sess. S. Doc. 234. Washington, 1904.

Journal of the Senate of the United States. 47 Cong., 1 sess. Washington, 1882.

Massachusetts. Debates in the Massachusetts Constitutional Convention, 1917–1918. Vols. I and III. Boston, 1919.

—— Journal of the Constitutional Convention of the Commonwealth of Massachusetts. Boston, 1918.

New York. State Constitutional Convention Commission. The Con·

stitution and Government of the State of New York: An Appraisal. New York, 1915.

—— State Constitutional Convention. Documents of the Constitutional Convention of the State of New York. Albany, 1915.

—— Problems Relating to Legislative Organization and Powers. Albany, 1938.

—— Revised Record of the Constitutional Convention of the State of New York: April 5 to August 6, 1938. Albany, 1938.

The Organization of Congress. Hearings before the Joint Committee on the Organization of Congress. 79 Cong., 1 sess. 4 parts. Washington, 1945.

The Organization of Congress. Summary of Hearings before the Joint Committee on the Organization of Congress, March 13–June 29, 1945. 79 Cong., 1 sess. Washington, 1945.

President's Committee on Administrative Management. Administrative Management in the Government of the United States. Washington, 1937.

Register of Debates, 18th to 25th Congresses, 1824–1837. Washington, 1824–1837.

Report of the Committee on the Judiciary on Senate Bill No. 150. Report No. 16. Senate of the Confederate States of America. Richmond, 1864.

Report of the Minority of the Committee on the Judiciary on the Senate Bill No. 150. Senate of the Confederate States of America. Richmond, 1864.

Senate Reports. 46 Cong., 3 sess. No. 837. Washington, 1881.

War of the Rebellion: Records of the Union and Confederate Armies. Series 1. Vol. XLVI. Washington, 1895.

Wisconsin Legislative Reference Library. "Interpellation of Hon. Mark S. Catlin, Sr., Senate Chamber, March 12, 1941" (typewritten).

—— "Interpellation of State Officers in Wisconsin." February, 1946 (typewritten).

Wisconsin Statutes, 1955. 23rd Edition. Madison, 1955.

BOOKS AND ARTICLES

Acheson, Dean. A Citizen Looks at Congress. New York, 1956.

American Political Science Association. Committee on Congress. The Reorganization of Congress. Washington, 1945.

American Political Science Association. Committee on Political Parties. Toward a More Responsible Two-Party System. New York, 1950.

Ames, Fisher. Works, ed. by Seth Ames. 2 vols. Boston, 1854.

Bagehot, Walter. The English Constitution and Other Political Essays. New York, 1907.

Bailey, Stephen K. The Condition of Our National Parties. A Fund for the Republic Occasional Paper. New York, 1959.

Bailey, Thomas A. The American Pageant. Boston, 1956.

Bauer, Elizabeth Kelley. Commentaries on the Constitution, 1790–1860. New York, 1952.

Belmont, Perry. An American Democrat. New York, 1940.

—— "Cabinet Officers in Congress," *North American Review*, CXCVII (January, 1913), 22–30.

—— Survival of the Democratic Principle. New York, 1926.

Benson, Ezra Taft. "Legislative-Executive Relationships in the Administration of Programs as Viewed by the Executive," in Legislative-Executive Relationships in the Government of the United States, ed. by O. B. Conaway, Jr., pp. 57–64. Washington, 1954.

Black, Henry Campbell. The Relation of the Executive Power to Legislation. Princeton, 1919.

Blaine, James G. Twenty Years of Congress. 2 vols. Norwich, Conn., 1884.

Bourinot, John George. "Parliamentary Government in Canada: A Constitutional and Historical Study," in Annual Report of the American Historical Association for the year 1891, pp. 309–407. Washington, 1892.

Bradford, Gamaliel. "Congress and the Cabinet," *Annals of the American Academy of Political and Social Science*, II (November, 1891), 289–99, and IV (November, 1893), 404–24.

—— The Lesson of Popular Government. 2 vols. New York, 1899.

Bridgman, Raymond L. The Massachusetts Constitutional Convention of 1917. Concord, New Hampshire, 1923.

Brown, Willard. "Shall Members of the Cabinet Sit in Congress?" *Atlantic Monthly*, L (July, 1882), 95–99.

Brownlow, Louis. The President and the Presidency. Chicago, 1949.

Bryce, James. The American Commonwealth. 2 vols. London, 1889.

Burns, James MacGregor. Congress on Trial. New York, 1949.

Butler, Nicholas Murray. Across the Busy Years. 2 vols. New York, 1940.

Cater, Douglass. The Fourth Branch of Government. Boston, 1959.

Chesnut, Mary Boykin. A Diary from Dixie, ed. by Ben Ames Williams. Boston, 1949.

Childs, Richard S. "A State Manager Plan," *National Municipal Review*, VI (November, 1917), 659–63.

Cleland, Robert G. "Jefferson Davis and the Confederate Congress," *Southern Historical Society Quarterly*, XIX (January, 1916), 213–31.

Cleveland, Frederick A. "The Reorganization of the Federal Government—An Alternative Proposal," *Proceedings of the Academy of Political Science*, IX (July, 1921), 361–419.

"Cobb Correspondence," *Publications of the Southern History Association*, XI (September–November, 1907), 312–28.

Commager, Henry Steele, ed. Documents of American History. 5th ed. New York, 1949.

Corwin, Edward S. The President: Office and Powers, 1787–1948. New York, 1948.

——, and Louis W. Koenig. The Presidency Today. New York, 1956.

Coulter, E. Merton. The Confederate States of America: 1861–1865. Baton Rouge, 1950.

Curry, J. L. M. Civil History of the Government of the Confederate States. Richmond, 1900.

Davis, Jefferson. The Rise and Fall of the Confederate Government. New York, 1881.

Dodge, Edmund Arthur. "Cabinet Officers in Congress," *Sewanee Review*, XI (April, 1903), 129–43.

Eaton, Clement. A History of the Southern Confederacy. New York, 1954.

Elliott, William Yandell. The Need for Constitutional Reform. New York, 1935.

Farrand, Max, ed. The Records of the Federal Convention of 1787. 3 vols. Rev. ed. New Haven, 1937.

Fenno, Richard F. The President's Cabinet: An Analysis in the Period from Wilson to Eisenhower. Cambridge, Mass., 1959.

Finletter, Thomas K. Can Representative Government Do the Job? New York, 1945.

Fisher, Sydney G. "Cabinet Officers in Congress," *Overland Monthly*, IX (February, 1887), 209–13.

Ford, Henry Jones. "The Cause of Political Corruption," *Scribner's Magazine*, XLIX (January, 1911), 54–61.

—— The Rise and Growth of American Politics. New York, 1898.

Fowler, Dorothy Ganfield. The Cabinet Politician: The Postmasters General, 1829–1900. New York, 1943.

Galbreath, C. B. "Ohio's Contribution to National Civil Service Reform," *Ohio Archaeological and Historical Quarterly*, XXXIII (April, 1924), 176–204.

Galloway, George B. Congress at the Crossroads. New York, 1946.

—— Congress and Parliament. Washington, 1955.

Godkin, E. L. "Cabinet Officers in Congress," *The Nation*, XXXII (February 17, 1881), 107–9.

Hamill, Katharine. "This Is a Bureaucrat," *Fortune*, XLVIII (November, 1953), 156–58, 181–88.

Hamilton, Alexander. Works, ed. by Henry C. Lodge. 12 vols. New York, 1907.

Hard, William. "One Immediate Reform," *The Nation*, XVIII (April 9, 1924), 397–98.

Harlow, Ralph Volney. The History of Legislative Methods in the Period before 1825. New Haven, 1917.

Hayes, Rutherford Birchard. Diary and Letters, ed. by Charles Richard Williams. 4 vols. Columbus, 1924.

Heller, Robert. Strengthening the Congress. Washington, 1945.

—— Strengthening the Congress—A Progress Report. Washington, 1947.

Herbert, Hilary A. "Cleveland and His Cabinet at Work," *Century*, LXXXV (March, 1913), 740–44.

Herring, Pendleton. "Executive-Legislative Responsibilities," *American Political Science Review*, XXXVIII (December, 1944), 1153–65.

—— Presidential Leadership. New York, 1940.

Hinsdale, Mary L. "The Cabinet and Congress: An Historical Inquiry," *Proceedings of the American Political Science Association*, II (1905), 126–48.

—— A History of the President's Cabinet. Ann Arbor, 1911.

Houston, David F. Eight Years with Wilson's Cabinet, 1913 to 1920. 2 vols. New York, 1926.

Hull, Augustus Longstreet. "The Making of the Confederate Constitution," *Publications of the Southern History Association,* IX (September, 1905), 272–92.

Hyneman, Charles S. Bureaucracy in a Democracy. New York, 1950.

Jefferson, Thomas. Writings, ed. by Andrew A. Lipscomb and Albert Ellery Bergh. 20 vols. Washington, 1903–4.

Jones, Roger W. "The Role of the Bureau of the Budget in the Federal Legislative Process," *American Bar Association Journal,* XL (November, 1954), 995–98.

Kefauver, Estes. "The Need for Better Executive-Legislative Teamwork in the National Government," *American Political Science Review,* XXXVIII (April, 1944), 317–25.

——, and Jack Levin. A Twentieth-Century Congress. New York, 1947.

Korngold, Ralph. Thaddeus Stevens. New York, 1955.

La Follette, Robert M., Jr. "A Senator Looks at Congress," *Atlantic Monthly,* CLXXII (July, 1943), 91–96.

Laski, Harold J. The American Presidency. London, 1940.

Lasswell, Harold Dwight. Power and Personality. New York, 1948.

Latham, Earl. The Group Basis of Politics. New York, 1952.

Learned, Henry B. The President's Cabinet. New Haven, 1912.

—— "Relations of the Legislature and the Executive," *The Nation,* C (February 11, 1915), 166–67.

Leupp, Francis E. "The Cabinet in Congress," *Atlantic Monthly,* CXX (December, 1917), 769–79.

Lipson, Leslie. The American Governor from Figurehead to Leader. Chicago, 1939.

Long, John Davis. Papers, 1897–1904, ed. by Gardner Weld Allen. Boston, 1939.

Longaker, Richard P. "Was Jackson's Kitchen Cabinet a Cabinet?" *The Mississippi Valley Historical Review,* XLIV (June, 1957), 94–108.

Loring, Augustus Peabody. "A Short Account of the Massachusetts Constitutional Convention, 1917–1919," *New England Quarterly,* VI, Supplement (January, 1933), 101 pp.

Lowell, Abbott Lawrence. "Ministerial Responsibility and the Constitution," *The Atlantic Monthly,* LVII (February, 1886), 180–93.

Lubell, Samuel. The Future of American Politics. New York, 1952.

Luce, Robert. Legislative Problems. Boston, 1935.

Maass, Arthur. "In Accord with the Program of the President? An Essay on Staffing the Presidency," Public Policy, III, 77–93. Cambridge, Mass., 1953.

McBain, Howard Lee. The Living Constitution. New York, 1928.

McCarthy, Charles. The Wisconsin Idea. New York, 1912.

MacDonald, William. A New Constitution for a New America. New York, 1921.

Maclay, William. Journal, ed. by Edgar S. Maclay. New York, 1890.

Madison, James. Journal of the Federal Convention, ed. by Erastus Scott. 2 vols. Chicago, 1894.

—— Writings, ed. by Gaillard Hunt. 9 vols. New York, 1900–10.

" 'Make Democracy Safe for the World' Says Governor McCall of Massachusetts," *The New York Times Magazine* (July 22, 1917), pp. 1–2.

Maverick, Maury. In Blood and Ink. New York, 1939.

Mills, Ogden L. "Participation of the Executive in Legislation," *Proceedings of the Academy of Political Science*, V (October, 1914), 134–37.

Montague, Andrew J. "The Cabinet before Congress," *World's Work*, XLIX (February, 1925), 358.

—— "A More Effective Cabinet" (Address before the Pennsylvania Bar Association, June 27, 1911) in Report of the Seventeenth Annual Meeting of the Pennsylvania Bar Association, pp. 239–58. Philadelphia, 1911.

National Municipal League. Committee on State Government. A Model State Constitution. 3d, 4th, 5th eds. New York, 1933, 1941, 1948.

Patterson, C. Perry. Presidential Government in the United States. Chapel Hill, 1947.

Plumer, William. Memorandum of Proceedings in the United States Senate: 1803–1807, ed. by Everett Somerville Brown. New York, 1923.

Price, Don K. "The Parliamentary and Presidential Systems," *Public Administration Review*, III (Autumn, 1943), 317–34.

"Proceedings of First Confederate Congress—First Session," *Southern Historical Society Papers*, XLIV (June, 1923), 3–206.

Randall, James G. Constitutional Problems Under Lincoln. New York, 1926.

Rawle, William. A View of the Constitution of the United States of America. 2d ed. Philadelphia, 1829.

Redfield, William C. "From Congress to Cabinet," *Outlook,* CXXXIV (June 6, 1923), 133–37.

Reed, Thomas B. "Should the Cabinet Officers Have Seats in Congress?" *The Illustrated American,* XXII (July 31, 1897), 137–38.

Richardson, James D., comp. A Compilation of the Messages and Papers of the Confederacy. 2 vols. Nashville, 1904.

—— A Compilation of the Messages and Papers of the Presidents. 20 vols. New York, 1897–1922.

Rowell, Chester H. "Next Step in Washington," *World's Work,* XLIX (February, March, 1925), 400–8, 553–60.

Rowland, Dunbar, ed. Jefferson Davis, Constitutionalist: His Letters, Papers, and Speeches. 10 vols. Jackson, Mississippi, 1923.

Sait, E. M. "Participation of the Executive in Legislation," *Proceedings of the Academy of Political Science,* V (October, 1914), 127–33.

Sandburg, Carl. Abraham Lincoln, The Prairie Years and the War Years. One volume ed. New York, 1954.

Schwab, John Christopher. The Confederate States of America. New York, 1901.

Secret Journals of the Congress of the Confederation—Foreign Affairs. 4 vols. Boston, 1821.

Shuman, Howard E. "Senate Rules and the Civil Rights Bill: A Case Study," *American Political Science Review,* LI (December, 1957), 955–75.

Snow, Freeman. "Cabinet Government in the United States," *Annals of the American Academy of Political and Social Science,* III (July, 1892), 1–13.

Stephens, Alexander H. A Constitutional View of the Late War between the States. 2 vols. Philadelphia, 1870.

Stimson, Henry L., and McGeorge Bundy. On Active Service in Peace and War. New York, 1948.

Story, Joseph. Commentaries on the Constitution of the United States. 3 vols. Boston, 1833.

Taft, William Howard. "Financial Retrenchment and Governmental Reorganization," *Proceedings of the Academy of Political Science,* IX (July, 1921), 420–26.

—— Our Chief Magistrate and His Powers. New York, 1916.

Truman, David. The Governmental Process. New York, 1951.

Union [Republican] Congressional Committee. "Congressional Record of George H. Pendleton, Candidate for Vice President." Washington, 1864.

University of Chicago Round Table. Streamlining Congress. Number 356. Chicago, 1945.

U'Ren, W. S. "State and County Government in Oregon and Proposed Changes," *Annals of the American Academy of Political and Social Science*, XLVII (May, 1913), 271–73.

Von Abele, Rudolph. Alexander H. Stephens. New York, 1946.

Washington, George. Writings, ed. by John C. Fitzpatrick. 39 vols. Washington, 1931–44.

Welles, Gideon. Diary, ed. by John T. Morse, Jr. 3 vols. Boston, 1911.

White, Horace. "Cabinet Officers in Congress," *The Nation*, XXVIII (April 10, 1879), 243–44.

White, Leonard D. The Federalists. New York, 1948.

—— Introduction to the Study of Public Administration. New York, 1948.

White, William S. The Citadel. New York, 1957.

Willoughby, W. F. Principles of Legislative Organization and Administration. Washington, 1934.

Wilson, Woodrow. "Cabinet Government in the United States," *International Review*, VII (August, 1879), 146–63.

—— "Committee or Cabinet Government," *Overland Monthly*, 2nd series, III (January, 1884), 17–33.

—— Congressional Government. New York and Boston, 1885.

—— Constitutional Government in the United States. New York, 1908.

—— "Responsible Government Under the Constitution," *Atlantic Monthly*, LVII (April, 1886), 542–53.

Young, Roland. The American Congress. New York, 1958.

Younger, Edward, ed. Inside the Confederate Government: The Diary of Robert Garlick Hill Kean, Head of the Bureau of War. New York, 1957.

Zurcher, Arnold J. "The Presidency, Congress and Separation of Powers: A Reappraisal," *Western Political Quarterly*, III (March, 1950), 75–97.

NEWSPAPERS AND MAGAZINES

Dates refer to the periods for which the papers were examined.

Boston Daily Advertiser, 1879–1881. Boston.

Boston Evening Transcript, 1918. Boston.

Boston Gazette and Country Journal, 1789–1790. Boston.

Boston Herald, 1901, 1906, 1918. Boston.

Cincinnati Commercial, 1864–1865; 1879–1881. Cincinnati.

Cincinnati Daily Enquirer, 1878–1881. Cincinnati.

Cincinnati Daily Gazette, 1865, 1878–1879. Cincinnati.

Daily Advertiser, 1789–1790. New York.

Daily Dispatch, 1862–1865. Richmond.

Daily Morning Chronicle, 1864–1865. Washington.

Daily National Intelligencer, 1864–1865. Washington.

Daily Richmond Enquirer, 1863–1865. Richmond.

Daily Richmond Examiner, 1862–1865. Richmond.

Gazette of the United States, 1789–1790. New York.

Harper's Weekly, 1879–1881. New York.

Literary Digest, 1922. New York.

Nation, 1864–1945. New York.

New York Daily Gazette, 1789. New York.

New York Herald, 1879–1881. New York.

New York Times, 1862–1945. New York.

Sacramento Daily Record-Union, 1879–1881. Sacramento.

Washington Daily Globe, 1864–1865. Washington.

Washington Daily Times, 1864–1865. Washington.

Washington Post, 1879. Washington.

Index